INTRODUCTION

I decided to start this *DA Delta Force* series of books since I had the rare opportunity to witness a phenomenon in which an extraordinary group of prosecutors were assigned to the DA's Major Crimes Division. The members of this group were incredibly talented and dedicated to seeing criminals prosecuted to the full extent of the law. These attorneys were entrusted with the toughest and most challenging cases. The news media has a knack of cherry-picking only a few of the 60,000 felonies prosecuted by the Los Angeles County District Attorney's Office DA's Office (LADA's Office). The vast majority of the felony trials never receive the slightest coverage by the media.

Over my 43 years I worked for the LA DA's Office, I became aware that you the public never hear about some of the most fascinating cases passing through the judicial system. When I retired from the LA DA's Office, I had the opportunity to continue to work there part-time by assisting the Major Crime Division attorneys with the preparation of their cases. This gave me an opportunity to interact with these extraordinary attorneys. So my perspective of these incredible attorneys is not from being their supervisor or co-equal, but like a fly on the wall watching them meticulously prepare and prosecute their intriguing cases.

Years ago before retiring, I tried my share of homicide cases and was thought to be an effective litigator. As a matter of fact, I prosecuted the first capital case under the new Death Penalty law. However, I have had the pleasure of watching and working with these highly gifted prosecutors in the Major Crimes Division and must admit they are clearly in a league all by themselves.

I look upon Major Crimes Division as being a stable of thoroughbred horses that are eager to prove themselves. However, even within the ranks of the Major Crimes attorneys, there are those who stand out from the rest. My first book on the DA's Delta Force was titled *Prosecutrix Fight for Justice*, which highlighted the extraordinary trials handled by Eleanor Hunter. The next book of the series was *The Top Gun Prosecutor*, which underscored the exceptional career of John Monahan.

Yet there are so many more great Major Crime prosecutors I would like to highlight and that is why this present book, *The Best of the Best DA* focuses on two more amazing prosecutors: Tony Manzella and Hoon Cheng. The best way to illustrate how talented they are is to follow them through a couple of cases they prosecuted.

In this book we start with prosecutor Tony Manzella, one of the most remarkable attorneys of all time. The reason I can heap such praise on him is that he and I joined the DA's Office at the same time. I have seen him as a prosecutor as well as a high priced Defense attorney. There has never been another attorney like Tony Manzella. When he retired from private practice, he came back to the DA's Office to litigate the toughest hardcore gang cases. He was so good he was picked up by the Major Crimes Division to concentrate his attention on the Mexican Mafia cases.

We review a case from San Pedro, in which he was assigned, where the Mexican Mafia had targeted a prolific drug dealer who wasn't paying his 10% tax to the prison gang. To teach the dealer a lesson, they used a serial killer to gain the confidence of the drug dealer so they could gain entrance to his residence in order to blow his head off.

Tony Manzella had the problematic task of finding witnesses willing to testify against Mexican Mafia members. You, the reader, will walk in Tony's footsteps as he methodically built a case against the killers. You will be surprised as to how Tony skillfully gained the confidence of certain witnesses in order to see that justice would be done.

After being successful with that Mexican Mafia case he gained the reputation as the can-do gang prosecutor. When the homicide detectives were being inundated with so many gang homicides they invited Tony to LAPD Northeast division to see if he could figure a way to build a prosecution that would stand up in court. Tony spent over a month analyzing dozens of LAPD Murder Books and gave the detectives a list of things they needed to do. You, the reader, will have the opportunity to follow Tony as he joined up with a group of seasoned homicide detectives in creating a solid case against the members of the Mexican Mafia.

You will follow Tony through five trials that took almost six years. You will see how he developed a winning strategy by turning their infamous 'Green Light' into laser beam focused on the destruction of the Mexican Mafia.

Then we move on to another outrageous gang case, that of Timothy McGhee, better known as the Monster of Atwater Village. Even though Tony Manzella was originally assigned the case, he wasn't able to try it since he was engaged in the lengthy Mexican Mafia case. This McGhee case had to be handed off to a prosecutor who was highly skilled in handling gang cases as well as a quick learner. Hoon Chun had come up through the ranks of the Hardcore Gangs Division before he was transferred to the highly prestigious Major Crimes Division. Hoon had gained incredible experience when he was co-prosecutor of the gigantic Asian Boyz, case which involved a dozen gang members who terrorized the San Fernando Valley.

Hoon took on this Timothy McGhee case even though it was fraught with one problem after another. You, the reader, will have the opportunity to follow Hoon as he has to steer the case from one disaster to another. This defendant had a reputation for killing off any witness who even considered testifying against him in court. Hoon was faced with a group of reluctant witnesses, so he had to find ways to use forensic evidence to build a case to present in court.

The final case we will discuss was one handled by Hoon that involved a paraplegic accused of murdering a USC student in the most bizarre manner. I told Hoon that there was no way he was going to convince 12 jurors to convict such a disabled person of murder. This book will show how wrong I was. Hoon figured out a way to use the parents of the paraplegic to end up being the key witnesses against their son. You, the reader, will learn from this book how Hoon used his ingenuity to convict a killer affiliated with the vicious Mara Salvatrucha gang.

After reading about these four fascinating cases, you will come to the same conclusion: that Tony Manzella and Hoon Chun definitely should be included as the BEST OF BEST DAs.

PROSECUTOR ANTHONY 'TONY' MANZELLA

The Gomez & Grajeda Case

(Remember to Pay your TAXES to the MEXICAN MAFIA)

CHAPTER 1 SHOOTING OF THE DRUG DEALER

It was a typical July evening in the beach community of San Pedro. The residence had their windows open to catch a gentle breeze coming off the Pacific Ocean. The hectic daily chores were over and everyone was chilling out with some type of soothing beverage. A drug dealer, Robert Dunton, was meeting with associates in his fortified house. He had his security guard, Robert Acosta, five feet away from him, so he felt secure. Contrary to the public image of drug dealers, this dealer wasn't doing drugs this particular evening but was sitting around enjoying a Pepsi Cola (not a Coke) in the usual red, white, and blue aluminum can. He had dined on fine take-out cuisine from Wienerschnitzel, as displayed by the empty bags and napkins on the coffee table in front of him. He and his associates were discussing what could be done to improve the drug business in the San Pedro area. Dunton boasted to his visitors that he had out-smarted the Mexican Mafia (better known as EME) and had figured out how to avoid paying their mandated dope sales tax.

Dunton was pleased with the money he was earning from his drug crews, who were selling all types of drugs throughout the harbor area. One of his visitors that evening was Ruben Gomez, a small-time dealer who had recently had been released from prison and was finding it difficult to resume his dope business. Gomez and Dunton had known each other for years and could be described loosely as friends. Gomez this evening had brought along with him Arturo Grajeda, who was well known as being from a prominent gang family in the San Pedro neighborhood.

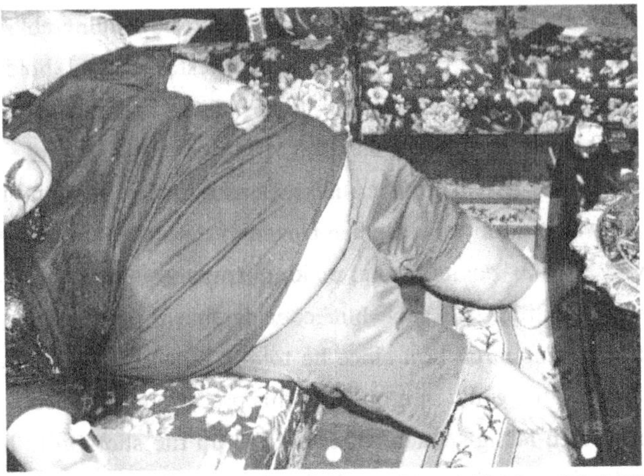

Victim Robert Dunton was shot to death while he was seated on his sofa on July 1, 1997

When the police arrived, they found Dunton's body still seated on the sofa with brain matter still oozing out of the head and falling on his shoulder. The detectives recognized that this was an over-kill homicide in which the murderer was trying to send a message to others. The detectives' job was to determine what was the message and who was sending it.

CHAPTER 2 TAXES FOR MEXICAN MAFIA (EME)

The old saying is that there are only two things that are predictable in life, and they are "Paying Taxes" and "Dying." However, the Mexican Mafia (Better known as EME) has a new slant to that saying in that "If you don't Pay your Taxes, you will Die". One of the fundamental rules or decrees of EME is that gang drug dealers have to pay taxes to the Mexican Mafia. The rate is generally 10% of whatever the seller collects from his sales of drugs. Over the years, some drug dealers have felt that the paying of the EME taxes is cutting into their profits from the narcotics business.

On the other hand, EME needs the tax money to conduct the business of their organization and provide their leaders, who are in prison, with spending money in order for them to live well behind bars. Therefore, EME recognizes it has to take onerous measures to persuade drug dealers to continue to pay up their taxes. To gain compliance, EME has had to order numerous brutal killings of non-complying dealers in order to send the message to the rest of the dealers to pay their taxes and not to even think of messing with the Mexican Mafia.

Sometimes there are disputes as to the exact amount of taxes owing. Even in legitimate businesses, it is hard for the IRS or Tax collectors to know how much gross revenue a certain business generates. Some businesses keep two sets of books, and the same is true in the narcotics business. There are times when the Mexican Mafia believes they aren't getting what they think is their fair share. This can lead to disputes with EME, which result in unfortunate consequences for the dealer.

Therefore, most dealers realize it is in their best interest to stay on good terms with the EME tax collectors if they don't want to be visited by one of the EME enforcers.

The Mexican Mafia is one of those organizations that the public has heard about but really doesn't understand. Just by the name alone, one doesn't think of it in a positive light. Most people's best guess is the EME is some type of prison gang. Some people place more emphasis on the "Mafia" part of the name and think they are the Mexican version of the Italian Mafia. Those people think EME is headed by some type of "Godfather." There are some similarities between the Italian and Mexican Mafias; in particular, both organizations oversee criminal activities from the top down.

Others try to romanticize it, believing it was established to help downtrodden immigrants to adjust to American values. Few people take the time to learn more about its existence and the myriad activities it is involved in. Part of the lack of knowledge about EME is due to the fact that it is a secretive association that purposely stays in the shadows of society. As a result, the image of EME is clouded in mystery and misinformation.

In order to learn the facts about the group, one has to go back to 1957 when EME was founded. Initially, it started with 13 Hispanic street gangs that stretched across the Los Angeles metropolitan area. Its genesis was a group of inmates at the old Deuel Vocational Institution who wanted to create an alliance to protect themselves from the other gangs that existed in the prisons. The idea was for the Hispanic gangs to put aside all their rivalries upon entering a prison. However, to gain the cooperation of the numerous gangs they used very violent gangsters to put the fear in the newcomers to comply with the tenets of their new organization.

One of the objectives of EME was to control the black market activities that existed within each of the prison facilities. By using violence, they were able to win over the cooperation of others. It wasn't long before the group had used force to gain control of the entire state prison system.

EME tries to bring some cohesive organization to criminal activities both inside and outside of prison. For example, on the streets it isn't good for business if there are too many gangs trying to sell narcotics in one particular territory. This causes too much competition, forcing prices to drop and causing a reduction in profits for all concerned. When there are too many dealers in one area, there can be violence between the gangs, causing the police to conduct investigations that might cause problems for the gangs and could impede EME receiving their tax money.

Back in 1993, the EME recognized that the local gangs were engaged in too many deadly rivalries that were self-defeating to everyone. Unfortunately, many of the high-level officials had received lengthy prison sentences, which meant that the EME hierarchy was concentrated in the max prison facility which was located in Pelican Bay near the Oregon border. They, as a group, realized that all the chaos on the streets needed to stop. That was when the EME *carnales* decided to set new rules for gang members to follow. It was described as the Blue Tsunami, in which EME ordered the following:

First, no more drive-by shooting between the local gangs.

Second, all local gangs were to swear allegiance to EME.

Third, all Hispanic gangs in California were to pay 10% on their sales of narcotics.

These rules were announced at a meeting held in Elysian Park. All the Hispanic gang leaders in the Los Angeles area showed up at the meeting. EME had one of their leaders who had just recently been released from prison to explain the new rules and how they would be applied to all the Hispanic gangs. Initially, some of the gang leaders didn't understand why they had to pay taxes so the EME leaders in prison could enjoy the comforts of prison life, which included drugs, snacks, electronic gadgets, and spending money.

For many, it seems confusing as to who are the exact members of EME. All its members are affiliated with a local gang, and for various reasons these members make up to the ranks of EME. This might be compared to the Masons and Shriners. Someone who has become an active Mason can go on to a higher level by becoming a Shriner. In other words, all Shriners are still Masons but not all Masons are Shriners. (By using this analogy, the author is not implying that Shriners are similar in any way to the Mexican Mafia.)

The EME members fit into three categories. The top echelon is called the Carnales and many of them are in prison. A new Carnale is sponsored by at least one existing Carnale. The sponsor is responsible for the actions of the new member. Below the Carnale position is the so-called Associates, who may be leaders in the local gangs. Finally, the bottom tier is the EME Soldiers or crew workers. These are the ones who actually carry out the edicts passed down by the Carnales. There is no such thing as a card-carrying member, and often the levels of membership become blurred over time.

(A good resource on the organization and operation of EME is a book written by Tony Rafael titled ***The Mexican Mafia***.)

CHAPTER 3 "GREEN LIGHT" DOESN'T MEAN GO

When one talks about the EME organization, most people think of their "Green Light" system. This term means that the top structure of EME has agreed that a certain person should be killed. There is a formal procedure that must be adhered to in order for a "Green Light" to be issued against a certain person. If a gang member kills someone without going through the procedure of obtaining a "Green Light," that could result in that person's death. The top Mexican Mafia officials want to have complete control over who lives and dies, and they don't take it lightly when someone doesn't abide by their rules.

Many "Green Lights" are issued when someone doesn't pay their taxes to EME. It's obvious that the organization must have money coming in continually to operate. Other reasons for a "Green Light" are when one encroaches into some other gang's territory. Another big reason is if someone is thought to be an informant for law enforcement. Sometimes the person isn't an informant but has just attracted the attention of the police. In those situations, people may be "Green Lighted" unfairly. EME may misread the facts and kill someone who isn't being cooperative at all, but they don't want to take a chance that a mole has penetrated their inner circle.

There are some chivalry reasons for "Green Light" when one member interferes with someone else's woman. This doesn't have to involve rape but may deal with someone dating some member's girlfriend when that person is in prison. EME looks upon a woman as being the property of the member who has dated or lived with that woman. Therefore, EME discourages the stealing of the affection of women linked to members who are serving time in prison.

There are numerous reasons why "Green Lights" are turned on for various members of the gangs. The fear of the "Green Light" is what maintains the order that the organization demonstrates in its daily operations. But what does a "Green Light" really mean? Since many of the top officials of EME are in prison, how are they able to carry out the killing of the person who is "Green Lighted"? The answer is that a "Green Light" is like a contract to kill someone. It means that it is the duty of every member to kill that individual if they have the opportunity to do so without getting caught. Most members know that it will be highly beneficial to their standing in the gang if they carry out the "Green Light" for the overall good of EME.

"Green Lights" are communicated to members through a coded piece of paper. It is hard to understand without some form of interpretation. If it fell into the wrong hands, few people would realize that is the official order to kill dozens of people. It contains a great deal of information such as whether the lights are turned on or off on certain individuals.

The written "Green Light" lists are almost impossible to read. They are often

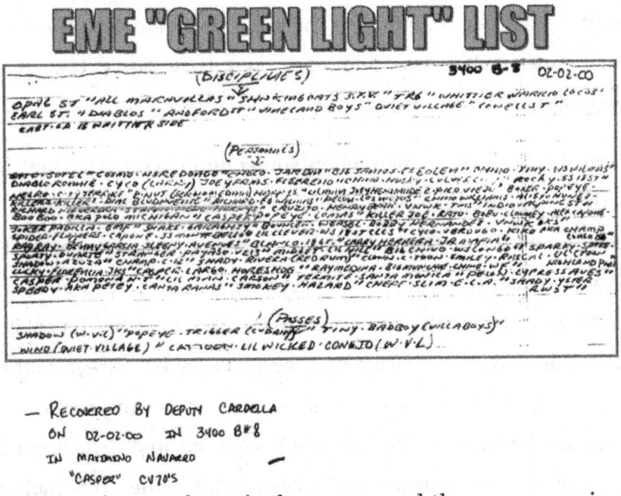

divided into three sections and one is the names and the accompanying information next to the names.

One of the people on the "Green Light" list was Ruben Gomez. Even though he had been considered a soldier for the Mexican Mafia, he had gotten into trouble with EME in that he didn't pay his EME tax when he was operating his drug business. When Gomez was released from prison, he was paroled to Los Angeles County. One might think that after spending so much time in prison that he would think of changing his life style, especially since he knew there had been a "Green Light" issued against him.

CHAPTER 4 GOMEZ THE ROBBER

Gomez never would be labeled a flourishing drug dealer. It may have been because the profit from his drug dealing business either ended up in his veins or snorted up his nose. That may explain why he didn't have money to pay EME their taxes. Gomez tried to make up one excuse after another, but the bottom line was he owed substantial money to the EME tax collector. When he was sent back in prison, Gomez had a sense of relief because EME would have to realize that while he was in prison, he didn't have the capability to pay them the taxes he owed.

Over the years he had done so much for EME that Gomez thought he was owed some slack. However, the leadership of EME didn't see it his way. Their feeling was that there were rules to follow and if not, the violator had to suffer the consequences. It didn't take long before there was a "Green Light" list with the name Ruben Gomez on it. Gomez didn't think it was fair, but the words 'fair,' 'just,' and even the word 'mercy' don't exist in the vocabulary of the EME Carnales.

When Gomez was released from prison the pressure was on to avoid any EME members until he could acquire enough money to pay off what he owed EME. The only skill set that Gomez possessed was the ability to rob people.

PATEL ROBBERY

On May 25, 1997, victim Rajandra Patel was 50 years old and had a good job as a Quality Control Engineer in Orange County. He just happened to be in the wrong area at the wrong time. Mr. Patel caught the attention of Gomez because he was wearing several gold chains. He was also wearing a Rolex watch. Eventually, Mr. Patel paid for some item and Gomez was all eyes. He noticed that Mr. Patel had a large roll of bills that he pulled out of his pocket. When Mr. Patel paid his bill, he stuffed the rest of the money back into his pants pocket.

Mr. Patel was displaying all the trappings that Gomez was looking for in a victim that would make an easy and lucrative robbery. When the opportunity arose, Gomez came up to the victim and used a knife to rob him of his jewelry, watch, and cash. These items would seem to be a sufficient reward for the robbery; however, he wanted more. The defendant stabbed the victim in the face and immediately threw him in the trunk of his car.

Then Gomez drove around trying to sell the victim's jewelry and watch. At some point, Gomez found out that the so-called expensive Rolex watch was just a fake and was worthless. Then he tried another approach by trying to get the victim to give up his PIN# so that he could withdraw money from the victim's account at an ATM. In order to get the victim to reveal his PIN#, Gomez resorted to torturing the victim.

Either the information wasn't correct or somehow the ATM idea didn't work out. Gomez was frustrated that this victim wasn't proving to be a good hit. He went back to the trunk of his car and pulled the victim out. Out of desperation and not wanting witnesses, he had no choice but to shoot him in the head. Since he had stopped in an isolated area, he rolled the victim's dead body over to the side of the road and drove away dissatisfied that he hadn't obtained anything worthwhile which he could use to pay off EME.

The entire robbery was a disappointment to all concerned. The victim ended up dead over a fake Rolex watch. It might have been a good idea to wear a fake expensive watch so if he got robbed it wouldn't be any great loss. Mr. Patel liked to wear gold necklaces to give the appearance that he was a successful individual. However, the glittery jewelry was noticed by the wrong person for the wrong reason. Unfortunately, it cost the victim his life.

ESCARENO ROBBERY

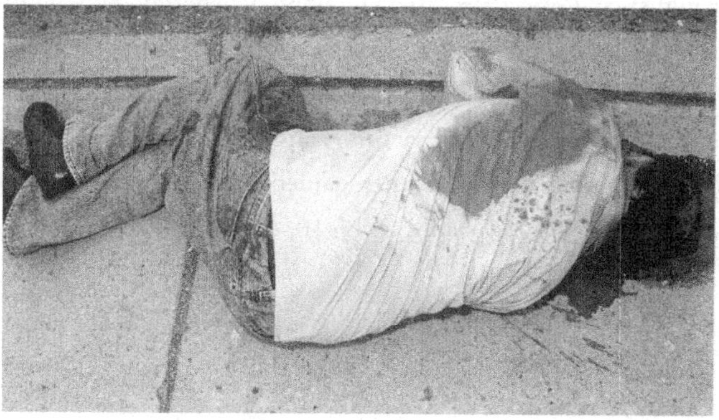

Victim Rajandra Patel robbed and shot on May 26, 1997

Several days later, Gomez was still desperately looking for new victims. He may have learned from his first experience that everything that glitters doesn't turn out to be gold. This time he wasn't looking for someone with jewelry and watches which all could be fake and worthless to sell. He decided to look for someone who had nothing but cash. From experience, he knew that drug dealers are the best source of cash. Since drug dealing was his old business, he knew just the right places to find the dealers. He drove over to where drug activity was commonly conducted. He cautiously started strolling around trying to fit in.

Jesus Escareno came out of an apartment building and started to walk through an empty parking lot until he reached a car in the last row. He opened the driver's door and sat down inside. With the use of both his hands he started to remove the 'club lock' on his steering wheel. Gomez was watching from a distance and could see that no one else was visible. Gomez exited his car and walked around Mr. Escareno's car and confronted him demanding money.

To his disappointment, Mr. Escareno wasn't a drug dealer and didn't have any money. The victim was a 21-year-old restaurant worker on his way to socialize with friends, so he was dressed like a Mexican cowboy with his cowboy hat and cowboy boots. He didn't have any weapon nor in any way did he pose a threat to Gomez. At most, the victim was a disappointment by not being a dope dealer with a lot of cash that Gomez could steal. Gomez's reacted by taking his shotgun and pointing it at Mr. Escareno's head. He pulled the trigger, thereby fatally wounding the victim.

Most robbers' reaction would be an initial dissatisfaction and then to walk away and continue the search for a better victim. Why was it necessary for Gomez to kill the victim for no apparent reason? Gomez gained nothing from this killing, and he was still in search of a more rewarding candidate to rob.

LUNA ROBBERY

Victim Jesus Escareno robbed and shot on June 9, 1997

Gomez was obsessed with locating a drug dealer who was full of cash. This time he drove around the most common drug dealing locations. Eventually, Gomez recognized a low-level drug dealer he had known over the years. He wasn't a high roller but he was someone who would have some cash. His name was Raul Luna, an Army veteran who hadn't been successful at any of his endeavors.

Gomez approached Mr. Luna and attempted to rob him. This time Gomez was slightly successful since Mr. Luna did have a small amount of cash. Gomez had to be disappointed with the small amount and Mr. Luna was even more disappointed since he was losing the money he needed to pay his distributor at the end of the day.

Gomez was so discouraged that he was never going to get enough money to pay off his "Green Light." He rose up his shotgun and pointed it at the victim's head. Without a word being said Gomez pulled the trigger and the shotgun blew away half of the victim's neck. This one shot was fatal and the victim was pronounced dead as he lay in a pool of blood in the dirt.

CHAPTER 5 HOW TO TURN OFF 'GREEN LIGHT'

Gomez made inquiries as to what he could do to get the "Green Light" turned off of him. At the same time, the Mexican Mafia was having difficulty in the San Pedro area with a big drug dealer, Robert Dunton, who wasn't paying his drug taxes to EME. This type of behavior couldn't be tolerated, since this made the Mexican Mafia look weak and unable to enforce its rules that every gang drug dealer had to abide by. Everyone had to pay their fair share of taxes for the so called protection they received from the Mexican Mafia.

EME had assigned one of its best hit men, Arturo Grajeda, to kill Mr. Dunton, who was being defiant and not paying taxes. What made this even more difficult for EME was the fact that this drug dealer had so well fortified his home and himself that he really had become one of the 'Untouchables.' Mr. Dunton had high fences and solid gates with surveillance cameras to make it impossible for anyone to enter his residence without his consent.

On top of that, he had an armed security guard always at his side. Grajeda thought of himself as a sophisticated hit man, but it infuriated him that he couldn't get close to this particular drug dealer. It was well known that EME was irritated that they couldn't get someone close to Mr. Dunton. It made EME look impotent that a man who weighed over 500 pounds couldn't come within the sites of EME.

When Gomez became aware of the EME dilemma, he stepped up to the plate saying that he was an acquaintance of Mr. Dunton and could easily get inside his property. Gomez thought that this was the perfect time to approach EME with 'Let's Make a Deal.' All Gomez wanted was the "Green Light" to be turned off of him if he was able to get a hit man in Dunton's residence. EME had to weigh who they disliked the most and who they wanted to eliminate the most.

EME didn't like being in this type of position; however, they couldn't afford to have such a large dealer refusing to pay his taxes. The Mexican Mafia begrudgingly agreed to lift the "Green Light" on Gomez on the condition that he, Gomez, would assist in carrying out the "Green Light" against Dunton.

The pressure was on Gomez. He made contact with Dunton and convinced him to allow him to meet with him to discuss business. Dunton immediately contacted his bodyguard Acosta to make sure he would be available to be present at any such meeting.

As stated earlier, Gomez was able to convince Dunton to allow him to bring Grajeda with him. The other unknown was the fact that Acosta the bodyguard somehow allowed Gomez to bring a shotgun into the residence.

CHAPTER 6

INVESTIGATING DRUG DEALER'S MURDER

For six months after Ruben Gomez was released from prison, he was roaming the streets of South Los Angeles killing people in order to make money to support himself. At the time, LAPD homicide had no idea who was committing these indiscriminate murders. There was no distinctive pattern and all the murders occurred where there were no witnesses. Gomez was doing his crimes in different neighborhoods against people who didn't know who he was. There was no one who seemed to be able to stop these unprovoked killings.

It was around 4:00 a.m. on July 1, 1997, that a LAPD dispatcher received a 9-1-1 call to go to Mr. Dunton's residence in San Pedro. When the police responded they found that Dunton and Acosta had been shot with a shotgun and that Dunton's body was seated on a sofa and Acosta was lying on the floor. A CSI technician dusted various parts of the apartment for latent prints. Gomez's prints were matched to latent prints found on the table top, the inside of the kitchen door, and the doorframe of the hallway; his palm prints were found on the back of a chair.

Also found in the apartment were several expended shotgun shells. One was found next to the sofa where Mr. Dunton was seated.

The next day after the double shooting, Gomez showed up at his cousin's house in Long Beach carrying a six-shot pump-action shotgun. The cousin hadn't seen him in eight years, so she thought his appearance was strange. After letting him in the house, she immediately went next door to a neighbor and called the police. In short order, the police arrived and arrested Gomez. When they searched the room where Gomez had entered, they found a shotgun.

The detectives concentrated on Dunton's residence and wanted to interview neighbors or anyone who was around at the time of the double homicide. Surprisingly, they learned that a druggie was staying in one of the other bedrooms. The detectives interviewed him and he gave inconsistent statements as to who was present in the residence at the time of the shooting. He did say that Gomez was present in the apartment during the shooting; however, the doper had gone into another room to shoot up drugs and didn't know who did the shooting. Eventually, after several stories, this witness said that Grajeda was present.

Several days after the murders, Acosta's girlfriend found a note in Acosta's handwriting tucked inside a family Bible which read:

6-30-97

Tuesday morn, Monday nite

Went meet Shady La Rana (Grajeda's moniker)

Don't like meeting at Hueros (Dunton's moniker)

Robert Acosta Spider

From this note, it appears that Acosta was uncomfortable with this meeting at Dunton's residence where Grajeda was going to be present. Acosta didn't know who to turn to but put his thoughts in a family Bible where the note would be found by the user of the Bible.

The detectives came across another witness who claimed to have taken Grajeda to Dunton's residence earlier in the day. This witness related that Grajeda told him that he was going to take Dunton out since he hadn't been paying his taxes to EME. Several days later this witness confronted Grajeda as to what really happened at Dunton's apartment at the time of the shooting. This witness said that Grajeda acknowledged that he had killed Dunton and Acosta.

CHAPTER 7 DETECTIVES MET WITH DA

In order to convict both Gomez and Grajeda, an extraordinary prosecutor would be needed. This case was complicated by the fact that it involved at least five murders with separate crime scenes. Since EME members were involved, the witnesses would be hesitant to testify in open court where EME members would be present. Another factor the prosecutor would be faced with was the fact that some of the victims were drug dealers who would be less than sympathetic in the eyes of the jurors. Some jurors might take the position that the drug dealers had created their own problems, and those jurors would be less likely to convict.

Tony Manzella had just finished prosecuting one of the EME Carnales who ordered the death of a person which resulted in a massacre of a family including young children. Tony called Sal LaBarbera, the head detective of South Bureau Homicide, to see if they had any pending EME cases that would fit the requirements for the DA's Major Crimes Division. The detective mentioned the Gomez and Grajeda matter that they were still investigating. However, he admitted that it was full of monumental problems but he was more than happy to let Tony review it.

Tony and his paralegal, Ruth, got in Tony's BMW and drove down to the South Homicide Bureau to examine the police reports. After a short briefing, Tony grabbed a stack of reports and started glancing over them. After he had digested the content, he would hand it to Ruth, his paralegal, and tell her to take notes summarizing the report. After several hours, Tony went over to Sal's cluttered desk and asked him when he could meet with the numerous detectives assigned to each of the homicides.

Tony's request was like music to the ears of a seasoned homicide detective who wasn't used to prosecutors coming to their Homicide Bureau to review cases. Sal didn't want to lose this opportunity and said that he would have all the assigned homicide detectives in his office at any time. Tony looked over to Ruth and asked what his schedule was for the next day. She reminded Tony that he had a sentencing hearing in the morning but was free for the afternoon.

Tony thanked Ruth for the info and said, "Let's make it tomorrow at 1:00." Tony apologetically asked if he could take copies of the Dunton Acosta homicide. He admitted to Sal that he was a little confused as to the time sequence of events. Sal was shocked and surprised someone from downtown was taking an interest in any of their cases. His response was, "Take whatever you need."

At that time, LAPD South Homicide Bureau was averaging one new homicide case every day. Most of them were gang shootings, which consumed much of investigation time but resulted in no criminal charges being filled. The next day at five minutes before 1:00 p.m. Tony and Ruth again returned and walked into the lobby of the South Homicide Bureau where he and Ruth were immediately escorted back to Sal's office, which was jam-packed with detectives. Because of the size of the group, it was decided to move everyone to the conference room. These homicide detectives picked up their green three-hole Murder Books and hurriedly congregated in the conference room, sitting at its long table.

Initially, some of the newer homicide detectives were wondering who the hell was this hotshot prosecutor who wanted to meet with them about their unsolved murder cases. Since Tony had had a court appearance in the morning, he was wearing a striped dress shirt with a crimson tie and a tweed sports coat. He is medium weight and height, giving the appearance of a man in his 50s although in truth he was in his 60s. His face is topped off by a full head of salt and pepper hair. His horn-rimmed glasses kept sliding down his nose, and in an automatic response his index finger pushed them back in place.

He held his briefcase in his left hand as he walked around the table and leaned slightly forward as he extended his right hand to shake hands with each of the detectives. He greeted everyone with a restrained smile and made pleasant small talk with a jovial chuckle. As the 'meet and greet' ended Tony took charge by asking specific questions about each of the homicides.

Tony's approach to filing criminal charges can best be summarized as follows: the prosecutor needs to start thinking like an investigator while the detectives need to start thinking like a prosecutor. Through the years, Tony has learned that prosecutors and detectives don't have to be at odds with each other. What prosecutors and detectives need to do is start thinking like the other side.

Homicide detectives as a group, tend to be suspicious by nature. They often have to deal with the low life of society as well as those who have a reason to hide the truth. Over time homicide detectives become accustomed to prosecutors having negative personalities. All prosecutors say, 'No you can't do that.' Or 'No you don't have enough for a search warrant,' or 'no you don't have enough for a criminal filing.'

However, this prosecutor 'Tony' wasn't saying anything negative but asking questions about things not in their police reports. The detectives were confused since they weren't used to Tony's personal approach. After several hours, Tony had made suggestions as to what further investigation and interviews would be helpful. By the end of the afternoon, these detectives were just getting acquainted with one of the most extraordinary prosecutors to ever work for the Los Angeles District Attorney's Office.

The detectives took Tony's suggestions and were able to uncover more evidence. After several weeks of these joint meeting between Tony and the detectives there appeared to be sufficient evidence to justify criminal charges being filed. As a result of everyone's effort, Tony was able to file five murder charges against Gomez and two murders against Grajeda.

CHAPTER 8 WHO IS TONY MANZELLA?

The detectives of the LAPD South Homicide Bureau had to wonder how did this **'Tony Manzella'** take all these 'sow ears and make a silk purse' out of them. Was this prosecutor some type of magician to make magic happen? The answer is that he had developed incredible litigation skills, at the same time amassing extraordinary experience trying difficult cases both as a prosecutor and Defense attorney.

To learn about Tony's background, one has to traverse a continent and visit the state of New Jersey. That was where his grandfather landed when he arrived in America from Naples, Italy. Tony's roots extend deeply into a working-class neighborhood in New Jersey. His father did well in school and ultimately became a lawyer. However, it wasn't easy for his father to practice law since he didn't want to be involved with cases involving the Costa Nostra. As a result, Tony gain firsthand experience with organized crime, but this was definitely in a different format than EME.

As a child Tony excelled academically, and after high school graduation he was able to qualify for and attend the Air Force Academy in Colorado Springs. After graduating from the Academy, he went on to law school at Georgetown, where he found a natural talent for the LAW. Upon leaving law school, he applied for a position with the local DA's Office in New Jersey. Although his father had an active law practice in the state, he wasn't aware how political the DA's Offices were on the east coast. When Tony was told that he needed to contribute $5,000 in order to get an interview with the local DA's Office, he knew it was time to look elsewhere.

At that point, he headed to the West Coast and settled in Los Angeles. In 1967, he applied for a job with the LA DA's Office, where no political contribution was required. I, the author, came into the DA's Office shortly before Tony. I remember when he and I were doing preliminary hearings in the old Hall of Justice. We both thought we were awesome attorneys since we were winning all of our preliminary hearings. What we, as neophyte prosecutors, didn't quite understand was the fact that any attorney could get a ham sandwich held to answer at a preliminary hearing. The burden of proof is much lower than what is required for trial.

It wasn't until later when both of us advanced to the Trial Division that we realize that convincing 12 jurors beyond a reasonable doubt that the defendant was guilty was a much more challenging task than doing prelims. Prosecuting felony cases was where Tony honed his legal skills. He wasn't afraid to take on any type of case, even those that were fraught with problems. He surprised his supervisors and won a number of unwinnable cases.

It wasn't long before the DA's administrators were favorably impressed with Tony's adroit command of the courtroom. He was brought in to assist in the ***Manson Family*** trial, which turned out an invaluable learning experience for Tony. Being a part of such a successful prosecution gave him confidence that he could handle anything assigned to him.

The question was, what made Tony such an exceptional attorney in the courtroom? One factor was that he had an innate understanding of criminal law. At that time, the rules of Search and Seizure were in their infancy and extremely confusing. He had a brilliant mind that was able to grasp the issues and he could expound on the case law that supported that legal issue. He may have been one of those fortunate individuals who have a photographic memory, or just a person who had an instinctive knack for the law.

Besides his knowledge of the law, he had an innate talent of being able to quickly assimilate the facts of any case and compartmentalizes them into blocks of evidence. This talent made him extremely effective when he was cross-exanimating Defense witnesses. When it came to arguing to the jury, he was a master of breaking down the relevant facts into simple terms that the jurors could understand. That was when his blue-collar North New Jersey accent came in handy for him. Even though he always appeared in his immaculate three-piece suit, his tone was down to earth, projecting an authenticity to the jury.

After years of trying one case after another, the DA's Office wanted him to move up into the management ranks. However, Tony resisted and wanted to stay in the courtroom. In the mid-1970s Tony was presented with an opportunity to be a full-time litigator in a civil law firm in downtown Los Angeles. He came to the realization that private practice could give him incredible financial rewards while allowing him to stay in the courtroom doing what he loved.

This transition for Tony worked out well for him, and he quickly rose through the ranks of the law firm to become a full-fledged partner. His old friends in the DA's Office looked on with envy as Tony's career went skyward. He had amassed a reputation as being a WINNER and was considered one of the top litigators in Los Angeles. As a result he made a ton of money.

At the same time, Tony was asked to teach law at the highly regarded Loyola Law School. What this meant was besides being an ace litigator he was a legal scholar on cutting edge case law. He continued to teach law for many years, and many of his students became prominent attorneys while others became judges on the Superior Court. Tony became a unique attorney who was thoroughly knowledgeable as to the law while having practical experience of trying cases in the courtroom.

He had reached the pinnacle of success for one who pursued a legal career. Tony was one of those who thoroughly enjoyed the legal process. He approached a trial like a chess match. He was fascinated by trying to anticipate his opponents' next move and how he was going to confront it. For Tony, a trial was a matching of wits. He believed that an attorney had to be prepared for any option that would or could arise during a trial.

After years of private practice, he became slightly disillusioned. "You take money from one rich guy's pocket and transfer it to another rich guy's pocket." Over time he felt less satisfied trying civil cases for the law firm. Then one day he remembered how much he enjoyed prosecuting cases at the DA's Office. At the same time, his law firm was undergoing significant changes. He had reached a place in his life where he didn't need to earn more money. His children were grown and his wife was well established in her professional career.

He floated a trial balloon to see if he could return to the DA's Office in order to be in the courtroom prosecuting cases. In 1994, the DA was Gil Garcetti, who recognized that the DA's Office needed strong prosecutors for the big cases. The DA's Office couldn't compensate Tony as to what he was making at his civil law firm. However, the money or salaries were a non-issue for Tony.

As the issues were being worked out, Tony was explaining to people at his law firm what he had planned to do. One of the paralegals, named Ruth, who was about to retire mentioned to Tony that she would love to accompany him over to the DA's Office. Since Tony is one of those people who understand the importance of teamwork, he agreed to bring her along to the DA's Office. Because of civil service rules, the DA's Office couldn't hire her as a paralegal.

Tony liked the idea of having Ruth as his sidekick, and he agreed to pay her half of what he was being paid by the DA's Office. The end result was that the DA's Office acquired an incredible, dynamic duo; however, it was unclear what cases they would be assigned to do.

When Tony and Ruth arrived, they were given several gang cases to handle. As messy as these cases were, Tony approached them by working hand and hand with the detectives. It wasn't long before Tony was back in the groove. He said prosecuting cases was like riding a bicycle: it all comes back after riding around the block just one time.

CHAPTER 9 LEARNING EXPERIENCE FROM MACIEL CASE

It wasn't long before Tony had his so-called 'sea legs' back. In Tony's situation, he really does have 'sea legs' since he is a consummate sailor on the weekends when he relaxes on his 42-foot sailboat, which he takes pride in keeping in immaculate condition.

However, when the DA's Office first brought Tony back as a prosecutor it found itself in a difficult situation. One of their top prosecutors, John Monaghan, was prosecuting an EME case in the Pomona Courthouse when a reliable informant explained that EME had a contract to kill the prosecutor personally or kill members of his family.

Immediately the DA's Office had to move John Monaghan and his family from their home and place them under 24-hour protection. Monaghan was finishing up the trial of the two killers and was about to start trial on the EME Carnales who ordered the killings. The DA's Office, for the safety of prosecutor Monaghan and his family, decided to reassign the main part of the case to someone else.

Depending on how one looks at it, Tony was the fortunate or unfortunate one who was assigned to the case of Luis Pelon Maciel, a high EME official who had ordered a "Green Light" on Gustito Aguirre. Aguirre was a long-time member of EME who was growing older and was looking for a way to drop out of the gang life. The police had obtained a search warrant for Aguirre's house, where they found a cache of illegal weapons hidden under the closet floor. At this stage in his life, all he wanted was to see his adorable daughter safely grow up. He recognized that if he returned to prison he would never see his daughter grow up. He wanted to quit EME and start a new life somewhere else

Maciel was in prison, but he directed two EME soldiers to carry out the hit on Aguirre. These EME killers spotted Aguirre on the street, and as they approached him he ran into a friend's house. The killers were able to corner Aguirre and execute him on the spot. In the process, the assassins came into contact with a couple in the apartment with their children. The assassins knew that EME permitted killers to kill anyone present who could be a witness to the original execution. They quickly turned the guns on the couple and killed them both.

What happened next created an unbelievable controversy. The one shooter turned his gun on the screaming five-year-old and fired, killing him. Without giving it any thought, the shooter turned to the six-month-old who was to the side and with rapid fire riddled the tiny infant's body with lead.

Because the killing of the children was so unnecessary, the police were able to obtain sufficient evidence from witnesses. The two shooters were prosecuted by John Monaghan, who at the time was in charge of the Hardcore Gang Unit in the Pomona DA's Office. (John Monaghan was featured in your author's book titled ***The Top Gun Prosecutor).*** Monaghan was fearless in the prosecution of both killers.

So that is the long and short story how Tony Manzella ended up prosecuting one of the bosses of EME. What was extraordinary about this prosecution was the obvious fact that no one wanted to testify against Luis Pelon Maciel, an EME Carnale. This was especially true due to the fact that Maciel held such a high position in EME. Tony didn't waver under the pressure and was able in presenting the evidence to figure out a way to convict Maciel of first-degree murder even though he was locked up in state prison at the time of the killing.

What was even more remarkable was the fact that Tony asked the jury to impose the death penalty on Maciel, which the jury recommend without any hesitation. The result of this Maciel case was that Tony learned the key to prosecuting EME cases. He realized that the tenets of EME possessed the seed for its self-destruction. Since EME is so prone to issue "Green Lights" on its wayward members, those people recognize that they are the walking dead. Their only hope to survive is to work with law enforcement and enter the witness protection program. Tony recognized how these disenchanted EME members can be used to build strong cases against the leadership in EME by giving these witnesses their only hope for life through Witness Protection.

Tony is a unique attorney who recognizes the dynamic effect of a trial. To him, it is like a chess match and the challenge is to anticipate his opponent's next move and be prepared for it. This is why for Tony it is so important to be prepared for any contingency. In Tony's mind, he figures out all the options and is prepared for whichever one the opposing counsel selects. What Tony had learned from 20 years of private practice was how to master this chess match.

Tony having grown in New Jersey where he saw the Cosa Nostra take over and control the community. Tony could see how the Mexican Mafia was trying to assert itself and get a foothold in the various barrios in Los Angeles. He understood how important it was to stop the spread of the authority of EME. Tony felt the battle against EME was a consequential fight. Some people compare EME to a giant octopus trying to strangle a community, and Tony saw his role as the person with a meat clever trying to cut off one of its tentacles.

CHAPTER 10
PREPARING FOR TRIAL

Tony worked with the detectives to coordinate evidence to see if they could build a case against Gomez. It was clear that no one knew how many homicides Gomez had committed. Their objective was to cull through those homicides that had some connecting evidence to Gomez. Then at some point, Tony and the detectives had to agree which murders had a chance of resulting in a conviction. Some of the killings looked suspicious but realistically no hard evidence had been forthcoming. At that point, Tony took those weaker cases and placed them in another stack on his desk and pushed them to the back. He didn't want to waste his or the detectives' time on a case that didn't have any prospect of leading to a conviction.

This could be a form of so-called 'tough love.' Some detectives spin their wheels on cases that have no likelihood of ever having enough evidence for court. Tony recognized that some detectives become personally attached to their homicide cases and they just continue to spend precious time on cases that seem to fall into the big 'Black Holes' in space. Tony has a sixth sense of knowing what cases have potential and which ones are futile. Not all detectives appreciate hearing "No, your case is never going to fly."

Tony had spent weeks reviewing reports and going over photos and potential evidence. As to the robbery/murders cases involving victims Patel, Escareno, and Luna, Tony filed murder charges against Gomez. As to the killings of Dunton and Acosta, both Gomez and Grajeda were jointly charged with those murders. Gomez was already in custody on a parole hold, and it was only Grajeda that needed an arrest warrant.

Within a short time, Grajeda was arrested and both defendants were proceeding through the court system. Both received appointed Defense attorneys who needed time to prepare for trial. During this time, Tony was meticulously building his legal case for trial. He believes in establishing a solid foundation for every piece of evidence he presents to the jury. Tony believes in the teamwork approach. As stated earlier he spends an inordinate amount of time with each detective. He is the type of attorney who wants to know everything and doesn't want to have any surprises pop up during trial. When surprises happen during trial the game plan has to change, which throws things out of balance.

After Tony obtained enough information that was necessary from the detectives, he returned to his office in the Criminal Courts Building on the 17th floor. His actual office in the Major Crimes Division is slightly larger than a postage stamp but a mere fraction of the size of his office at his old law firm. When he was a senior partner, his office windows revealed the entire landscape of Los Angeles and Hollywood. However, his DA's office was windowless, with just enough room for two county-issued desks facing each other and a couple of dented file cabinets stuck in the corner. Tony didn't complain but merely smiled and said that he was certain one of the desks in the room was the same one he had 30 years ago when he was a novice deputy district attorney.

In that jam-packed office, both Tony and Ruth went to work. Tony started setting up a complete Discovery file for the Defense. In order to prevent the Defense from later claiming that they had not been given a certain report or document, he had Ruth 'Bates-stamp' each page on the bottom. When Tony turns over all documents to the Defense, he requires the Defense attorney to sign a document showing that he has reviewed and declares that he received all the Bates-stamped documents. (A Bates Stamp is an automatic stamp which is used to number the pages of documents in sequential order.) As more documents become available, the Bates Stamp is set at the next number in the series and continues to mark the pages in order.

Tony then started preparing all the pretrial motions he would be filing with the court. He also anticipated what motions the Defense would make and he had Ruth prepare the Response. Since Tony had been teaching at the law school for years, he had Points and Authority prepared for almost every predictable legal battle.

Tony and Ruth, his paralegal, almost seem inseparable. Some have claimed that Ruth is Tony's secret weapon. There is no way one person can possibly read and remember thousands of pages of police reports and transcripts of interviews. After Tony has read the material, he gives it to Ruth, who files it in a set of binders she organizes by subject matter. When Tony needs a report or piece of evidence in court, he respectfully turns to Ruth, who immediately hands him the item.

Since this dynamic duo has been working together for many years, Ruth can anticipate what Tony will need before he has even said a word. At times Tony has to stop and smile at how the two of them think in unison. Having this type of working rapport frees Tony up to concentrate on what is going on in court and not worrying about the logistics of finding things.

Other prosecutors claim that it is unfair that Tony has a paralegal at his beck and call. None of the other prosecutors have their own paralegals, and if they have access to one that paralegal is shared with the other prosecutors. Unfortunately for the other prosecutors, none of them are rich enough to personally pay for the services of a paralegal like Tony, who pays half of his salary to Ruth who doesn't receive a penny from the DA's Office.

Even though both Tony and Ruth are married to others, they have a unique bond of helping each other out. The bottom line is that they both enjoy what they are doing because when they work together, they operate like a fine-tuned Ferrari ready for a race. I, the author, have known and worked with Tony for over 30 years. Later when I was working in Major Crimes Division, my office was across from them. As a result, I could see and hear how they worked together and complemented each other.

One example of how they were inseparable was when Tony came down with laryngitis and he couldn't speak a word. He was in the middle of trial and they had crucial witnesses scheduled to testify. The judge didn't want the case delayed and was constantly putting pressure on both attorneys to finish up their part of the case. Tony whispered into the microphone, on the counsel table, that he would continue calling witnesses by using Ruth's voice. The judge thought for a minute whether he could legally permit Ruth, a non-attorney, to ask questions to a witness in open court in front of a jury. As the judge was hesitating, Tony leaned forward to the microphone. He uttered, in his almost inaudible voice, that all the questions would be his and he would write them out on a piece of paper and Ruth would be merely using her voice to read them.

The impatient judge replied, "Okay, as long as it doesn't delay the trial." Within a few minutes, the jury was back in their seats and Ruth was asking questions of the witness on the stand. Every few moments, Ruth would pretend to look down on a note pad and then ask her question. She was so knowledgeable about what questions to ask because days before she had typed up all the questions for Tony. After several minutes Ruth was rattling off questions on her own. The judge didn't seem concerned, and Tony leaned back in his chair. A big grin came over Tony's face as he pondered the thought that he had been replaced by 'Ruth the Paralegal.'

CHAPTER 11 TRIAL

Tony understood the dynamics of the courtroom. He understood the importance of drama. Merely having all the facts in an attorney's favor doesn't assure that he will win his case before a jury. All the jurors have watched dozens of movies and TV series, and in their own minds they have an image of what they expect a judge and attorneys should look like. That is why Tony believes in dressing the part he will be playing. Jurors want to see a prosecutor look formal as though he is representing the government.

When Tony walks through the courtroom doors, he is decked out in a three-piece dark suit. His tie isn't flashy but bold and solid. He is accompanied by Ruth in her business suit with her short dark hair neatly combed back. When the two of them enter the courtroom, no one has any doubts which side they are on. However, what sets the tone for the courtroom is the large two-rack cart that Tony pushes in front of him. The bottom rack is neatly arranged with folders all in alphabet order. The top rack contains green three-ring binders with the numbers one through ten on them.

Tony is well known for his so-called 'LawMobile.' There is a myth in the Criminal Courts Building that when Tony wheels his cart in the courtroom the juries get the impression that these defendants must be guilty. Even though that isn't true, when Tony and Ruth sit at counsel table, they park the LawMobile between them so both of them have at their fingertips easy access to all the facts and law that applies to the case.

This is a photo of Tony's LawMobile parked in his office ready to go to court. The author's office was across from Tony's office and on many occasions I could hear Tony coming and going to court by the squeaky wheels on his LawMobile. I offered to bring in oil to stop the clatter from the cart. However, Tony resisted claiming that the noise caused people to get out of his way like at the airport where the carts purposely make noise as they careen through the boarding area.

Early in the year 2000, the trial commenced in Judge William Ponders' courtroom on the 9th floor of CCB (Criminal Courts Building). Jury selection began with both sides trying to find the perfect set of jurors for their side. However, both sides exercised preemptive challenges to knock off the jurors they thought would favor the other side. Eventually, both sides ended up with jurors that they may not like but felt they could live with. Since the DA's Office was seeking the Death Penalty as to defendant Gomez, the jury selection process was protracted.

Tony loves the jury selection process since it is made up of a subjective gut reaction. Since Tony had picked hundreds of juries, he had an excellent intuition as to determining which jurors were likely to convict. The term 'profiling' has received a bad rap when it is done for racial reasons. The courts prohibit any type of racial profiling. However, every human being uses profiling in everything they do. This is particularly true when a person meets someone new. Of course, every good salesperson looks at a potential customer and profiles whether they are likely to buy their product or not. Tony knows how to listen to potential jurors as they answer questions. He is also looking at the person's body language as well as their disposition of interacting with their fellow jurors.

After all sides had accepted the jury, Judge Pounders didn't waste any time and asked the prosecution to give its Opening Statement. Tony stood up and looked at the jurors and in a soft but serious voice began telling the story of what his case was all about. After several minutes, he started explaining the charges against the two defendants. Tony knew that the jurors would get confused as to which charges applied only to Gomez and which involved both defendants.

Tony used this visual to help the jurors become familiar with each of the defendants.

First Tony held up a poster board for the jurors to see which contained photos of both defendants with their name spelled underneath. Tony knew he couldn't afford any of the jurors to mix up who was who. Tony remembered when he first talked to the detectives at the Homicide Bureau, he became confused himself regarding the charges.

Tony picked up a poster-size chart leaning against his LawMobile and carried it over to the courtroom's large blackboard (courtroom blackboards are really white which use black Marks-a-lots). He leaned the so-called 'Charges Chart' against the board and walked jurors through each line. First he started explaining the Charge and code sections that applied and next mentioned the name of the victim. He finished off each line by mentioning the date of the crime and which defendant was charged with that crime.

PEOPLE v. RUBEN GOMEZ and ARTURO GRAJEDA

COUNT	PENAL CODE	CHARGE	VICTIM	DATE	DEFENDANT
1	211	Robbery	Xavier Salcedo	2/25/97	Gomez
3	187(a)	Murder	Rajandra Patel	5/26/97	Gomez
4	211	Robbery	Rajandra Patel	5/26/97	Gomez
5	207(a)	Kidnapping	Rajandra Patel	5/26/97	Gomez
6	187(a)	Murder	Jesus Escareno	6/9/97	Gomez
7	211	Robbery	Jesus Escareno	6/9/97	Gomez
8	187(a)	Murder	Raul Luna	6/10/97	Gomez
9	211	Robbery	Raul Luna	6/10/97	Gomez
10	187(a)	Murder	Robert Dunton	7/1/97	Grajeda & Gomez
11	187(a)	Murder	Robert Acosta	7/1/97	Grajeda & Gomez

This is the Charges Chart Tony used in his Opening Statement & Argument.

When Tony was certain that the jurors understood the basic facts of the case, he moved on to explain when exactly each murder occurred. In order to convict Gomez of all the robbery/murders charges, Tony needed to show how they were all clustered together within a period of three months. In order not to lose any of the jurors, he placed three charts listing the months all in a row on the blackboard. Tony took his gold Cross pen out of his pocket and used it to point to the 25th day of the month of May. By that time, all the jurors' eyes were focused on the little square on the bottom that said, 'Patel last seen.'

Then Tony walked the jurors through the rest of the month of May and then over to the next chart with the month of June when most of the criminal activity occurred. The jurors could now visualize when the various crimes occurred as well as when evidence was found. Also, the calendars showed the dates when defendant Gomez made statements to others. Those statements would be instrumental in the prosecution of the case.

1997 MAY 1997

Sun.	Mon.	Tues.	Wed.	Thur.	Fri.	Sat.
				1 Lucado moves in w/ Huero	2	3
4	5	6	7	8	9	10
11	12	13	14	15	16	17
18	19	20	21	22	23	24
25 Patel last seen	26 Patel's body found	27	28 Patel's car found	29	30	31

1997 JUNE 1997

Sun.	Mon.	Tues.	Wed.	Thur.	Fri.	Sat.
1	2	3	4	5	6	7
8 Patel murder weapon recovered	9 Escareno shot	10 Luna shot	11 Escareno car found	12	13	14
15 Gomez moves in w/ Huero	16	17	18	19	20	21
22	23 Grajeda starts visiting	24	25	26	27	28
29 Boxer visit	30 Grajeda & Gandara visit					

1997 JULY 1997

Sun.	Mon.	Tues.	Wed.	Thur.	Fri.	Sat.
		1 Dunton & Acosta shot	2 Gomez arrested	3 Grajeda admission to Gandara	4	5
6	7	8	9 Gomez calls Arce	10	11	12
13	14	15	16	17 Arce visits Gomez at county jail	18	19
20	21	22	23	24	25	26 Grajeda speaks w/ Kimberly Bivins
27	28	29	30	31		

This shows the various months when the murders occurred. Tony used this to show the shortness of time between the murders.

The prosecution's Opening Statement gave the jurors an understanding of what they would be hearing from civilian and expert witnesses over the next two months of the trial. In order to tell the prosecution side of the story, Tony called several civilian witnesses who might be described as having questionable backgrounds. One of the key witnesses admitted he was shooting up drugs in another room when he heard the blasts of the shotgun. Tony used him because this witness placed Gomez and Grajeda in Dunton's apartment at the time of the shooting. This witness didn't want to testify to seeing the actual shooting but claimed he came out afterward and saw the two victims shot to death. He was the person who ran to a drug store to call the police and tell them about the shooting.

After Tony's direct examination, both Defense attorneys attacked the prosecution's key witness's credibility, especially since he had told numerous versions to the detectives. Tony smiled to himself, realizing that when it was time for him to argue the case to the jurors, he would explain that in hell you don't find stellar witnesses like Mother Teresa. Another prosecution witness claimed that he had taken Grajeda to Dunton's apartment in the late afternoon and Gomez and others were present. This witness went on to say that later Grajeda admitted to taking care of Dunton and Acosta since they weren't paying their EME taxes.

Again, the Defense hammered on the fact that this DA witness was trying to get a favor from the prosecutors on a sentencing matter he was facing in another court. Tony took the Defense's credibility attack in stride. At the end of the case, Tony would argue that everything that this second witness testified to was corroborated by other independent evidence.

When Tony put on his next civilian witness, he thought it doesn't get any better than this. The witness was Acosta's girlfriend, who testified that she found a handwritten note by her boyfriend in her family Bible. The note illustrated how concerned Acosta was in having to meet with Gomez and Grajeda.

However, Tony couldn't wait to put on Gomez's cousin. She testified that when she saw Gomez bring a shotgun into her place, she immediately called the police, who came out and arrested Gomez. Tony wanted the jury to understand what a brave act Gomez's cousin had performed. Her actions of getting Gomez off the streets undoubtedly saved many lives.

The next group of witnesses pertained to forensic evidence involving finding Gomez's fingerprints at the crime scene and on the recovered shotgun. Then a ballistics expert explained to the jury that the shotgun matched up to the expended shotgun shells found in Dunton's apartment.

With the civilian witness and forensics witnesses out of the way, Tony sat back in his chair knowing his next group of witnesses would mesmerize the jurors. He called Sgt. Valdemar to the witnesses stand. He stated that he was retired from the Los Angeles Sheriff's Department and had been assigned to head up the Prison Gang Unit. Tony asked him to explain the workings and operation of prison gangs, in particular the Mexican Mafia.

For the next hour, Sgt. Valdemar captivated the jurors by telling them what a large footprint EME has over the prison system throughout the country. He discussed how the leadership is housed in the prisons but they continued to operate in every barrio through the use of EME associates and soldiers. Next, he spelled out how vital it was for EME to be able to collect taxes from every Hispanic gang conducting drug business. EME couldn't afford to have drug dealers refuse to pay up. They as an organization have to respond harshly to any wayward dealer.

This witness was followed by Special Agent Duarte from the California Department of Corrections. He testified that defendant Grajeda was an associate of EME and Gomez also was a member or East Side Wilma gang, which owed its allegiance to EME. He used photos of both defendants' tattoos to corroborate the fact that they were gang members.

For some perverted reason, jurors seem to look forward to the testimony of the medical examiners from the Coroner's Office. It may be due to all the TV programs involving forensics. Tony didn't disappoint the jurors and walked the medical examiner through each killing, asking about which injuries were fatal and the possible order of each shot. The bottom line was all five victims were dead and their killings had been done in a brutal fashion.

After a few more witnesses Tony announced that the 'People Rest.' That meant the Defense attorneys could present any evidence that could exonerate either defendant. Grajeda's attorney tried to present evidence of an alibi. He called a woman who said that she was at a friend's home where Grajeda was present. She said that she never saw the defendant Grajeda leave the house during the time of the shooting. Her testimony was compromised when she said that on two occasions that she had left the house briefly. Since Grajeda hadn't been arrested immediately, she couldn't be certain that she was referring to the date of the homicide. Her effectiveness was compromised by her not remembering the critical date.

Finally, the prosecutor and the Defense attorney had rested their cases. Next was the time for Argument. Tony, like all attorneys, loves to argue; however, most attorneys don't understand the subtleties of giving an effective Argument. With Tony's wealth of experience, he knows that jurors have a short interest span. Years earlier, in the 1960s and 1970s when Tony argued to jurors, they were more respectful of the DA since back then jurors were more supportive of law enforcement. However, today jurors are more skeptical of all attorneys and especially suspicious of law enforcement.

Tony, as a result, recognizes that today's jurors require more attention when trying to argue to them. This is why Tony uses the same visual in his Argument as he used in his Opening Statement. He summarizes all the DA witnesses and leaves the jurors with these words: 'With all this evidence against the defendants, they CAN'T be not guilty."

Grajeda's attorney tried to focus the jurors on the testimony of his alibi witness. Gomez's attorney tried to be the devil's advocate in that the DA hadn't proven their case beyond a reasonable doubt. As to the robbery/murders, he hammered on the fact that there weren't any eyewitnesses. One of the robbery/murders was thin on evidence and he clearly pointed that out to the jurors.

Eventually, both sides were finished arguing their case and it was time for Judge Pounder to read the jury instructions. After which the case was truly in the hands of the jury. It was a matter of time waiting for the jury's verdict. From Tony's perspective, everything went the way that Tony and Ruth had planned it. The preparation paid off and there were only a few glitches, and those that did occur were quickly handled and the case had moved forward.

After considerable deliberation, the jury buzzed indicating they had a verdict. At that point, Tony realized that there was no hung jury, meaning that these two killers could be either back on the street within minutes or in prison for the rest of their lives. Tony had a momentary thought that maybe he should have permitted both

Gomez and Grajeda to plead guilty to second-degree murder, which would have guaranteed they would be off the streets for 15 years.

When the courtroom clerk read the guilty verdicts against Gomez, Tony felt relieved. Tony didn't feel any regret when the jury came back with a not guilty verdict as to one of the robbery/murders. However, Tony's ears were waiting to hear the jury's decision as to Grajeda, the person who didn't pull the trigger but was merely aiding and abetting in the murders. When he heard the word GUILTY as to the murders of Dunton and Acosta, Tony leaned back in his chair and looked over to Ruth with a big smile saying, 'Well, we did it.'

Since the jury found the special allegation true, that meant that Grajeda would receive a sentence of life in prison without the possibility of parole. Although Tony and Ruth had finished the criminal proceedings against Grajeda, they still had to proceed with the Death Penalty phase of the case for Gomez.

CHAPTER 12 SHOULD GOMEZ RECEIVE THE DEATH PENALTY?

With that all behind Tony, he started to litigate the real issue of the case, and that was whether the defendant Gomez should receive the Death Penalty. Tony knew from experience that downtown Los Angeles juries seldom return a verdict of Death. His challenge was to persuade all 12 jurors that Gomez was one of those rare individuals who truly deserved and earned the Death Penalty.

The Death Penalty phase of the case began as to Gomez. Tony made an Opening Statement to the jury explaining how they would be considering whether the Aggravating evidence against Gomez substantially outweighed whatever Mitigating evidence Gomez's attorney would present in court.

Tony knew that it was next to impossible to convey to jurors what their job was in deciding whether to recommend a sentence of Life or Death. Since I, your author, had been involved with trying one of the first cases under the new Death Penalty law, I personally knew firsthand the challenge of explaining the entire process to jurors. As a result, I gave Tony one of my old visual aids that I had used to illustrate to the jury the factors that they could and could not consider in determining the appropriate sentence.

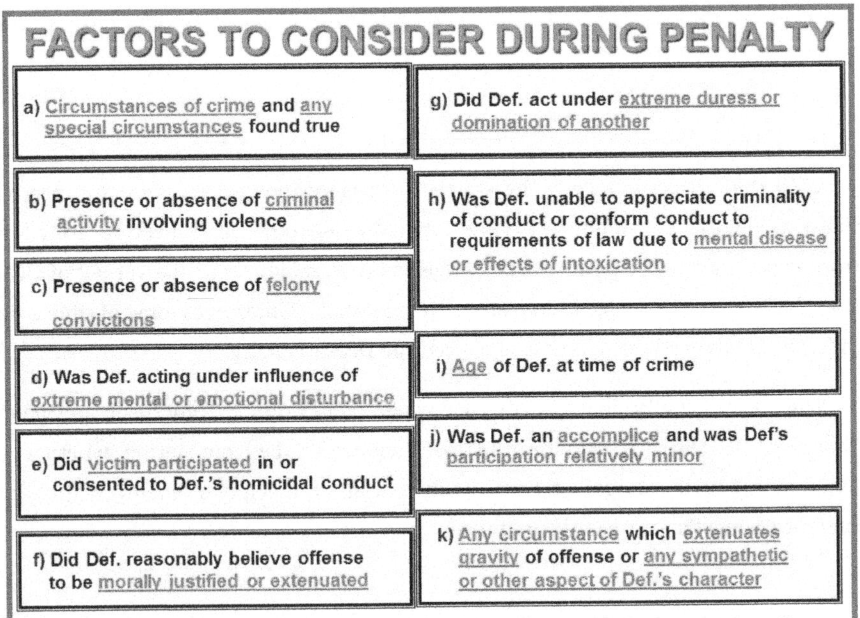

This was the visual Tony used to explain the Aggravating and Mitigating factors that the jurors could consider

When it came time to present evidence, Tony introduced numerous prison documents proving what crimes and dates Gomez had been convicted of violent acts. Also, he introduced prison and jail records showing Gomez had been involved in various acts of violence while in custody.

In order to prove up certain acts of violence, prison guards and jailers were called to testify to various attacks he had made on guards and inmates.

When it came time to argue, Tony pulled out a chart showing the jury what factors that they could consider as Aggravation. Tony emphasized three points under a) Circumstances of Crime. One of these was the "Frequency," as the defendant had killed five people in a period of 37 days. Next, he touched upon "Callousness" in that Gomez shot the victims in the head or throat, the shots were fired at close range, and he used a shotgun or semi-automatic pistol. Finally, he finished this part of his Argument by discussing the defendant's "Motive," which was Greed done in a Cowardly manner.

AGGRAVATION

a. Circumstances of crime?

Frequency

- Killed five people in 37 days

Callousness

- Shot in head (throat)
- Contact or close range
- Shotgun and semi-automatic pistol

Motive

- Greed
- Cowardice

b. Criminal violence?

Jorge Lucho robbery 4-4-91
Chad Millan stabbing 1998
Urine on Vanderleek 11-99
Montoya head butting12-99
Montoya slashing 12-99
Threats against jail and transportation deputies 12-99

c. Felony convictions?

12-91 Assault by state prison inmate with deadly weapon on 10-08-91

12-91 Possession of deadly weapon by state prison inmate on 11-02-91

In the Death Penalty phase Tony used this to chart to show the Aggravation evidence against defendant Gomez

Tony knew that the jurors might not be able to identify with some of the victims in the case. Some jurors most likely wouldn't think it was a great loss that Dunton the big drug dealer and his bodyguard Acosta were killed for not paying their taxes to the Mexican Mafia. As some jurors might say, "Oh Well!" Tony realized that he had to have the jurors direct their attention to the other criminal activity that defendant Gomez had been involved in starting back in 1991.

The next visual aid that Tony turned to was titled "Chronology" which was a poster-size chart showing Gomez's criminal activities. This list gave the facts starting with the dates and the type of crime he was involved in. It also listed all the time he spent in state prison and what violent acts he committed while in custody.

CHRONOLOGY

04/04/91	Jorge Lucho robbery
06/12/91	Received at state prison
10/08/91	Assault by state prison inmate
11/02/91	Possession of deadly weapon by state prison inmate
1992	State prison
1993	State prison
1994	State prison
1995	State prison
1996	State prison
01/10/97	Paroled from state prison to Los Angeles county
02/25/97	Salcedo robbery
05/25/97	Patel murder
06/09/97	Escareno murder
06/10/97	Luna murder
07/01/97	Dunton/Acosta murders
07/02/97	Arrested
06/01/98	Chad Millan stabbing
11/20/99	Vanderleek attack
12/14/99	Montoya head butting
12/15/99	Montoya slashing
12/21/99	Threats

This visual was used by the prosecutor to show all the acts of violence by Gomez.

Tony wasn't naive as to how unpopular the Death Penalty was among certain members of society. He knew that many people made the argument that merely placing a person in prison without the possibility of parole was sufficient to keep society safe from any monstrous, violent person. Tony then showed the jury the next chart, showing how dangerous Gomez is both in and out of prison.

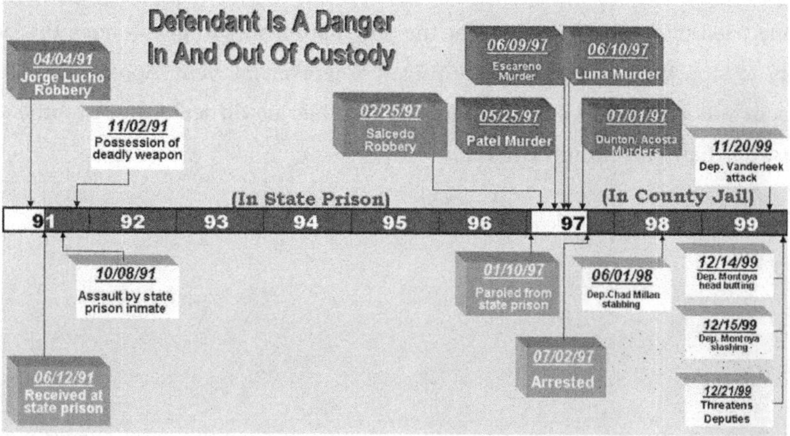

This is the Visual that Tony used to show how Gomez was a danger in and out of custody.

Tony wanted a more dramatic way to get the jurors' attention in regard to how dangerous Gomez was to society. What Tony did was create a theme for the case, that being "Defendant Is A Danger In And Out Of Custody." Tony used this chart in his closing argument. He wanted to dramatically show the jury that the other alternative, which was "Life in Prison Without Possibility of Parole," was too dangerous. This would put other inmates and guards at risk for as long as defendant

Gomez would live. That period of risk could include however long Gomez lived, such as for the next 40 to 50 years.

With this Timeline, the jurors could see that in 1991 the defendant went to state prison for robbery. Even then, society wasn't safe from the defendant's violence in that during that time he Possessed a Deadly Weapon and also Assaulted another inmate. Then finally after five years in prison, he was placed back into society on parole. Within about a month of his parole, he committed another robbery. Within the next several months he murdered five people. After his arrest and while being held in County Jail, he stabbed a guard, and on several other occasions he attacked more guards.

Tony tried to show the jurors that the only option was to give Gomez the Death Penalty to stop the reign of violence he left wherever he went. Apparently, Tony's argument was persuasive enough since the jury had no difficulty in recommending the Death Penalty for RUBEN GOMEZ.

CHAPTER 13 TONY'S SUCCESSFUL PROSECUTION

After the case was over, Tony wouldn't say whether this was the "Perfect Case" that he had always wanted to try. He took it all in stride and immediately started discussing some legal points with Ruth about their next case. For Tony, trying a case in court isn't a personal thing. He doesn't do it to prove to others how good he is or how smart he is. He is truly the consummate trial lawyer.

He understands the LAW and RULES OF EVIDENCE. He has mastered his craft of how to be persuasive to 12 lay jurors. By trial and error, he has learned that the side that wins isn't the one who shouts the loudest or longest. His effectiveness is not due to an ego that has to win at all costs. He and Ruth have combined in a teamwork effort to build cases from the ground up with old-fashioned preparation. Thank God, Tony came back to work on the prosecution side. Also, Tony will admit that he doesn't mind the fact that his efforts result in some BAD DUDES being taken off the street, making for a safer community.

PROSECUTOR ANTHONY 'TONY' MANZELLA

The Mexican Mafia Case

(Gigantic Case, Huge Impact & Massive Headaches)

CHAPTER 14 NOT A GOOD DAY FOR MUPPET

One might call him a wannabe gangster at the rookie age of 15. Randy Morales, better known as Muppet, was the type of kid who wanted to size up what was going on in the barrio. Quickly he learned that the dope dealers were the ones who had all the money. They cruised around in flashy cars and were surrounded by gorgeous women eager to please. When these dealers mingled with others they were always treated with the utmost respect. Muppet wasn't a slow learner. He could see that if he wanted to have the good life and be held in high esteem, he needed to learn how to be a drug dealer.

Muppet was smart enough to gravitate to those who had made it. Alex Aguirre was a highly successful drug dealer who just happened to be a Carnale in the Mexican Mafia (better known as the EME.) Muppet followed Alex around like a puppy dog in order to learn the details of the drug business. After spending months watching Alex run his lucrative drug business, Muppet felt he was ready to try his hand selling dope. Like any naïve kid, he thought he could make some fast money selling cocaine. He eased into the business slowly, dealing in small amounts. It became apparent to him that there was more profit when dealing in larger quantities. There was a graduation process he went through, and he was able to do mid-level deals.

August 21, 1995, he was transporting a substantial amount of coke for a transaction that would be exceedingly profitable for him. However, this time something went wrong. As he was driving to the deal, he was stopped by a traffic officer. The officer asked Muppet if he had any objection to him looking in his car. Muppet was starting to sweat since he didn't know how to handle such a request.

Should he say 'No?' If he did that, the cop would be suspicious that he was in possession of something illegal. If he said 'Yes,' what were the chances his search would be thorough enough to find his dope? He had to make a split-second decision as to what to say. He had stuffed the large amount of cocaine up under the passenger seat. What was the likelihood that this traffic officer would check under the passenger seat?

Muppet's response was, "Why not, as long as it doesn't take too long since I have to get to school." The officer walked around the car and reached into the glove box and shuffled through a stack of disorganized papers. He continued to check out the passenger side of the car. Within minutes, the officer pulled out a large sandwich bag filled with dozens of little bindles of white powdery substance.

Muppet didn't know how to respond to the officer as he came over to Muppet and cuffed his hands behind him. He was taken to the police station to talk to the narcotic detectives. Since he was a juvenile, Muppet was transported to Los Padrinos Juvenile Detention Center. There he was interrogated by the detectives. They explained to him what type of sentence he was facing for carrying such a large amount of cocaine. He was told that he could end up in the Youth Authority camp for several years. Muppet lacked any personal knowledge of what really happened to first-time juvenile offenders. The detectives put the fear of God in him by telling him that by having such a large quantity he likely wouldn't see his family for a long time.

Muppet had to wonder where he went wrong. Alex, the big drug dealer, hadn't discussed with him how he should act when caught by the police. Muppet the rookie drug dealer had reached one of those moments in life when he was all by himself and he was faced with the biggest decision of his life. The detectives sufficiently petrified Muppet, who now felt forsaken by his homies. The detectives stepped away, indicating that they had to do the paperwork to book him into custody. Muppet, the infantile gangster, was all alone in a police interrogation room. The detectives made sure the door was locked from the outside when they left. Muppet sat by himself in this drab room whose dirty-white walls seemed to be closing in on him. His adolescent mind was racing a hundred miles per hour in hopes of finding a way out of this situation.

Muppet thought of his parents who had tried to protect him. Recently his parents had moved from the gang-infested neighborhood called the Avenues to a better part of the San Fernando Valley. Could he count on them to come to his aid? For several years he had ignored their warnings of the dangers of running with the gang members. His folks wouldn't be sympathetic toward him for being arrested for possession of drugs for sale. His only thought was how his fellow gangsters would handle this type of situation. He remembered some of his homies had bragged how they were able to talk their way out of drug busts by claiming to help the police. He had been told that all the detectives were interested in was catching the so-called big fish.

His mind considered shady characters he knew that he might be willing to give up their names to the police. When the detective came back into the interrogation room, the one detective continued to harp on the fact that he, Muppet, was in big trouble. That detective alluded to the fact that Muppet was a shrewd guy who knew plenty of stuff going down on the streets. One of the detectives suggested that maybe they could help him if he would be willing to help them. Muppet's mind was filled with all the bad dudes he had come across while distributing dope. Could he tell them some names of dope dealers?

Teenager Muppet didn't know how to bargain as an informant. His mind came back with the infamous gangster saying, "A Snitch Belongs in a Ditch." Was he supposed to initiate the conversation as to names he could possibly give to the police? But before he could find the right words to say anything, the one detective started complaining about all the homicides in the Northeast area. The detectives seemed obsessed with the recent shooting of the Sanchez brothers that occurred about two weeks earlier. Muppet remembered some facts of the shooting of those brothers. He didn't think of it as some big deal since the Sanchez brothers were members of a rival gang in Highland Park. Also, Muppet didn't have much sympathy for the brothers since they refused to pay the mandatory 10% taxes to the Mexican Mafia.

The one detective continued to rail about the double murder and seemed to be interested in prying any information out of Muppet. Out of frustration, the detectives were about to terminate the interrogation since they weren't getting any info out of Muppet. Muppet didn't want to waste this opportunity so he wanted to test the waters, but how was he supposed to give information without ending up in a DITCH?

Muppet said he could tell them who was involved, but he wanted to make sure that no one else would ever find out he said anything. He seemed almost paranoid in his fear that someone would find out that he was a snitch. The detectives assured him that whatever he told them would be kept totally confidential. Muppet wasn't buying their promise to keep quiet. He went so far as to say he would talk to them as long as his statements were not written down or tape recorded.

The detectives nodded in agreement and the one put his pen down that he had been using to take notes. The other detective went over to turn off the tape recorder. Then there was a pause in the room as the detectives said, "Okay tell us what you know." Muppet realized that the ball was in his court and he turned his head from side to side looking to see if anyone was around. How was he going to explain what he knew without saying too much?

Muppet leaned over the table and in a hushed voice that was barely audible said that he had heard that it was Javier Marquez, better known as 'Gangster,' who had murdered Yogi and Wicked from Highland Park. The detectives were well familiar with those monikers for Sergio Sanchez and Herman Sanchez. The detectives wanted some form of corroboration that supported what Muppet was saying. The detectives had been burned by arrestees saying anything just to be released. Their question was, how do you know that 'Gangster' did it?

Muppet was so concerned about giving up a name that he wasn't thinking in terms of having to verify the information he had just given them. Muppet's response was that Javier had personally told him shortly after the shootings that he had shot five dudes and planned to shoot more Highland Park gang members. The justification that Javier gave was that the Highland Park gangsters were refusing to pay the Mexican Mafia taxes on their portion of the profits that they made on the sale of narcotics.

The detectives were well aware of the rivalry between the Avenues gangs and the Highland Park gangsters. They were familiar with drive-by shootings between the gangs, but killings done for the benefit of the Mexican Mafia were less common. The more the detectives questioned Muppet, the more they could see that he seemed to have second thoughts about being a Snitch. He emphasized that no way, no how, would he ever testify against Javier. The detectives were pleased that they had gotten the info of Marquez involvement in the killings, but this wasn't going to help them in trying to prosecute Javier for the killing of the Sanchez brothers. Without more information, the detectives stood up and thanked Muppet and assured him that they wouldn't say anything about what he had told them. They agreed not to file any criminal charges for the dope that was found in his car.

Life went on for everyone. The detectives wrote their reports regarding what Muppet had told them. They clearly stated in their report that Muppet wanted the information he had given them to be kept confidential. Javier Marquez was arrested several days later on August 25, 1995, on other charges and not until six months later was he charged with the Sanchez brothers murders. The prosecutor in this Marquez case was in the DA's Hardcore Gangs Division, and he turned over all the police reports he had on Javier Marquez. One of those reports was the so-called Chronological Record that the detectives had written about Muppet's arrest and the information he had given them about Marquez being involved in the Sanchez Brothers shootings. (Although the detectives had told Muppet that they wouldn't mention his statement, they were required to reduce to writing all information they received regarding any and all homicides)

One of the detectives who had filed the murder charges against Marquez was required to go over all the police reports and redact all the names of informants. This task is carried out by the detective using a black Marks-A-Lot pen to cross through the name of the informant. Needless to say, the police detectives aren't thrilled about spending hours blacking out the appropriate names. This can't be left to the clerical staff to do since they wouldn't know which names to cross out.

Every LAPD homicide has what is called the Murder Book, which is given to the prosecutor and copies are given to the Defense attorney. Often these Murder Books will be three or four inches thick depending on how long the detectives have been investigating the case. In other words, the Javier Marquez Murder Book consisted of hundreds of pages, including all types of reports that were generated during the investigation of the crime and the apprehension of the suspect.

CHAPTER 15 TAKING MUPPET FOR A RIDE

When Marquez's attorney received the redacted Murder Book, it was made available to whoever the attorney wanted to give it to. It was unknown when the police report got in the hands of Marquez, but it was sometime after March of 1996. What was unknown to authorities was the fact that **Muppet's name had NOT been redacted from the Murder Book**.

It wasn't long before Javier Gangster Marquez knew who had snitched him off. 'Gangster' by his moniker implied he was a hardened gang member who was considered to be one of the EME associates. Since he was in custody, there was no way he could get out to take care of Muppet. First he had to get the permission from the Carnales in EME to agree that Muppet should be killed. In short order, the EME authority agreed to issue a Green Light on Randy Muppet Morales, listing him under the name "Puppet." (This was a misspelling of Muppet's moniker.)

When a Green Light was issued it was up to anyone who was in close contact with Muppet to do him in. Since Muppet had moved back with his family, he no longer was living in the Avenues area. Because he was no longer around, it was less likely that the Green Light could be carried out. His parents had moved to Tujunga in the San Fernando Valley to get him out the gang atmosphere. However, Muppet couldn't stay away from his homies who he had grown up with. So every opportunity to return to the old neighborhood, he took advantage of it.

On October 5, 1996, he learned that a friend of the family had to go down to the Avenues area so he talked her into giving him a ride. By the time he reached his old neighborhood it was early Saturday evening. The main commercial streets going through the Avenues territory are San Fernando Road and Eaglerock Boulevards. Other roads were given numeric names, all ending with the word Avenue. This barrio started at Avenue 30 and extends all the way up to Avenue 43. Strangely enough with all these Avenues, the most active street was Drew Street, which is only two city blocks long. For whatever reason, Drew Street became known as the place to go if one wanted to buy drugs.

Besides the narcotics dealing, Drew Street had a reputation for prostitution activity, which was so perplexing since it was located within a stone's throw from the LAPD Northeast station. The other unique feature of Drew Street was that it practically makes up the southern border of the Forest Lawn Cemetery, where Michael Jackson, along with dozens of other Hollywood celebrities, is buried. One would think that Drew Street would be one of the quietest and safest streets in Los Angeles. The truth was that it was a hot bed of illegal activity run by the various sects of the various Avenues gangs.

When Muppet was dropped off in the barrio, he migrated to Drew Street, where he ran into several of his old homies. He was eager to converse with them to find out what was going on. After a short time, Muppet saw his old friend George Chato Vidales and went over to him and asked for his gun. A week earlier Muppet had loaned a gun to Chato Vidales for some type of job he was doing. Chato responded that he didn't have the gun since he had left it at his house. Muppet was disappointed and said that he wanted his gun back since he needed it. That was when Chato indicated that he would see if he could get a ride over to his place, which was in El Sereno several miles away, so he could pick up Muppet's gun.

Within minutes they had come across Gerardo 'Criminal' Reyes, who they asked if he had 'Wheels.' Criminal said he didn't have a car but his girlfriend, Diana (better known as Kilo Lady), had a minivan he could borrow since he had to pick up some groceries for a friend. Within minutes Reyes lined up the van and pulled up to Muppet and Chato and he told them to jump in. Two other buddies, Carlos and Ponce, were standing around and were invited to join them. Carlos wasn't old enough and asked 'Criminal' if they could stop somewhere and buy beer for everyone.

After driving a few blocks, the van stopped and Carlos handed over the money for the beer. Chato exited the van and promptly entered this tiny 'mom and pop' mini-store. He maneuvered through the over-stocked shelves to get to the beer cooler in the back, which was full of Corona and Dos Equis beer in bottles. His eyes scanned all the various types of beer and tried to figure out which one to buy. Since all the guys hadn't stated a preference what beer to get, he looked for the cheapest and got a couple of six packs.

When he got back to the minivan, he handed the beers to all the homies. Since the beers were ice cold, everyone promptly grabbed one. No one complained as to the choice of beer. The van continued down the street when they saw Jimmy Drac Maxson cruising toward them in his 'tricked out' Mustang. Both cars pulled over to their respective side of the street. Chato immediately got out and ran over to talk to Drac. Drac asked, "What's up?" Chato in a low voice while glancing to both sides said, "We are going to 'check out' Muppet.

That comment set Drac back with a dazed look. Since Drac had grown up with Muppet, he considered him one of the Avenues homies. Drac didn't know what to think and made a cautionary statement, "Have you run this by Lil Pee Wee Aguirre since those guys are close?" Chato assured him that there was a Green Light out on Muppet and it was their duty to carry it out. Their conversation continued on other topics as though there was no big deal to the fact that they were on their way to kill one of their own.

Drac's his last words to Chato were, "Make sure that Lil Pee Wee is on board with this shooting." Chato responded that it had been approved all the way up. Chato turned his head and proceeded back across the street. That was when 'Criminal' Reyes told Chato to do the driving. Since Chato had never driven a minivan, he didn't hesitate to get in on the driver's side and put the car in drive. 'Criminal' Reyes moved to the passenger seat. They made a stop along the way to deliver some groceries to a friend of Reyes' girlfriend.

CHAPTER 16 TIME TO CHECK OUT MUPPET

By now everyone in the van had had several beers. One could say that everyone in the car was starting to feel the buzz. Little did Muppet know that he was willingly being transported to his death by his homies, who all felt like they were all one big family. His friends didn't want the police to suspect them in the demise of one of their own, so there was a mutual agreement that Muppet's body should end up in El Sereno, which is in their rival's territory. That way the police would assume that the killing was committed by one of the El Sereno gang members.

Since Chato had lived near the El Sereno area, he was given the assignment to find a suitable isolated area to do the dastardly deed. Since El Sereno is an older, well-developed area on the east side of LA, Chato knew it would be a challenge to find a completely desolate street. However, he remembered that there was a section of Remstoy Drive that was devoid of houses on either side, which gave the area an eerie deserted look. Chato was driving and was able to maneuver the minivan on the sharp curve that leads up the hill.

The seating inside the minivan had Chato driving, 'Criminal' Reyes in the passenger seat, Carlos stretched out in the middle bench seat, and Ponce and Muppet in the rear seat. The weight of the five guys caused the minivan to bog down as it attempted to move up the hill. As the van strained to make it up the incline, Chato yelled out that he had to take a leak and pulled the van to the curb, where he stopped. Since everyone had been drinking, this seemed like the ideal place to stop for a relieving break. All the guys exited the vehicle and each made a beeline to the side of the curb facing uphill.

Since they all had been drinking, everyone was in a jolly mood. What could be a more idyllic way to spend Saturday night than with your buddies? There was a feeling of fellowship and belonging. This could have been a fraternity outing with those who would be willing to do anything for their brother in a time of need. This area of Remstoy Drive had no streetlights, making it difficult to see your surroundings. Not a sound could be heard except for someone's dog howling in the distance. Since they were on the hillside, a slight breeze whiffled down the street giving off the sweet scent of night blooming jasmine growing on the hillside.

As the guys spread out to piss in their own private space, no one noticed that 'Criminal' and Carlos had fallen behind the others. 'Criminal,' without making a sound, pulled a handgun out of his waistband and held it to his side. Muppet leaned slightly forward as though finished urinating. 'Criminal' took one step forward and raised his gun up to the rear of Muppet's head. Criminal squeezed the trigger and there was a loud shot, causing the others to jump slightly. Everyone glanced in the direction of Muppet seeing his body fall forward as if in slow motion and hitting the pavement with a thud. 'Criminal,' like a good assassin, took two more steps to lean over Muppet and pointed the gun straight at his head and without any hesitation shot him at point blank range five more times.

The shooting seemed cold and calculated. Minutes before, 'Criminal' was exchanging pleasantries with Muppet then seconds later he was carrying out his duty to eliminate this low-life Muppet who had ratted on one of their own. Throughout the shooting, Carlos was standing to the side of 'Criminal' with his gun at the ready position just in case he was needed. However, Carlos's backup wasn't necessary since 'Criminal' was more than a good shot at such close range.

Immediately after the shooting, Muppet's body made some slight movement, but within less than a minute Muppet's boyish existence was no longer. His homies were fixated on looking at his body as the only motion was a steady stream of blood slowly oozing from his head flowing down the gutter. One of the homies realized that, for their own sake, they needed to get out of there and yelled to the others, "Let's go!" 'Criminal' was still holding the gun in his hand and recognized it was time to go. He took several steps over to the vehicle and took the passenger seat in front as the others piled into the back of the minivan. Chato got behind the wheel and revved up the engine and put the minivan in gear.

The vehicle lurched forward as he made an abrupt U-turn in the middle of the street. The guys in the back were having difficulty trying to close the side door of the van. They pulled the sliding door but they couldn't get it to engage, so the dome light in the van stayed on. Chato's only reaction was to push the accelerator all the way to the floorboard, which gunned the engine but didn't cause the wheels to spin. Everyone was so busy in getting away that no one looked back at their old homie Muppet, whose body lay unceremoniously curled up on the dirty asphalt gutter.

Although Chato was familiar with the street, he miscalculated their speed on the sharp curve on Remstoy Drive as he drove by the corner house. The noise of the shooting had aroused the residents of the house, who looked out to see the red minivan race by showing the occupants to appear to be gang members with shaven heads. Since they purposely did the shooting in El Sereno Gang territory, Chato accelerated the minivan to reach the safety of the Avenues barrio.

Shooting one of their own created a mixed bag. 'Criminal' was pleased that he was able to carry out the Green Light for EME. He was able to meet the challenge and performed a difficult but necessary task. He held his head up high because he had done something worthwhile that bestowed credit on his local gang. The other homies milled around with the Drew Street crowd experiencing mixed feelings since they all liked Muppet as a good friend to hang out with. A melancholy feeling came over them, which they took care of with several more beers.

The next day Chato saw his friend Maxson and he confirmed that the 'check out' of Muppet went well. Maxson asked how Lil Pee Wee had taken the information of the taking out of Muppet. Maxson reminded Chato that Lil Pee Wee grew up with Muppet and they were very close boyhood friends. Chato admitted that he wasn't sure that Lil Pee Wee would be pleased with their questionable act. Chato gave the matter some thought but quipped back that he knew that EME had a Green Light on Muppet and somehow that would protect him from any retaliation.

CHAPTER 17 UNSOLVED GANG MURDERS PILE UP

No one seemed to lose any sleep over Muppet's passing. His mother was saddened by his death. She had warned him many times not to associate with the Avenues Gangs. Even though Muppet's parents were recently divorced they had tried so hard to steer Muppet from the gang culture. His father was a hard worker who had worked himself up to a good job with one of the local cities in the area. Although his parents didn't have much money, they managed to scrape together enough for Muppet to attend Immaculate Heart parochial high school. The hope had been that Muppet would have come to the realization that gang life had nothing to give him.

The parents were determined that Muppet grow up away from the gang culture. Therefore, the family moved away from the gang-infested Avenues area. Although the new home was in a safer community, some five miles away, it didn't take Muppet long to figure out the bus routes that would transport him back to the Avenues part of town where he felt at home.

Muppet's death didn't shake Los Angeles to the core. There wasn't any news coverage of Muppet's death. The reason was that *it wasn't news*. The mere fact of finding a shot-up young gang type was all too common and didn't justify any news coverage. The only point of interest was whose homicide detectives would end up having to investigate this shooting. Since the body was found in the El Sereno area, initially it was assigned to the Newton Station detectives. However, when the police later determined that Muppet was an Avenues gang member, the LAPD administration decided to transfer the investigation of the case to Northeast Division detectives.

By the late 1990s the homicide team at Northeast had 17 gang shootings that hadn't been solved. One of the detectives assigned to this massive number of gang killing was Andy Teague. His desk was stacked high with green binder Murder Books. He continually followed up with any active lead or interview in hopes of solving this avalanche of murder cases.

CHAPTER 18 GANG LIFE

The so-called Avenues Gang in reality is made up of several street gangs, such as the 43rd Street Gang and the Cypress Gang, which all occupied that portion of northeast Los Angeles that had numbers to designate the various streets. The Avenues Gang had existed for years and had roots back to the original Hispanic gangs in the 1940s with the infamous Zoot Suit gang. The Avenues Gang was well respected in the gang world since they had numerous ties to the Mexican Mafia (EME). As a matter of fact, the Avenues Gang had more top officials in the EME organization than any other local gang.

No one knows for certain how many members there are in the Avenues Gang. The police have gang officers who have personal contact with the various local gangs, and it was estimated that there were 600 active members in the early 1990s and by 2000 it had grown to 1000. For a gang to grow, there has to be leadership and young recruits who are willing to use violence to protect their territory. That meant that gang members had to be ever vigilant of other gangs trying to take over part of their territory.

The Avenues Gang had a rivalry with other gangs in the area such as the El Sereno Gang, Lowell Street Gang, and Dogtown Gang. It was almost a daily battle to chase or attack rivals out of the Avenues Gang territory. This constant friction between gangs was why northeast detectives had so many homicides to investigate.

Gangs mean different things to different people. Many see gangs as a poor man's fraternity in which young men learn about bonding with others. It is felt that a sense of belonging is important, especially in urban environments.

Certain groups in society like to idealize and romanticize gangs and conveniently overlook the violence created by the rivalries. A wonderful example of this was created in the musical and ultimate movie ***Westside Story***. Leonard Bernstein wrote the music and Stephen Sondheim worked on the lyrics of this sensational story about gangs in the New York barrio, which included two rival gangs: the Sharks and the Jets. Supposedly it was a takeoff on Shakespeare's Romeo and Juliet.

No one can forget the famous ***Westside Story*** song, 'Maria:'

The most beautiful sound I ever heard
Maria, Maria, Maria, Maria
All the beautiful sounds of the world in a single word
Maria, Maria, Maria, Maria, Maria, Maria, Maria
I've just met a girl named Maria
And suddenly that name will never be the same to me
Maria, I've just kissed a girl named Maria
And suddenly I've found how wonderful a sound can be

It is strange how gang violence is glorified in certain forms of American culture. One of the songs from the ***Westside Story*** illustrates how many members of the public have a misconception that violence is acceptable under certain conditions. The following song glosses over the violence in a romantic way.

'The Jet Song'

When you're a Jet,
You're a Jet all the way
From your first cigarette
To your last dyin' day.

When you're a Jet,
If the spit hits the fan,
You got brothers around,
You're a family man!

You're never alone,
You're never disconnected!
You're home with your own:
When company's expected,

You're well protected!

Then you are set
With a capital J,
Which you'll never forget
Till they cart you away.
When you're a Jet,
You stay a Jet!

Granted this is just a musical or movie, but it somehow condones violence where the gang members gain a friendship and loyalty from others. However, the homicide detectives may not see all the lofty goals that gang membership provides. What the detectives experience when they are assigned another murder to investigate is the victim's family constantly calling to find out why their son's case hasn't been solved. The detectives feel the pressure from headquarters which wonders why those detectives haven't been sharp-witted enough to solve this epidemic of homicides in this part of the city of the Angels.

There is a reason why gang killings don't get solved. Most gang cases have little in the way of forensic evidence. Although many of the killings are done with a gun, forensics can't help if the gun is never recovered. Most shooters realize the first thing to do is dispose of the gun so it can't ever be compared to the projectiles or shell casings recovered from the crime scene. In order to solve a gang shooting, the detectives need eyewitnesses who saw the shootings. However, most gang violence is done by drive-bys or in isolated areas where there are no witnesses. Even if there are witnesses, seldom will anyone be willing to come to court to testify against a gang member.

People who live in the gang territory know that testifying against gangsters is a one-way ticket to the morgue. However, at times there may be fellow gang members with the victim at the time of the shooting. They will be uncooperative with law enforcement. Their response is that their gang will take care of the problem on their own terms. Undoubtedly, they will retaliate on their own saving the detective and court system from having to spend time trying to prosecute the original shooter. This may explain why the number of homicides increases and few are ever solved.

CHAPTER 19 A MEXICAN MAFIA INFORMANT

The Northeast homicide detectives realized that they had another layer of difficulty in solving their numerous homicides. It became clear that the Mexican Mafia (EME) was deeply involved in the local gang activities. You, the reader, learned in the previous Gomez and Grajeda case, that EME will use deadly force to encourage drug dealers to pay their taxes. However, there is an even more deadly rule and that involves any gang member becoming an informant for the police.

That is where the EME saying, "A Snitch belongs in a Ditch," originated. Needless to say, this tenet had to be strictly enforced in order for EME, a prison gang, to survive. Because EME is involved in illegal activities, their members are going to come in contact with law enforcement. When a gang member is arrested by the police, they will naturally put pressure on the arrestee to give up information about EME activities and its membership. In order to discourage gang members from talking, EME makes it well known that any person who provides information to law enforcement will suffer a brutal, torturous death.

Another EME tenet that is similarly enforced is that no member can drop out of the organization. In other words, once an EME member, it is for life. EME can't afford to have older members leave and reveal confidential information about the organization. There are no dropouts from EME. This rule can be overly harsh for old timers who have outgrown the gang banging and want to become a family man.

It is understandable why EME deals so harshly regarding drug dealer taxes and informants; however, it less clear why they are harsh regarding sexual activity. Outwardly, they are opposed to any homosexual activities; however, this seems strange since many of the EME members are spending the rest of their life in a prison without having any contact with females. They are clearly opposed to anal sex.

Also, EME members are to respect women. It is strictly forbidden to have any sexual relations with another EME member's girlfriend or wife. Regarding the tenet about women, some might say that chivalry is still alive and well in EME. Another positive aspect of EME is the high reverence for children. There is no tolerance for child molesting by any member or any person of the general public. Often EME will severely discipline any member who purposely kills or even accidentally kills a child.

In addition, EME is opposed to a street gang committing drive-by shootings. EME realized that such gang banging was counterproductive for all gang members. Also forbidden is for any gang member to develop an alliance or friendship with any African American gang. Another area where gang members can run afoul of the EME rules is fighting against each other. EME instructs all members not to raise up a hand against another member without prior approval from the EME leaders.

Over the years EME has created an elaborate procedure for disciplining its members. The method is called Green Lighting. The EME Carnales (leaders) decide who should be disciplined and how severe that discipline should be. They have a list prepared citing the names of those who have been wayward. In one portion of the Green Light list are the names of members who the organization has agreed should be killed. If the Green Lighted person is anywhere within the area of a member, it is the duty of that member to carry out the killing of the Green Lighted individual.

If a member doesn't make an attempt to carry out the Green Light, then EME Carnales can impose a Green Light on the person who failed to do their duty. Often the only reason a gang member commits a killing of a fellow gang member is out of fear that he might end up on the Green Light list himself.

For EME to continue to exist, it must rely heavily on the local soldiers to carry out the edicts from the Canales, who are mainly in prison. If the soldier is in the prison system, he may be required to transport 'kites' from the Canales to other members. However, those soldiers on the outside of prison are the ones who are expected to carry out the killing regarding the Green Light list.

An illustration of how one doesn't want to have a Green Light directed at them can be seen as to what happened to actor/director Edward J Olmos after he made the movie ***American Me*** in 1992. He wanted to make an authentic movie about the history of the Mexican Mafia. Olmos's aim was to show the good and bad of Chicano gangs in Los Angeles. It told the story of how the EME founder was killed when he went back to prison and indicated that he didn't want to continue to be a member of EME. As indicated earlier, that was one of the tenets of EME in that one can't drop out of EME even including one of the founders of the organization. For whatever reason, Olmos changed the facts of the story so the founder was killed by his own gang members, when in fact the killers were from a rival gang.

Even though Olmos had gone out of his way to consult with the EME leadership, the Carnales didn't like the fact that Olmos took a few liberties in telling the story. As a result, Olmos and others from the movie were Green Lighted and a contract was placed on their lives. Olmos didn't realize the hornet's nest he had created. For several months, Olmos lived in fear for his safety and the safety of his family. Fortunately, his production company paid off EME to have the Green Light turned off for Olmos.

Some would like the public to believe that the Mexican Mafia is a myth or just a group of hip gangsters who are locked up in faraway prisons. What some people miss is the fact that FEAR may not be visible but is real especially when someone's name ends up on a Green Light list. The person on that list doesn't know who will execute him or even when it will occur. Wealthy actor Olmos found out that when your name is on the Green Light list you are nothing more than the Walking Dead.

CHAPTER 20 ALAN DOWNEY A MEASLY DOPE DEALER

The detectives at the LAPD Northeast station couldn't understand why they were being inundated with one homicide after another. The shootings seemed to be professionally done in that the killers didn't leave any incriminating evidence behind. However, what was left in each murder was a wall of silence. There were no eyewitness accounts of what happened or any willingness to provide information as to who might be involved.

The police were unaware that the local Avenues Gangs had gained unbelievable stature in the violent gang world. What had happened behind the scenes was that FOUR of the Avenues Gang members became full-fledged Carnales of EME. When Alex 'Pee Wee' Aguirre was sent back to prison he joined his fellow Avenues Gang members, Alfred 'Tigger' Salinas, Big Rick 'Psycho' Aguirre, and Albert 'Boxer' Tolento. Now with the Avenues Gang having four Carnales in the top leadership of EME, they, as a gang, had gained enormous prestige and muscle in enforcing EME's rules.

As stated earlier in this book, for EME to survive it relies heavily on the collection of taxes from dope dealers. Needless to say, most dope dealers aren't overly thrilled in having to pay EME this so called 'sales tax.' In order to gain the dope dealers cooperation EME had to instill FEAR in the hearts of all the dealers to get them to willingly pay the tax. At times EME had to flex its muscle to teach wayward dope dealers the deadly consequence of non-compliance.

As the stack of homicide cases continued to pile up at LAPD's Northeast station, the detectives tried to figure out a new strategy in confronting the problem. Everything they did resulted in a stalemate and no workable leads were forthcoming. In desperation, the detectives asked the CSI team and the crime lab to retest items and make further comparisons of the forensic evidence that had been collected at the crime scenes. Shortly thereafter, the detectives received the word from the latent prints section of the crime lab that there had been a new match. A latent print examiner had found that a latent print collected from a vehicle at a crime scene came back to a Lil Pee Wee Aguirre.

At the time of the match, no one in law enforcement and certainly no one in EME had any idea this would be the turning point in ending the wave of murders in the Avenues community of Los Angeles. The irony of how Lil Pee Wee Aguirre's print got on the vehicle was that it occurred over a dispute with Alan Downey for not paying his EME taxes.

It all started out as a result of a misunderstanding as to who was the proper party to pay the EME taxes to. Alan Downey was an Avenues Gang member who grew up in the Avenues barrio of Los Angeles. He got to know Alex Pee Wee Aguirre, the older brother of Lil Pee Wee Aguirre. (The author recognizes that this may be confusing so we will refer to the older Aguirre as Alex and the younger brother as Lil Pee Wee) At the time, Alex was very much involved in the EME organization and activities. Within a short time, Alex would become a Carnale in EME. Alex grew a liking for young Alan since he was willing to help Alex with his drug dealing business.

Alex knew that Alan wanted to have his own drug dealing business. So Alex agreed to help Alan get started by giving Alan the exclusive right to sell all the dope in the boundaries of the City of Burbank. The understanding that Alex worked out with Alan was that he would purchase all of his dope from Alex at a premium price as well as pay Alex the 10% EME tax. Both Alex and Alan benefited by this agreement, and after a while this became a lucrative arrangement for both. Alan couldn't have been happier, since the City of Burbank was a great market for selling dope. Burbank was the home of much of the entertainment business, where drug use was prevalent and acceptable.

Alex and Alan's business arrangement seemed ideal until many of the buyers started complaining about the poor quality of the dope. For whatever reason, the coke Alex was selling to Alan had been stepped on too many times. (Often drug dealers to make more money will take the cocaine and mix it with milk powder to increase the quantity but in the process reduce the quality.) Alan was losing customers and had gained the reputation of selling bunk. In order to save his business, he started buying some of his coke from another dealer who had better quality dope. He continued to do business with Alex but started to buy more and more coke from another dealer by the name of Benny "Sleepy" Garcia. Alan continued to pay his taxes to Alex but told friends that "Alex's coke was shit."

Time went by and Alan continued to buy from both dealers; however, Alex was arrested and eventually convicted of RICO violations resulting in him being sent to Federal prison. Alex was no longer able to conduct his dope business. Alan, therefore, decided to buy all of his dope from 'Sleepy Garcia.' Alan decided there was no need to pay his taxes to Alex's drug dealing business since he wasn't buying anything from them.

Alex's dope business was too profitable to close down just because Alex was in prison. So his kid brother, 'Lil Pee Wee' Aguirre, stepped in to take over Alex's drug business. It wasn't long before Lil Pee Wee learned that Alan was no longer buying dope from his family's business nor paying the taxes to them for operating in the City of Burbank. Lil Pee Wee approached Sleepy Garcia and issued an ultimatum to Garcia that he had to kill Alan for not paying the taxes to EME.

Sleepy Garcia's reaction was that he wasn't going to kill Alan, at which point Lil Pee Wee attacked Garcia with a knife and told him that his name was going to put into the hat (placed on the Green Light list) if he didn't carry out his order. The reason why Garcia may have challenged Lil Pee Wee's order was the fact that Lil Pee Wee was only 15 years old and hadn't gained the sinister reputation that his brother Alex had.

Lil Pee Wee realized that he wasn't being taken seriously as a replacement for his brother Alex. That was when he decided to join with some of his fellow gang members to flex his muscle so he would be respected. He wanted his homies to realize that he was speaking and acting for and in place of his brother, a full-fledged EME Carnale.

Alan Downey was a young man who was energetic and not a mere small-time dope dealer. He liked driving nice cars but didn't have the money to afford a new car. Ingeniously, Alan worked out an arrangement with a local car repossessing company that he would assist with the repossessions. He would provide a certain amount of muscle while the repossessor hooked up the car to the tow truck.

Most repossessions occur when the buyer of a car defaults on their monthly payments. The job of the repossessor is to pick up the car and store it until the financial company decides what to do with it. Alan was compensated for his help by the towing company allowing him to use the repossessed vehicle until the bank asked for it back.

This meant that Alan got the privilege to drive the car free of charge for several days. This business arrangement was a win-win for everyone. No one would notice nor care that Alan put several hundred additional miles on the car.

CHAPTER 21 Lil Pee Wee Decides To Act

In August of 1995, Alan helped in the repossessing of a dark green Toyota and was given the vehicle to drive for his own use for several days. A side benefit for Alan was that he could do his drug dealing in a car and no one would recognize the car as being his. On August 14 during the early morning hours, Alan was peacefully driving this repossessed Toyota northbound on Eaglerock Boulevard. Coincidently, at that same time 'Lil Pee Wee' Aguirre and fellow gang member 'Gangster' Marquez were driving on the same street. Neither Lil Pee Wee nor 'Gangster' was particularly interested in this green Toyota. As they passed the Toyota, Lil Pee Wee glanced at the driver and could see that it was Alan Downey who was all alone driving the car. Since Lil Pee Wee was seated on the passenger side of their vehicle he had a clear view of Alan. Lil Pee Wee instructed 'Gangster' Marquez, who was the driver, to slow down as Lil Pee Wee reached for his gun.

The outside weather temperature was warm and both cars had their windows open. With a quick motion, Lil Pee Wee pointed his gun out the window as Alan was focused looking straight ahead. Lil Pee Wee fired one round, which struck the outside of the driver's side mirror and continued through the car, eventually striking the rear passenger window. Both cars were now side by side, and Lil Pee Wee pulled the trigger several more times.

Several of the later shots hit Alan on the left side of his head. Instantaneously, the Toyota made a jerking motion and started veering to the left as Alan's body leaned forward striking the steering wheel. The Toyota careened over the center divider of Eaglerock Boulevard. and crossed the southbound lanes without hitting any cars. It seemed as though everything was moving in slow motion as the Toyota continued over the curb causing the tires to blow out.

It all seemed like a surreal experience since the car didn't seem to stop until it slammed up against a cinder block wall on the west side of the street. The gunshots and the blowing out of the tires and the car crashing into the wall had created deafening sounds. Lil Pee Wee had to make an important decision as to what to do next. The smart thing was to get out of the area as quickly as possible before any witnesses could identify either of them or the car they were driving.

On the other hand, Lil Pee Wee had to consider whether he had really fatally shot Alan. Shooting from one car into another car is tricky business and it can be difficult to hit a target. Lil Pee Wee was a person who didn't want to take chances. He wanted to know for sure whether he had killed Alan or merely injured him. He shouted at his buddy 'Gangster' Marquez to make a U turn and directed him to pull up alongside where the Toyota had come to rest.

Marquez pulled up parallel to the Toyota. He could hear the engine still running with the headlights still on. Lil Pee Wee yelled "stop" as he leaped out and ran over to the passenger window of the Toyota. Looking inside the car, he could see Alan's body leaning down on the front seat. By this time blood was oozing out of his head. Without any hesitation, Lil Pee Wee placed his hand against the roof of the Toyota to steady his hand and fired several more bullets into Alan's body. This might be construed as the final coup de grace, but in reality Alan Downey was in no condition to do anything and had definitely taken his final breath.

At that moment Lil Pee Wee had demonstrated to the world that he might be only 15 years old

but he was capable of carrying out the orders of his big brother Alex, a true Carnale of EME. With great satisfaction, he nonchalantly returned to the car driven by 'Gangster' and said to him, "Let's get out of here." Lil Pee Wee showed no emotion for killing Alan, a fellow gang member he had grown up with. Everyone in the barrio knew the rules: if you didn't pay your EME taxes the sentence was DEATH even for an old homie.

Shortly thereafter, the police received word that a person was found lying in a car that had been involved in some type of traffic accident. When the officers noticed the bullet holes in Alan, the homicide detectives were asked to respond to a possible shooting on Eaglerock Boulevard. The victim looked like a possible gang member;

however, the Toyota didn't fit the usual description of a gang vehicle. When they learned that the car was in the process of being repossessed, they had questions for the repossession company as to how this victim got hold of such a car. The victim's identification was determined, and when the detectives located the victim's girlfriend at a local motel she sang like a bird.

She indicated that she had rented a room at a local motel where she and Alan were spending several days. She said that Alan got a call after midnight and left to go to the 'Big O' Bar, which was where Alan at the time was selling dope. Since it was getting late, she called Alan to see when he was coming back to the motel. He promised her that he would be back in five minutes. When he didn't return she called the 'Big O' Bar to find out whether Alan was still there or had left.

When she was told he had left much earlier, she began to be concerned for his safety. She called a colleague and expressed her concern. He agreed to go out looking for Alan. In less than an hour, this friend came by the motel and asked her to accompany him to check out a suspicious traffic accident. He wasn't certain whether that could have been the repo car that Alan was driving. The girlfriend got in the friend's car and they drove the short distance to where the car was still smashed into a cinder block wall on the side of Eaglerock Boulevard. As they slowly drove by the accident scene, the girlfriend had no doubt that was the repossessed Toyota that she and Alan had been using for several days.

The girlfriend admitted that Alan was dealing dope and recently was concerned about the fact he wasn't paying his EME taxes since he didn't know who the proper person was to give the money to.

CHAPTER 22 FORENSICS CRACKS THE CASE

Needless to say, the repossessed Toyota was covered with numerous latent prints. There were the original owners, who had used it for months. Alan and his girlfriend had been using it for several days. During that time, many of Alan's gangster friends had reason to leave their fingerprints on the car. Also, the repossessor had touched the car when hooking it up to the tow truck. The CSI team spent a lengthy amount of time trying to lift latent prints from the car. This seemed hopeless since it appeared that the shooting was a possible drive-by in which the shooter had no reason to touch or come in contact with the car.

Every latent print they lifted had to be eliminated from all those people who had knowingly come into contact with the car. Since the LAPD crime lab was severely understaffed, the homicide detectives had to wait forever to get back any results. They had one good print from the roof area of the Toyota, but it didn't come back as a match to anyone listed in the state or national fingerprint databases.

This shooting occurred in 1995 when Lil Pee Wee was only 15 years old. Needless to say, at that time juvenile fingerprints were not being entered into the fingerprint databases. It was not until around the year 2000 that the crime lab made a positive match to Lil Pee Wee. By that time, he was 20 years old and had been implicated in a number of murders. Det. Andy Teague was thrilled to have some hard evidence to present to the DA's Office for a homicide filing. Since Teague was a veteran homicide detective, he recognized that he was going to need a highly skilled and experienced prosecutor if they were ever going to get a conviction.

Teague was able to persuade the DA's Office to give the case to one of the top prosecutors in the Major Crimes Division. The police were pleased; however, as time went by this veteran prosecutor could see the difficulty in prosecuting a person who was a juvenile at the time of the killing. A plea bargain deal was arranged in which

Lil Pee Wee was basically permitted to plead guilty to Manslaughter for killing Alan Downey.

The detectives were more than disappointed since this was the only possible case, they had in which they had solid forensic evidence. The detectives tried to point out to the assigned prosecutor that a Murder conviction would send a loud message to the gangsters to stop the violence. The prosecutor's position was that the case wasn't all that strong. Lil Pee Wee could easily claim the fingerprint on the car occurred sometime earlier when he had stopped to talk to Alan while he was in the car parked on the street.

The detectives had to admit that they hadn't been able to come up with any eyewitnesses or obtain any incriminating statements from Lil Pee Wee. They recognized the weakness in their case against Lil Pee Wee, but they were not happy. His pleading guilty to a Manslaughter would be like a slap on the wrist for Lil Pee Wee. The Northeast LAPD Homicide squad felt utter exasperation. What else could they do?

CHAPTER 23 NEED A FIRST-RATE PROSECUTOR

During an investigation, when it seems that a detective has hit a solid brick wall the first thing he or she does is start to complain. The old-time seasoned detectives may take out his or her frustration by swearing up a storm. However, after the cursing has subsided the detective starts looking for a way over or under the wall. Was there some way around the impasse? That was what happened to Homicide Detective Andy Teague. He refused to give up and accept the Manslaughter plea bargain for Lil Pee Wee.

Det. Teague had heard from several of the South Homicide detectives that there was a hotdog older prosecutor who had recently sent several EME members to Death Row. Hard-nosed Det. Teague started asking around for the name of this impressive prosecutor. The best he could find out was that this attorney had some type of Italian name. He was also told that every time he appeared in court, he always wore a dark three-piece suit like a well-dressed mortician. Teague didn't know what to glean from the strange description. Since he prided himself on being a clever detective, it wasn't long before he determined this prosecutor was none other than Tony Manzella, prosecutor extraordinaire.

What Det. Teague learned from other homicide detectives was that this Tony Manzella was able to convict one of EME's top leaders, Luis Pelon Maciel (better known as Big Homie), of four counts of murder. Why the detectives were singing the praise of Manzella was the fact that Maciel ordered the killing of a former EME who had dropped out of the organization 20 years earlier. Maciel was enforcing the EME's policy of 'blood in, blood out,' by which EME members are not allowed to leave EME without feeling the pain of death.

Yet it was the detectives who worked the San Pedro area who had the most praise for Manzella. They couldn't stop talking about how he came over to their station and rolled up his sleeves and started reviewing their green Murder Books. He sat down with each of the homicide detectives trying to help them figure out what more was needed to be done. After considerable investigation, he was able to tie three robbery murders together against Ruben Gomez. He combined those cases with the double homicide involving a drug dealer who wasn't paying his EME taxes. Besides defendant Gomez, he added Arturo Grajeda as another defendant.

All of this admiration of Manzella intrigued Det. Teague. He wondered whether he was just a super-duper fast-talking attorney but not street smart. Teague asked more questions about how gang-wise was he. What he found out was that Manzella had worked closely with the county gang task force. There he met the top experts regarding the operation and membership of EME. Manzella had a knack for understanding the workings of EME while at the same time he was gaining incredible **expertise** as to how to prepare and present an EME case to a jury.

Manzella spent his weekends cruising on his 42-foot sailboat up and down the Southern California coast. When he was cruising the ocean on calm days, he had time to critically analyze the way EME operated. After giving it considerable thought, he discovered the Achilles' heel of EME. One of EME's tenets was that if someone wanted to drop out of EME they were given a Green Light. Therefore, those who had tried to leave were already Green Lighted, which meant that they had been sentenced to death. Manzella realized that any gang member who had a Green Light against him was part of the walking dead. That was the pivotal point when that person would be willing to testify in court if given a chance to relocate themselves and their families.

For a Green Lighted EME member, the prosecutor possessed the only hope to survive. All they had to do was tell the truth in court and they receive WITNESS PROTECTION. Understand that EME's use of the Green Light can be the prosecutor's best friend. Tony Manzella wasn't merely an outstanding litigator, he had discovered the key that could allow EME atrocities to be successfully prosecuted.

CHAPTER 24 DECISION TO TAKE ON EME

Det. Teague was sold that Tony Manzella would be the precise prosecutor for their stack of homicide cases. The question was how to get him involved in all of the Northeast gang homicide cases? One day when Det. Teague and his partner were downtown on the Lil Pee Wee case, they walked by Tony's office in the Major Crimes Division. Det. Teague was no wallflower and, on many occasions, could be described as overly assertive.

Det. Teague entered Tony's office and introduced himself. Tony was a little taken back wondering who Teague was. Tony was well mannered and immediately told Teague and his partner to sit down at Ruth's desk since she wasn't in. Teague sat down and laid out his concern about the handling of the Lil Pee Wee case. Tony sat behind his desk leaning back in his County-issued chair with his head resting against his clasped hands behind his head.

Tony listened intently and kept saying, 'Tell me more." Teague, like a fisherman, knew that he almost had Tony hooked. After a half hour of listening Tony could have stood up and said, "It was nice talking to you and I wish you luck on your cases. Goodbye."

For some unexplainable reason, Tony said, "I'll come up to Northeast station and take a look at your Murder Books." What Tony didn't realize at the time was that decision would change his life for the next five years as he took on the biggest Mexican Mafia case in the history of the Los Angeles DA's Office and LAPD. Possibly if Ruth had been present, she might have talked him out of getting involved.

However, Tony's decision would change so many lives, and as a result the Mexican Mafia would forever be crippled.

Tony is a man of his word, and within a couple of days he and Ruth drove his new BMW up to Northeast station. They walked into the lobby and there they were directed back to the Homicide squad room. Stacks of green Murder Books clutter the detectives' various desks. After a short greeting, the social formalities were over and Tony asked to see the Alan Downey Murder Book, which involved Lil Pee Wee Aguirre. Tony and Ruth were shown an empty desk and given two chairs to sit in. Tony removed his sport coat and rolled up his sleeves. At the same time, Ruth opened a briefcase and pulled out a yellow legal tablet and started copying down the information on the outside of the Murder Books which were piled high on the desk. Without any fanfare, Tony and Ruth started the laborious process of trying to figure out what pieces of the puzzle the cops had. At the same time, they were looking for the missing pieces they would need to build a case against the EME members.

Over the next two months, Tony read all of the 17 Murder Books, looking for a thread connecting them all together. Some of the cases had possibilities and others looked hopeless for a solution. Tony in his gentlemanly way would make a suggestion about what needed to be done as far as more interviews and more forensic testing. Usually, detectives are resistant to prosecutor's suggestions, but the Northeast Homicide detectives were so delighted to have a prosecutor working side by side with them they would have done anything. If Tony would have asked for a fresh cup of Starbucks coffee, they would have gone Code 3 to get it.

Each further investigation yielded some piece of incriminating evidence but not enough to lead to a filing of criminal charges. Tony rekindled his contact with the prison gang task force. He asked if there were any old EME members who had Green Lights on them. Tony knew if he could get one or two old EME members to testify, he would have enough to file charges. It all depended on what that EME witness knew and how credible he could be.

Then Det. Teague got the word that a prisoner, Trooper Ramirez, who was serving time in Calipatria State Prison, was willing to talk and testify. He had been Green Lighted for skimming and outright stealing EME tax money. Ramirez was the type who loved his local Avenues gang but didn't like EME, who he saw as being only interested in business. There was no question he knew a lot, but would he come across as a credible witness in front of the jury?

Det. Teague got the word that there was an Avenues Gang member in a federal prison back in Minnesota who claimed he could be helpful to Teague's investigation of all the shootings in the Avenues area. This was a long shot and became the pivotal point in building a case against EME. Would LAPD be willing to spend all the money required transporting three detectives and one DDA all the way back to Minneapolis? In every large organization there are 'bean counters' who spend their day saying "No" to every request that costs money.

No one knows for sure where the authorization came from, but all four of them were in the air on the LAPD King Air 200 twin turboprop flying to Minnesota. Either the 'bean counter' was off that day or more likely Det. Teague had conveniently forgotten to get prior permission. He had learned years earlier in his career it is easier to get forgiveness than permission.

When Tony met with the prisoner Jimmy Drac Maxson it wasn't long before he realized that Maxson knew so many crucial facts. The other thing was that whatever he told them could be corroborated. What was appealing about Maxson was that he didn't have a vendetta to get certain gang members. Also a plus was the fact that Maxson hadn't shot at anyone. All he wanted was to have the chance to restart his life so he could spend it with his young son.

After interviewing Maxson, Tony knew he had the piece of evidence that he was looking for. Now he had the lynchpin that could hold the entire case together. At that point, Tony's perspective had to dramatically change. If he didn't file criminal charges within the next couple of days, he would never be able to prosecute several of the actual killers. The federal authorities were about to deport 'Criminal' Reyes to Mexico. Also, Lil Pee Wee was within days of accepting the plea bargain in which he would plead guilty to Manslaughter, allowing him to escape the murder charges.

On the morning of May 25, 2001, Tony and Ruth hastily prepared the criminal complaint charging eight defendants of committing the murder of seven individuals. Before notifying the defendants of the filing of the charges, Tony contacted Lil Pee Wee's attorney asking him to bring his client to the Criminal Courts Building to resolve the plea to the Manslaughter. Tony told the attorney to meet him in the lobby on the first floor at 3:00 p.m. Since it was Friday, the lobby of the courthouse was almost empty except for a few jurors who were being excused for the weekend.

At 2:45 p.m. the Defense attorney drove into the courthouse parking lot and didn't have any difficulty finding a parking space. Both Tony and Ruth stood patiently waiting for the meeting and both Tony and Ruth were packing steel. As Tony tells it, he always carries his 'feather duster' in a shoulder holster. Ruth is more discreet with her firearm, but both know when you're in the business of prosecuting some of the coldest killers on the planet it is wise to be prepared.

At 3:00 sharp, Lil Pee Wee with his counsel walked in the door of the lobby of the CCB. At that time on a Friday afternoon there is a musty smell that permeates the lobby, caused by the janitors sweeping the granite floor with some type of disinfectant. Tony waved over to Lil Pee Wee's attorney and motioned for them to come over to where he was standing next to a built-in wooden bench. With a cocky strut, Lil Pee Wee followed his attorney over to Tony and Ruth. Tony started making small talk to the attorney. Lil Pee Wee stood nonchalantly with a smile like a person who had just won the Mega Millions Powerball Lottery.

From the other side of the lobby, Det. Teague and Det. King slowly and quietly walked up from behind Lil Pee Wee and uttered the words, "You're under arrest for murder." There was a moment of silence as the detectives slipped the handcuffs on Lil Pee Wee. From that moment on, Lil Pee Wee, who had just turned 20, would never be a free man again. His reign of violence in the Avenues area had come to a peaceful termination.

CHAPTER 25 CASE DIVIDED INTO FOUR SEPARATE CASES

The big challenge was the gigantic size of the case. One killer may be involved in several different murders. Another murder may involve several killers who acted together to carry out the crime. The challenge for the prosecutor was finding the thread to tie all these cases together. Tony decided to file criminal charges in seven separate murders that all had ties to the Mexican Mafia (EME). There were eight EME affiliates who were charged with these seven murders. Some were lieutenants and others were associates and some were just the EME soldiers from the local gangs. Tony realized that the prosecuting of all eight defendants at the same time would be a nightmare from the standpoint of security and coordination of witnesses.

CHARGING DOCUMENT

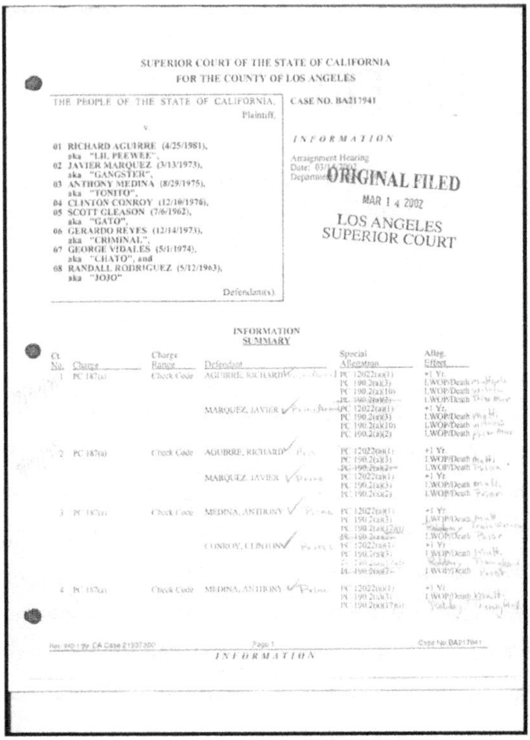

SUPERIOR COURT OF THE STATE OF CALIFORNIA
FOR THE COUNTY OF LOS ANGELES

THE PEOPLE OF THE STATE OF CALIFORNIA,
Plaintiff,

v.

01 RICHARD AGUIRRE (4/25/1981), aka "LIL PEEWEE",
02 JAVIER MARQUEZ (3/13/1973), aka "GANGSTER",
03 ANTHONY MEDINA (8/29/1975), aka "TONITO",
04 CLINTON CONROY (12/10/1976),
05 SCOTT GLEASON (7/6/1962), aka "GATO",
06 GERARDO REYES (12/14/1973), aka "CRIMINAL",
07 GEORGE VIDALES (5/1/1974), aka "CHATO", and
08 RANDALL RODRIGUEZ (5/12/1963), aka "JOJO"

Defendant(s).

CASE NO. BA217941

INFORMATION

Arraignment Hearing
Date: 03/14/2002
Department

ORIGINAL FILED
MAR 1 4 2002
LOS ANGELES
SUPERIOR COURT

INFORMATION
SUMMARY

Ct. No.	Charge	Charge Range	Defendant	Special Allegation	Alleg. Effect
1	PC 187(a)	Check Code	AGUIRRE, RICHARD	PC 12022(a)(1) PC 190.2(a)(3) PC 190.2(a)(10) PC 190.2(a)(2)	+1 Yr. LWOP/Death LWOP/Death LWOP/Death
			MARQUEZ, JAVIER	PC 12022(a)(1) PC 190.2(a)(3) PC 190.2(a)(10) PC 190.2(a)(2)	+1 Yr. LWOP/Death LWOP/Death LWOP/Death
2	PC 187(a)	Check Code	AGUIRRE, RICHARD	PC 12022(a)(1) PC 190.2(a)(3) PC 190.2(a)(2)	+1 Yr. LWOP/Death LWOP/Death
			MARQUEZ, JAVIER	PC 12022(a)(1) PC 190.2(a)(3) PC 190.2(a)(2)	+1 Yr. LWOP/Death LWOP/Death
3	PC 187(a)	Check Code	MEDINA, ANTHONY	PC 12022(a)(1) PC 190.2(a)(3) PC 190.2(a)(17)(i) PC 190.2(a)(2)	+1 Yr. LWOP/Death LWOP/Death
			CONROY, CLINTON	PC 12022(a)(1) PC 190.2(a)(3) PC 190.2(a)(17)(i) PC 190.2(a)(2)	+1 Yr. LWOP/Death LWOP/Death
4	PC 187(a)	Check Code	MEDINA, ANTHONY	PC 12022(a)(1) PC 190.2(a)(3) PC 190.2(a)(17)(i)	+1 Yr. LWOP/Death

Rev. 940-1/99 CA Case 21937300 Page 1 Case No BA217941

INFORMATION

As result, Tony worked out a schedule in which all seven murders and eight defendants would be divided into four separate trials. This was extraordinarily complicated to orchestrate, but this gave the prosecutor what he needed, which was time to prepare four manageable trials. Instead of having to deal with eight Defense attorneys at one time, he now had only two or three he had to contend with in any trial. He knew that each of the cases would require a gang expert to testify to the organization and the operation of EME. Even though this would require that some witnesses would have to testify four times, the subjects were such that there would be little danger of creating prior inconsistent statements by having a witness testify so many times.

The substantial part of each trial was going to be the testimony of three witnesses who were former gang members in the EME structure. They had already been Green Lighted for death by EME, so they didn't feel any increased threat by testifying. By testifying, they got some added protection from law enforcement. Tony spent considerable time going over the facts of each murder with these three witnesses. They were high enough in the EME organization that they had personal knowledge of each of the murders. They didn't participate in the actual murders but they overheard the defendants talking about the facts. The key to the case was making sure that every relevant fact that the witnesses testified to could be corroborated with some type of independent evidence.

CHAPTER 26 FIRST TRIAL AGAINST THE KILLERS OF MUPPET

Since Lil Pee Wee seemed to be at the center of this gigantic case against EME, many had assumed his case would be the first trial. However, for a variety of reasons it was decided the first trial would be the one with the most defendants and Defense attorneys. That sub-case involved the killing of Muppet by three defendants, 'Criminal' Reyes, Chato Vidales, and Jo Jo Rodriguez.

Tony was totally ready for trial. He had prepared all his exhibits that he would be introducing into evidence. For Tony, the key to success is thorough preparation. To show how prepared he was, he had written and even rehearsed his closing Argument even before the first day of the trial. I, the author, have never worked with any attorney who was so well prepared. Tony's reasoning of being so ready is that it frees him up during trial to concentrate on what is going on in the courtroom.

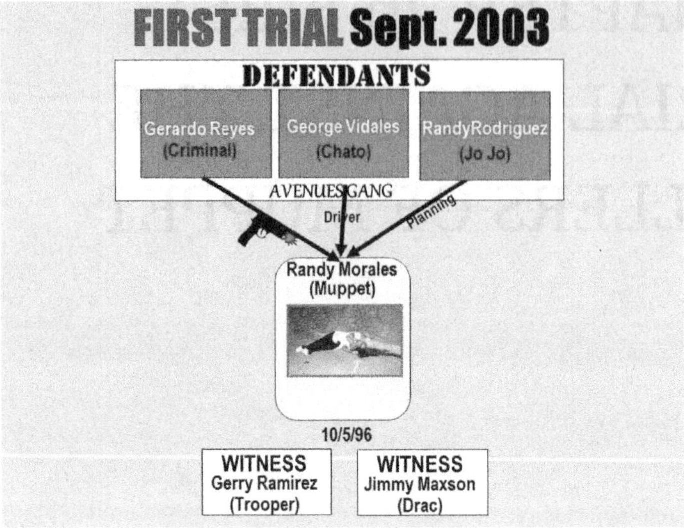

The first order of business for the trial was the selection of the jurors. Tony was looking for certain jurors he would like on his jury. He realized that it was unlikely that jurors would be overly sympathetic to gangsters, especially dealing with the Mexican Mafia. However, Tony wanted to have jurors who were compatible and would be willing to work together. Tony was always trying to avoid the juror who is the 'odd man out' type who wants to be the contrarian always taking the opposite side.

When all the jurors were accepted by both sides it was time for the Opening Statements. Tony wanted to use his time wisely since he needed to educate the jurors as to Gangs, the Mexican Mafia and introduce the jurors to the underside of life which would be foreign to them. Factually, this case would be described as simple and straightforward. This was the first trial and the defendants were the parties who were involved with driving the victim Muppet Morales to El Sereno where he was executed while urinating by the side of the minivan. It was decided that three soldiers of EME would carry out the killing.

Tony wanted the jurors to understand how far the killers had to drive to make it look like it was a shooting by a rival gang in El Sereno. Tony showed the jurors an exhibit that showed where the gang members picked up the van and drove over to El Sereno where the execution took place.

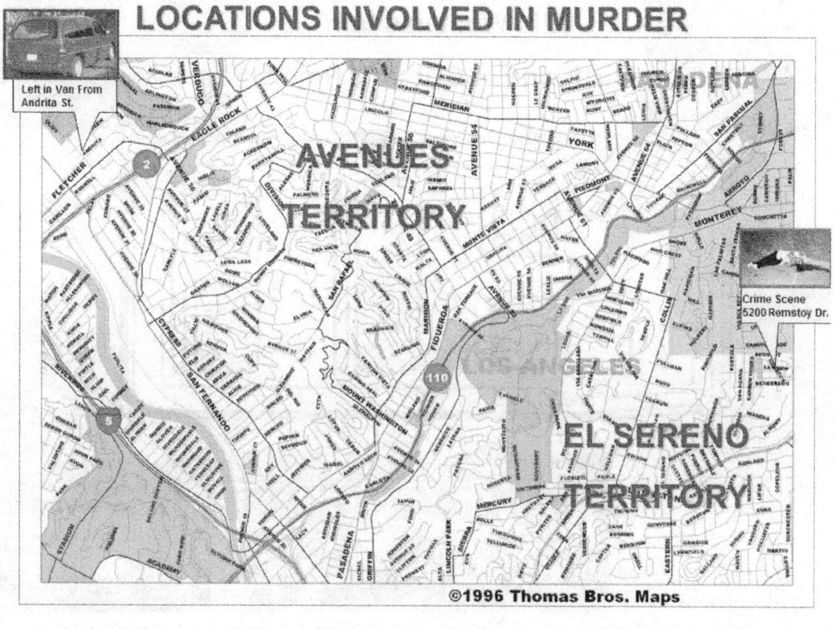

Next Tony used this exhibit to show the van that the gangsters drove. He knew that the witnesses might be confused as to where everyone was seated. So he placed a diagram in the center and photos of the van surrounding it.

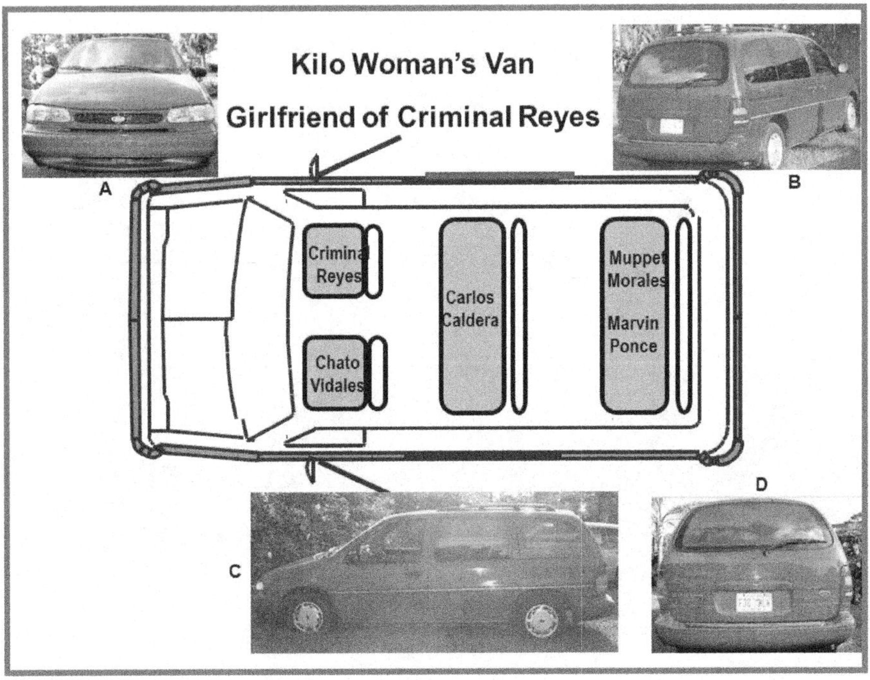

It was dark when the shooting occurred, and the witnesses were unfamiliar with the area. Tony used an aerial photo to show the general area and also indicates that it was an isolated area in an urban setting.

Tony recognized that the jurors had seen movies and TV programs that depict gang life. However, Tony knew that his witnesses would be referring to gang terms that the jurors wouldn't be familiar with. So he sat down with the gang experts to come up with the most common gang words that jurors needed to know to understand what the gang witnesses were testifying to.

Although the gun used to shoot Muppet was not recovered, Tony wanted the jurors to understand that the victim was shot six times with the same gun. He showed the six spent shell casings found at the scene to corroborate what the witnesses claimed happened.

He made a chart that the jurors could follow along as he explained each term. He would also use this when he had the gang expert testify as to the manner in which gangs and in particular the Mexican Mafia operated.

GANG TERMS

Carnal	Eme member, camarada and "brother"
"Taking care of business"	Engages in gang activity; does things which further the goals of the gang
Person is "down"	Person is committed to the gang, the gang's goals and the gang lifestyle
"The Bay"	Pelican Bay – a state prison
Cliqua	Gang, subset, clique
Brother	Eme member, carnal, camarada
YA	California Youth Authority – custodial facility
"In the hat"	An individual or a gang which is marked for death
"Green light"	Marked for death, either an individual or an entire street gang
Riga	Written instructions from an Eme member or members
"Kite"	Written communication between prisoners or inmates
"Pictures"/ photos	Money, cash

Most jurors would be familiar with the word 'Hit' to be a shooting or killing of someone. However, in this case Tony needed the jurors to know that 'Taxes' and 'Rent' are the terms used to explain the money that drug dealers need to pay for doing business in certain gang territories. Tony also came up with a plan to educate the jurors as to what they needed to know about the Mexican Mafia (EME) so they could properly decide the case.

GANG TERMS

To "check"	To beat and to discipline a gang member for a violation of Eme's rules or orders
"Work"	Activity done in furtherance of the gang's goals
"A good earner"	A gang member who makes money for the gang by selling contraband narcotics, by collecting taxes
"Taxes"	"Rent", money paid by drug dealers to the Mexican Mafia for the right to sell drugs within neighborhoods claimed by the Mexican Mafia
"Rent"	Same as taxes
Rata	A rat, a snitch, one who informs against other members of the gang, one who cooperates with law enforcement
I "did" someone	I shot someone, I killed someone
"Hit"	A shooting, a killing, a homicide

Tony knew that the jurors were going to become confused with the hierarchy of the Mexican Mafia (EME). In his Opening Statement he showed the jury a chart listing the names and monikers of the various gangsters. So Tony started out with an organizational chart of the part of the EME structure that they would be dealing with. The top level was the actual officers in the Mexican Mafia who would be mentioned during various parts of the trials.

The Avenues Gang had four of its members as official Mexican Mafia members. The main part of the prosecution would involve the 57th Avenue branch of EME overseen by Alex "Pee Wee" Aguirre. His lieutenants were Richie "Little Pee Wee" Aguirre and Randy "Jo Jo" Rodriguez. There were six so-called "Associates" under them. And under each one of the "Associates" was a group of EME soldiers that consisted of persons who were very active in their own local gang.

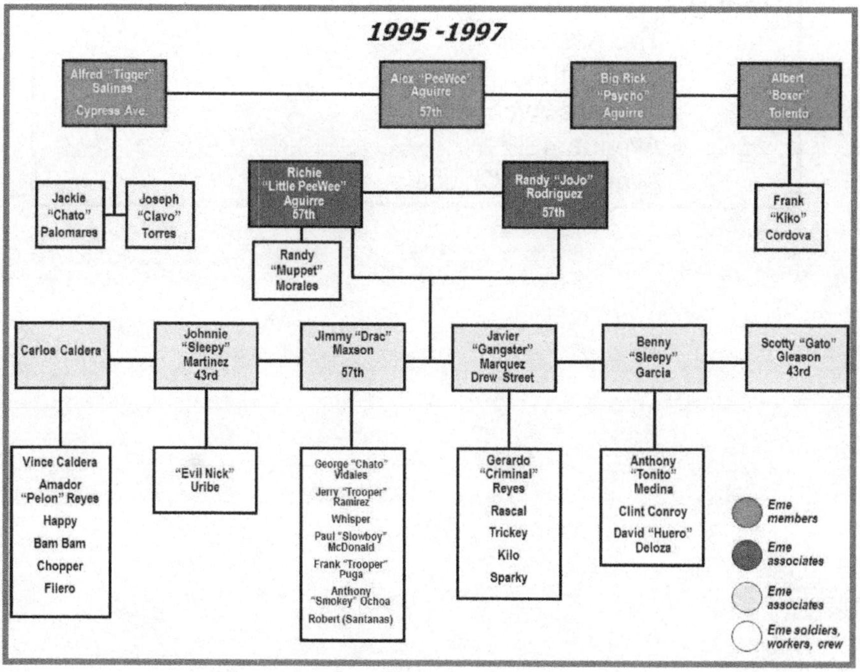

Tony knew that the jurors could get lost as to the differences between EME and the actual Avenue Street Gang. He used this chart to show the various cliques that made up the Avenues Street Gang.

STRUCTURE OF THE AVENUES GANG

- There are about 800 – 1000 members of the Avenues Street Gang
- The Avenues is one of the only street gangs to have *four* members who are also members of the Mexican Mafia – not including Gangster Marquez
- There are five cliques in the Avenues Street Gang:

  The Assassins
  Drew Street
  Cypress Avenues
  Avenue 43rd
  Avenue 57th Chicos

Many of the jurors had lived in Los Angeles for their entire life but they were unaware of what area constituted the territory of the Avenues Street Gang. This map was used by the gang experts to explain to the jury what were the boundaries of the Avenues Gang.

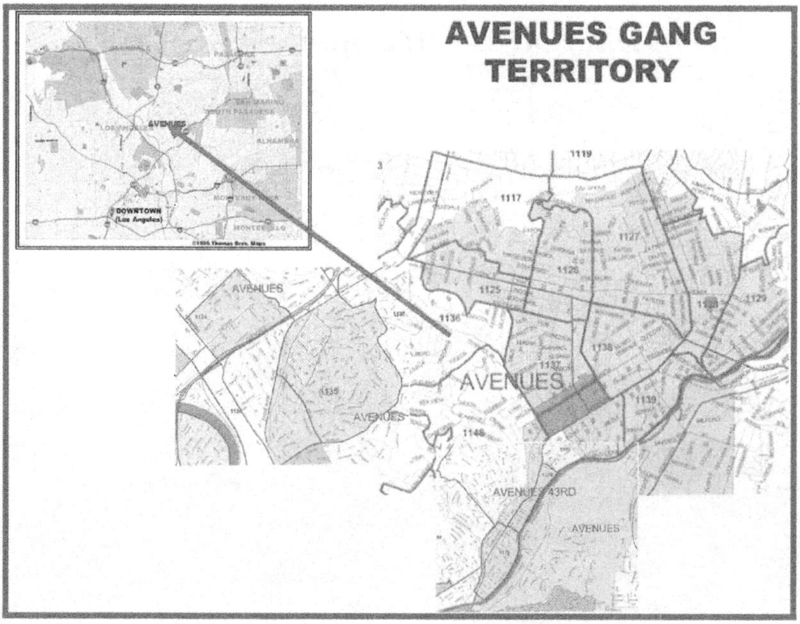

When the medical examiner testified, he referred to the Coroner's diagrams of the head to show the various entrance and some exit of projectiles. The medical examiner could show that the shooter was standing behind the victim when he was first shot in the head. By the time Tony got to the medical examiner, he had finished presenting the prosecution evidence to the jury.

SHOTS TO HEAD OF
VICTIM RANDY 'Muppet' MORALES

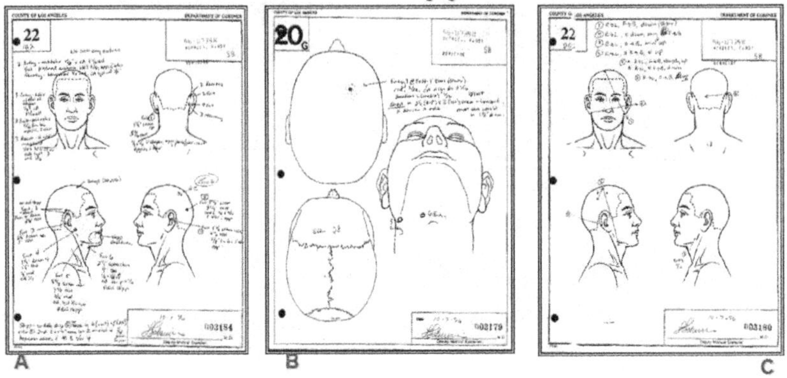

Next was the Defense's turn to present their evidence. Jo Jo Rodriguez's attorney presented evidence that his client had long hair on the date of the shooting. Since the prosecution witness claimed the people in the van were shaved-headed gangster types, this excluded his client. The other Defense attorneys disputed that their clients were involved. The Defense evidence was limited and took only several days.

CHAPTER 27
ARGUMENT

After both sides had presented all the evidence, it was time for the Arguments. Since the prosecution had the burden of proof, Tony was the first to argue. The case was being tried in 2003, when in fact the events occurred years earlier. Tony used this Timeline to try to get the jurors to remember the important dates. This chart helped to explain the order of events.

During the trial, the defendants were all dressed in suits with long-sleeve shirts. Many of the defendants' tattoos weren't visible. Tony needed to show that the

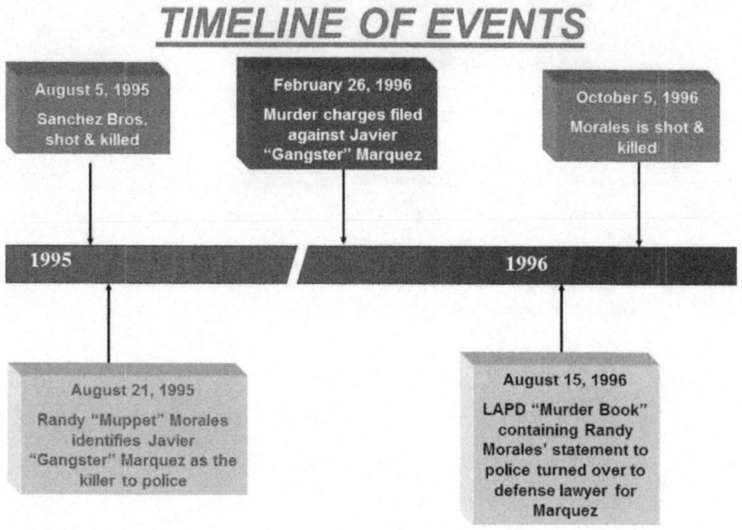

defendants were in fact members of the Avenues Street Gang. So he used the booking photos blown up on a poster board and had the gang expert witness testify to the meaning of the various tattoos. The Defense tried to keep the photos out, claiming that it would be prejudicial against them. However, the judge ruled that the tattoo photos could be shown to the jury to prove that they were members of the Avenues Street Gang.

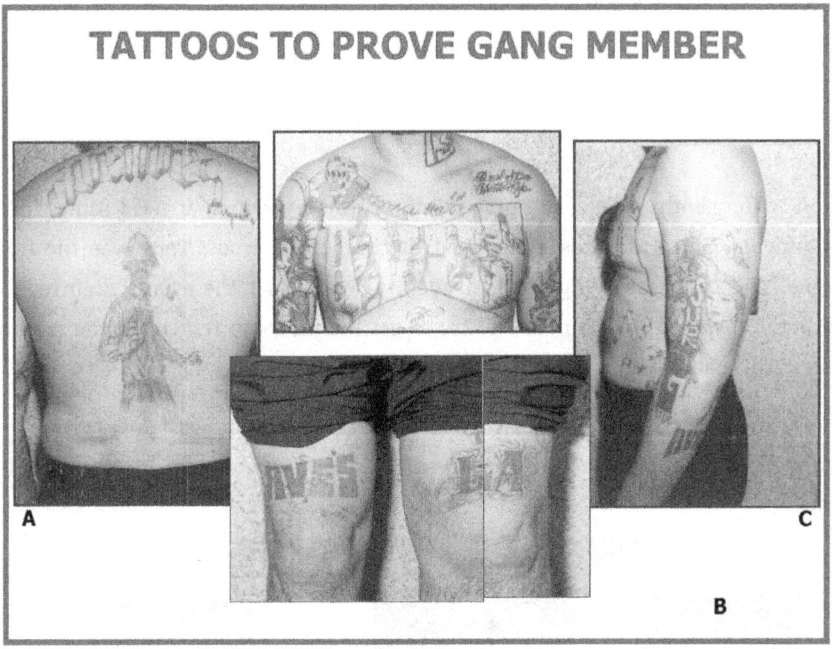

At time of trial, the defendants had let their hair grow out, covering up the tattoos on their skulls. Tony used the photos to show that in fact they were gang members even though they had changed their appearance.

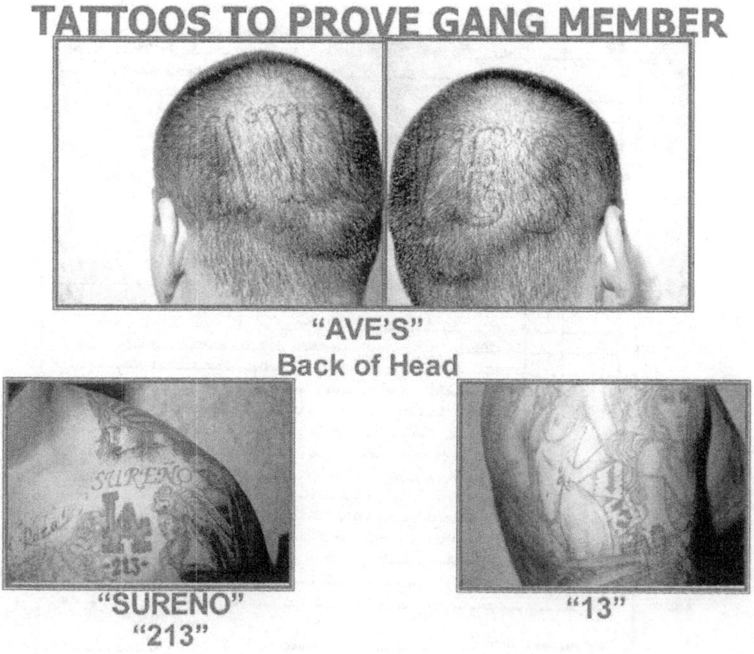

In order for the jurors to understand how Muppet's death was the result of someone not crossing out Muppet's name on a police report, Tony blew up the report to poster size. This permitted the jurors to see how the leaders of EME learned that Muppet had ratted on one of their leaders

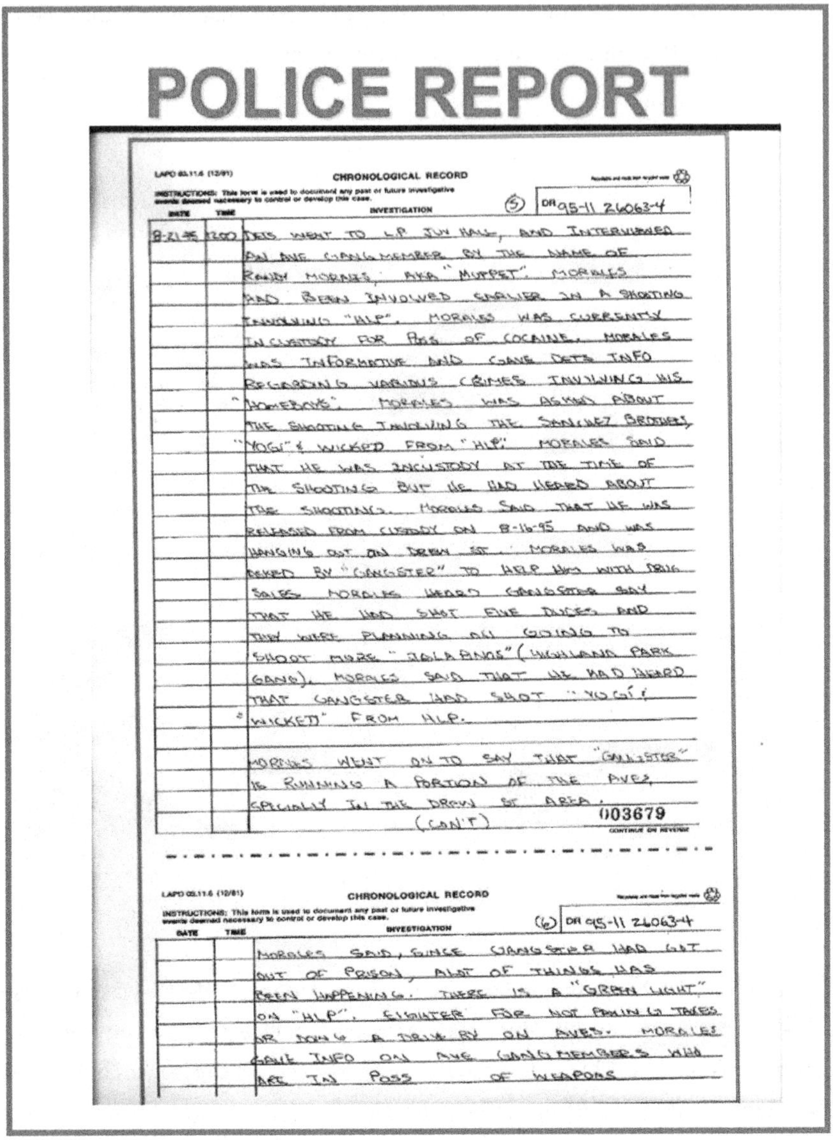

POLICE REPORT

LAPD 03.11.6 (12/81)

CHRONOLOGICAL RECORD

INSTRUCTIONS: This form is used to document any past or future investigative events deemed necessary to control or develop this case.

(5) DR 95-11 26063-4

DATE	TIME	INVESTIGATION
8-21-95	1200	DETS WENT TO L.P. JUV HALL, AND INTERVIEWED
		AN AVE GANG MEMBER BY THE NAME OF
		RANDY MORALES, AKA "MUPPET". MORALES
		HAD BEEN INVOLVED EARLIER IN A SHOOTING
		INVOLVING "HLP". MORALES WAS CURRENTLY
		IN CUSTODY FOR POSS OF COCAINE. MORALES
		WAS INFORMATIVE AND GAVE DETS INFO
		REGARDING VARIOUS CRIMES INVOLVING HIS
		"HOMEBOYS". MORALES WAS ASKED ABOUT
		THE SHOOTING INVOLVING THE SANCHEZ BROTHERS,
		"YOGI" & WICKED FROM "HLP". MORALES SAID
		THAT HE WAS IN CUSTODY AT THE TIME OF
		THE SHOOTING BUT HE HAD HEARD ABOUT
		THE SHOOTING. MORALES SAID THAT HE WAS
		RELEASED FROM CUSTODY ON 8-16-95 AND WAS
		HANGING OUT ON DREW ST. MORALES WAS
		ASKED BY "GANGSTER" TO HELP HIM WITH DRUG
		SALES. MORALES HEARD GANGSTER SAY
		THAT HE HAD SHOT FIVE DUCES AND
		THEY WERE PLANNING ON GOING TO
		SHOOT MORE "JOLA BNOS" (HIGHLAND PARK
		GANG). MORALES SAID THAT HE HAD HEARD
		THAT GANGSTER HAD SHOT "YOGI &
		WICKED" FROM HLP.
		MORALES WENT ON TO SAY THAT "GANGSTER"
		IS RUNNING A PORTION OF THE AVES,
		SPECIALLY IN THE DREW ST AREA.
		(CON'T) 003679

CONTINUE ON REVERSE

LAPD 03.11.6 (12/81)

CHRONOLOGICAL RECORD

INSTRUCTIONS: This form is used to document any past or future investigative events deemed necessary to control or develop this case.

(6) DR 95-11 26063-4

DATE	TIME	INVESTIGATION
		MORALES SAID, SINCE GANGSTER HAD GOT
		OUT OF PRISON, ALOT OF THINGS HAS
		BEEN HAPPENING. THERE IS A "GREEN LIGHT"
		ON "HLP", EIGHTER FOR NOT PAYING TAXES
		OR DOING A DRIVE BY ON AVES. MORALES
		GAVE INFO ON AVE GANG MEMBERS WHO
		ARE IN POSS OF WEAPONS

What the below visual showed was that the victim's pants zipper was open. This was zoomed in on showing a close-up of the zipper in the open position. This was strong corroboration to support the witnesses' contention that "Muppet" was merely urinating when he was shot.

The purpose of shooting him when he was urinating was obvious in that he was most vulnerable and wasn't able to defend himself.

Originally, Tony had prepared the below chart to illustrate the Conspiracy to kill Morales, aka "Muppet." This spelled out the various steps that went into the killing of "Muppet". However, at time of Argument Tony decided not to pursue the charge of Conspiracy since he felt that the Murder charge was more than enough. (Therefore the below visual wasn't shown to the jury.)

After both sides had argued, the jury was instructed as to the law that applied in this case. Then the judge excused the jurors to start their deliberation. They were out for two days and then indicated that they had a verdict as to one of the defendants. The judge had them give him that one verdict, which was a not guilty as to Jo Jo Rodriquez. As to 'Criminal' and Chato, the jury claimed they were hopelessly unable to return a unanimous verdict. As a result, the judge declared a hung jury on those two defendants and set a date for another trial.

CHAPTER 28 SECOND TRIAL

April 2004, Tony and Ruth started the retrial of 'Criminal' and Chato. Since Jo Jo Rodriquez had been acquitted of the charges, the case would proceed at a faster pace. Tony had given considerable thought as to the retrial of the case. He could have easily settled this case, and the two remaining defendants would have been ecstatic and the judge would have been pleased. He was so certain that both were guilty of killing Muppet and he blamed himself for not doing a better job of selecting the jurors.

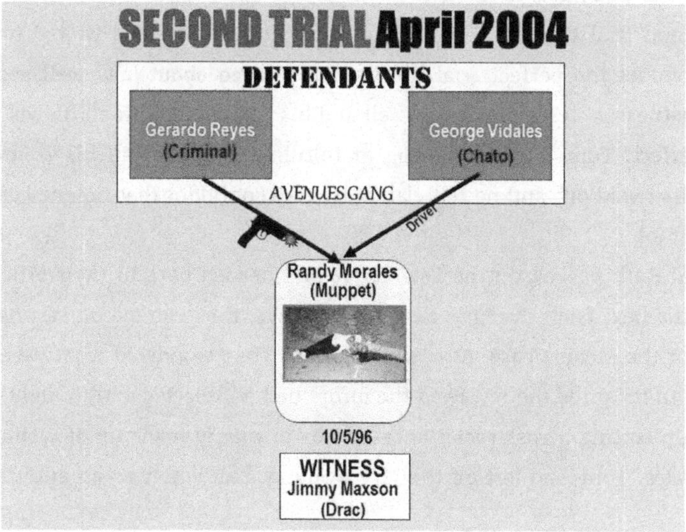

This new trial commenced and Tony delved through the new set of jurors' questionnaires to see if he could get a better fix on what type of juror they would make. Granted, the jury selection process certainly isn't a science but consists of a large amount of gut reaction based on the attorney's experiences.

When it came time to present the evidence, it was truly déjà vu of the first trial. Tony explained the murder of the Sanchez brothers by Marquez. Then he covered the interview that Muppet gave to the juvenile detectives in which he implicated Marquez. After that, Tony described how the police report wasn't properly redacted when it was given to Marquez's attorney. As a result, Marquez learned that Muppet had informed on him so he talked his former brother-in-law 'Criminal' Reyes to take care of Muppet.

The same witnesses were called regarding using the van, including Debbie R., who testified again that she saw the van speed by her house and noticed four shave-headed gangster types in the back of the van. The gang experts testified as to the operation of the Avenues gangs as well as EME. Their testimony was followed by Jerry Trooper Ramirez and Jimmy Drac Maxson, who explained the statements that both defendants had made to them.

This second trial was flawless for the prosecution. Tony had waited his entire career to conduct the perfect trial. He was so pleased about how well everything went. The witnesses' testimony went well and his argument with all his visuals was textbook perfect. Tony had the feeling of fulfillment in that all his training and experience had paid off, and he felt elated. He was confident that no one could have done a better job.

Tony and Ruth packed up the LawMobile and headed back to their office to get started on the next trial. Over the next several days, they worked on setting up the witnesses for the Medina case. After several days, Tony wondered what was holding up the jury. In his mind, he reviewed the jurors he had selected and thought it was a diverse group cutting across racial lines. It was primarily made up of women, with only two males. Tony had left on the jury a young man who was an entertainment lawyer who Tony believed would end up the foreperson because of his legal background.

After many days without a verdict, everyone in the courtroom wondered what could be hanging things up. After a week of deliberation, the jury announced that they were hopelessly deadlocked. The judge listened and seemed sympathetic to the jurors' dilemma. Then he told them to go back to the jury room and try harder to reach a unanimous verdict. The jurors tried but claimed that they had gone over all the testimony and still could not all agree on a verdict. Judge Fidler called them back into the courtroom and asked them if any more time would help to break the deadlock. The foreperson shook his head and crossed his arms in a defiant manner and admitted that no further deliberation would be of any benefit.

The judge declared a mistrial and then asked what were the numbers and for which position. The foreperson in a dejected voice said that it was 11 for guilty and one for not guilty. Tony sat motionless at the counsel table as though he was frozen in his chair. He couldn't believe how close they had come. The case was reset for a new trial date, and Tony headed out into the hallway to see if any of the jurors were still present. Several of the women jurors were standing near the restrooms. Tony in his inquisitive style approached them and asked what more did they think they needed to reach a unanimous verdict.

The women jurors were pleased to speak to Tony. They indicated that they all thought there was more than enough evidence to convict. Then they started divulging what happened in the jury room. Almost in unison they said that this young man who was the entertainment attorney felt that the prosecution hadn't proved their case. The women jurors couldn't explain why the attorney juror continued to object or disregard whatever the prosecution had presented.

Ruth was standing at Tony's side as he conversed with the jurors. Ruth noticed that Tony's face was turning beet red. She knew that wasn't a good sign and tried to nudge Tony over to the elevator. Eventually, Tony seemed to understand what they were saying. He thanked the jurors for talking to him and gave them a forced smile. He pushed the LawMobile into the empty elevator followed by Ruth and waited for the elevator door to close.

At that point, it seemed that Mt. Vesuvius had erupted. Tony started swearing like a stevedore saying, "That is the reason I don't like lawyers." He used other words to describe what he thought about this attorney juror. (Out of consideration for younger readers, we will not print the actual words Tony uttered in the elevator.) Ruth just silently stood in the corner looking down at her high heels. Tony continued to rant all the way to the 17th floor.

Needless to say, Tony was upset with the hung jury. He realized that these killers were likely to go free because most judges will not permit the prosecutor to try a case for a third time. Tony was well experienced and he blamed himself for not kicking that attorney juror off. He should have known that an attorney could easily think of himself as a contrarian and play the role of the devil's advocate. It took Tony the rest of the day for his blood pressure to subside. By the next day, Tony was refocused and trying to develop a strong argument that he could make to Judge Fidler to allow him to retry the case for the third time.

CHAPTER 29 IS THE THIRD TIME A CHARM?

Several of the other EME cases came to trial before the retrial of Reyes, Criminal, took place.

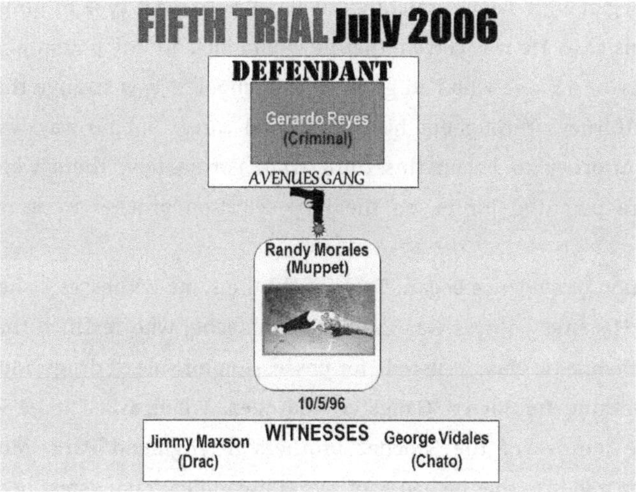

The hearing to decide whether to try Muppet's case for a third time began and Tony argued to Judge Fidler that in the last trial 11 jurors felt that the defendants were guilty. The prosecution needed only one more vote, which they would get in another trial. As much as the judge wasn't looking forward to hearing the case a third time, he reluctantly told Tony that he could try it one more time but that would be it. Tony was relieved that he had won the first battle with the judge. However, would Tony be able to pull a rabbit out of the hat or just created a giant headache for himself?

Tony realized that this was going to his final chance to get the murderers of Muppet. He started to assess the strengths as well as the weaknesses of his case. For the other trials, Tony relied heavily on witnesses Jimmy Drac Maxson and Jerry Trooper Ramirez. On cross-examination, Trooper wasn't very convincing. His testimony made it seem that he was committing acts of violence to get even with people he had a grudge against.

Tony wished he didn't have to rely on Trooper's testimony. The big question was who else could he get to testify having direct knowledge of what really happened in the killing of Muppet? For years, defendant Chato and his attorney had indicated that they would be amiable to some type of disposition. But any such disposition seemed to be elusive.

The third trial began with Tony scratching his head as to what type of jurors he wanted to decide this case. He was certain that he would kick off any potential juror who was an attorney or anyone who had gone to law school. It was strange that he had worked with attorneys throughout his entire legal career but no way was he going to trust an attorney to be on this third trial. Fortunately, there were no attorneys who were potential jurors, so the jury selection process went rather rapidly.

As the presentation of evidence began, Tony called the same witnesses as he had in the other trials. His first witness was Det. Mike Camacho, who testified that he interviewed Muppet while he was in custody for possession for sale of drugs. Muppet revealed he was working for Javier 'Gangster' Marquez. When asked if he knew anything about the murder of the Sanchez brothers in Highland Park, Muppet related that Marquez told him that he had shot five Highland Park gangsters because they weren't paying their EME taxes.

Other witnesses followed indicating that Marquez's attorney had been given a police report in which Muppet's name had not been redacted. (By this time you, the readers, are saying okay we have read all about it. We don't need to go over it a third time. I, the author, understand that and I will not put you through a rehash of the facts of the Third Muppet trial. However, I listed the first witness so you can feel the frustration Tony, Ruth, and the witnesses had to endure by trying the case for the third time.)

After all the witnesses had testified, Tony called his big gun, Jimmy Drac Maxson. This witness testified that on the night of the murder he saw 'Criminal' Reyes driving down Drew Street with Chato and Muppet in the red minivan. Maxson testified that Chato came over and told him that they were going to 'check out' Muppet. He testified that several days later he saw Chato, who told him that he didn't know they were going to kill Muppet. Following that conversation, he came in contact with 'Criminal' who told him, "I shot Muppet because he was a "rata" and Javier 'Gangster' Marquez said he had to go." Finally, Maxson told the jury that he had received a phone call from Javier (Marquez) from county jail in which he said to tell Richie 'Lil Pee Wee' Aguirre that Muppet was a rat and that Richie should 'let it go."

Then the Defense attorneys started their cross-examination of Maxson. Since they had been down this road twice before, they were well prepared to attack Maxson's credibility. Tony sat there at counsel table listening to his key witness being tarred and feathered. Some people would say, "It's what it is." After the Defense attorneys had sliced and diced Maxson, Tony got up and started his redirect examination by asking Maxson, "Did you ever kill anyone?" The witness answered with a loud "No." Next Tony asked why he didn't take advantage of the witness protection program. In a sober voice the witness said, "I didn't go because I would have had to leave my son behind." He put up his hands to cover his eyes as he started to tear up.

Tony's last question was, "Is there a Green Light on you?" Maxson in a soft voice almost whispered, "If they get me, or I let them get me, they'll kill me." After that Tony sat down at counsel table wondering whether had he done enough to convict 'Criminal' the shooter and Chato, who was the driver of the van. If Tony was a card player, what were his odds of getting a conviction as to both defendants? However, after Maxson testified, Tony was reassessing the situation.

The pressure was on Tony. Did he want to gamble and end up with a third hung jury and both defendants walking free? On the other hand, he could give Chato some type of deal to testify against his codefendant. Tony didn't know how good a witness Chato would make in court. How could he grant immunity to Chato without being burned?

The more Tony thought about using Chato as a witness, the more he recognized that it would give him an airtight case. Tony's mind reflected back to the days he worked on the infamous Manson Family case. He remembered that the DA's Office got caught granting immunity to one of the defendants who later changed her mind at time for trial not to testify.

Tony wondered if there was some way that he could be assured that Chato wouldn't renege on the deal. Tony came up with the idea to permit Chato to plead guilty to second-degree murder. If Chato testified truthfully as a witness then the DA would permit the Murder charge to be reduced to Manslaughter.

The Manslaughter sentence would be about six years in prison, and with Chato's amount of time served he could be a free man within months after his testifying.

Chato and his attorney agreed to the plea bargain and Tony notified the judge of a settlement. 'Criminal's' attorney was told of Chato's decision to testify against his client. Immediately 'Criminal's' attorney went back into lockup to break the bad news to 'Criminal.' Needlessly to say, 'Criminal' was shocked. 'Criminal' and Chato were blood brothers who were willingly do anything for each other. Suddenly the impact of the plea bargain hit 'Criminal.' What a comparison: if 'Criminal' were convicted he would be spending the rest of his life behind bars while Chato would be able to enjoy a free life. 'Criminal' must have felt how unfair life was for him.

'Criminal's' attorney left the lockup and went back into the courtroom and stated that he wanted to see all the statements that Chato had made to the police. Tony said that he would turn over to the attorney all the statements. Then 'Criminal's' attorney demanded a month's continuance so he could be ready to cross-examine Chato. Judge Fidler recognized that 'Criminal's' attorney did need some time to get prepared. Since the court had already invested several weeks in the present jury trial, the judge said, "All right, we will be in recess until Monday. At which time we will continue the trial."

When that Monday morning arrived, "Criminal' got a taste how unfair life could be for him. Instead of his homie, Chato, sitting next to him at the counsel table, Chato was sitting in the witness chair ready to answer questions. Tony was holding his breath as to how convincing a witness Chato would be. Apparently, Chato recognized the 'sweetheart deal' he was getting and tried to be as truthful as possible. He explained to the jurors that he started dealing drugs for Lil Pee Wee's older brother. He related how and when he got involved in the Avenues Street Gang.

Then he told the jury his knowledge and involvement with Muppet's death. It all started when he had asked to use Muppet's gun. At that time Muppet freely loaned his gun to Chato. Then on October 5, 1996, Carlos Caldera met Chato and told him that Javier 'Gangster' Marquez wanted Muppet killed since he had ratted on him. Carlos indicated that 'Criminal' Reyes had volunteered to murder Muppet; however, they wanted Chato to help out. Chato responded that he didn't want to be involved.

Carlos said that they knew that Muppet had loaned Chato his gun. Carlos wanted to set up a ruse by telling Muppet that he, Chato, didn't have his gun since he had left it at his home. Then he was to say that he could take Muppet over to his place to pick up the gun.

Sure enough, when Chato ran into Muppet over on Drew Street, Muppet said he wanted his gun back. At that point Chato did what he was supposed to do and told Muppet the story that he could arrange to have someone take Chato and Muppet to Chato's home to get the gun. Chato asked 'Criminal' if he could help out with the transportation. 'Criminal' said he would try to work something out.

'Criminal' was able to borrow his girlfriend's minivan. Her moniker was 'Kilo Woman' since she was known to deal drugs in large quantities. In less than a half-hour, 'Criminal' pulled the vivid red minivan up to the curb and parked on Drew Street. 'Criminal' yelled to Chato and Muppet to get in. Carlos came over to the group and said he had some money for beer but he needed someone with an ID to buy it. Since Chato was the oldest he agreed to buy the beer and Carlos gave him the money. 'Criminal' drove to the store and picked up some of the groceries he had promised his girlfriend that he would deliver to her friend. After that he was free to use the minivan for whatever he wanted to use it for.

'Criminal' then drove back over to Drew Street and picked up Carlos and another gang member, Marvin P. Chato told the jury that he was surprised when 'Criminal' threw the keys to the van to him and told him to drive. Chato said, "Whatever" and went to the driver's door and got in.

By this time Chato was driving the minivan and 'Criminal' was in the front passenger seat while Carlos was leaning back in the middle seat all by himself. The other guy, Marvin, was with Muppet in the rear seat just joking around. As they were driving, everyone inside the van grabbed a cold can of beer. Since it was Carlos who put up the money, all his homies gulped down the free beer. Chato drove slowly around, killing time as he headed toward his home in the El Sereno area. By then the guys had consumed most of the cold beer. As a result, someone asked if there was somewhere along the way where they could take a leak. Chato was familiar with the area and said he knew a suitable place to stop. He added that it has a great view of the city.

Chato had to make a hard left turn on Remstoy Street. This is a hairpin turn and then the street starts up a steep incline running along a hillside. He slowed down just as he got to an isolated area where there were no houses on either side of the road. Another benefit of this location was the fact there were no streetlights. Chato pulled to the curb and turned off the engine. He told the others that he was going to take a leak and if they wanted to they had better get out with him. Chato got out of the driver's side door and softly closed it. The side sliding door on the van opened and the the guys filed out. Muppet didn't know how much longer it was going to take to get to Chato's place so he followed the others to walk behind the van where the guys were standing next to the curb area. They all leaned toward the hillside trying to find a bush to piss on.

'Criminal' was the last person out of the van and he let everyone line up on the curb line. He stepped further into the street and positioned himself directly behind Muppet. For some reason, Muppet leaned slightly forward either to try to pull up his pants zipper or possibly tie his shoelace.

With one motion 'Criminal' pulled the gun out of his waistband and pointed it at the back of Muppet's head. Without one word being spoken, his finger squeezed the trigger and the gun went off. Muppet's head flew forward, He didn't fall down immediately but his tall body wavered slightly. 'Criminal' moved closer and pulled the trigger several more times as Muppet's body curled over as his legs gave way under him. 'Criminal' wanted to be absolutely certain that Muppet was dead. He shot Muppet at least six times to make sure he had completed his mission to kill the *ratta*.

Then all the homies took a long hard look at Muppet's body as it twitched slightly and the blood started to trickle down the asphalt street. Someone said, "Let's get out of here." Everyone except Muppet got back in the minivan. Chato gunned the engine and made a giant U-turn and headed back down the hill. The guys in the back of the minivan were struggling to close the side sliding door. Three of the guys were pulling on the door but they couldn't get it to latch.

As they were driving back to the Avenues' turf, 'Criminal' methodically wiped the gun off and placed it in a plastic bag. While they were driving 'Criminal' yelled at Chato to pull into a mini-mall. Near the alley were several large dumpsters next to the closed businesses. 'Criminal' pointed to one of the dumpsters and told Chato to stop next to it. 'Criminal' stepped out and dropped the gun wrapped in the plastic bag inside the dumpster.

Tony listened to Chato tell this story and wondered to himself why he hadn't made a deal with him sooner. Then it was time for 'Criminal's' Defense attorney to try to trip Chato up in his testimony. Chato was the most credible witness Tony had seen in any of his gang cases. Tony at that point knew that there was no need to call Jerry 'Trooper' Ramirez. He had too much baggage that could be distracting to the jurors.

With Chato's testimony coupled with Jimmy 'Drac' Maxson, there was no need to muddy the water with Trooper's testimony, since he was an easy target for the Defense. Tony couldn't have been happier with the deal he had made with Chato and his attorney. After Tony rested the prosecution's case, the Defense had their opportunity to call the other two persons that had been in the minivan. The Defense had subpoenaed both gang members, but neither would testify since they claimed their Fifth Amendment right not to incriminate themselves. When it was 'Criminal's' turn to testify he reluctantly turned down the opportunity. After Chato's testimony 'Criminal's' only hope was for some contrarian juror to hang his case just like they did in the first two trials.

However, this time, the jurors agreed with Tony and this time there was no hung jury. The jurors unanimously found the defendant Gerardo 'Criminal' Reyes guilty of all charges. Besides the fact that 'Criminal' would spend the rest of his life behind bars, it had to be extremely hurtful for him to see two of his fellow homies Chato and Maxson nail his coffin shut. IT WAS NOT A GOOD DAY FOR 'CRIMINAL.'

CHAPTER 30 THE OTHER EME CASES: MEDINA TRIAL

*(One of the purposes of this book is to highlight several remarkable prosecutors who did an incredible job trying to convict violent killers so they couldn't continue to victimize the public. The above story of the three trials of Muppet's case was interesting from the standpoint that Tony and Ruth had the **tenacity** to see it through even if it meant trying it three times. Many prosecutors would never have filed this case in the first place. Those who would have filed it would certainly have tried to plea bargain this case away early on.*

*However, the real story I wanted to convey to you, the reader, is how Tony and Ruth were willing to take on multiple Mexican Mafia cases consisting of six trials over a period of five years. Without a doubt, their efforts truly demonstrated more than tenacity. They as a team displayed the utmost in (you can use any of these words) **stamina, endurance, resilience, fortitude, grit, perseverance, and doggedness**. That is why I am going to continue to **briefly** discuss the other Mexican Mafia cases that they tried. I am NOT going to discuss (overwhelm you the reader) with all the details of the investigation, the preparation or the trial. All I would like to convey to you, the reader, just how remarkable Tony and Ruth were. The public isn't aware of the many extraordinary people who do their jobs to make us safer and they don't do it for the money, fame, or even a pat on the back.)*

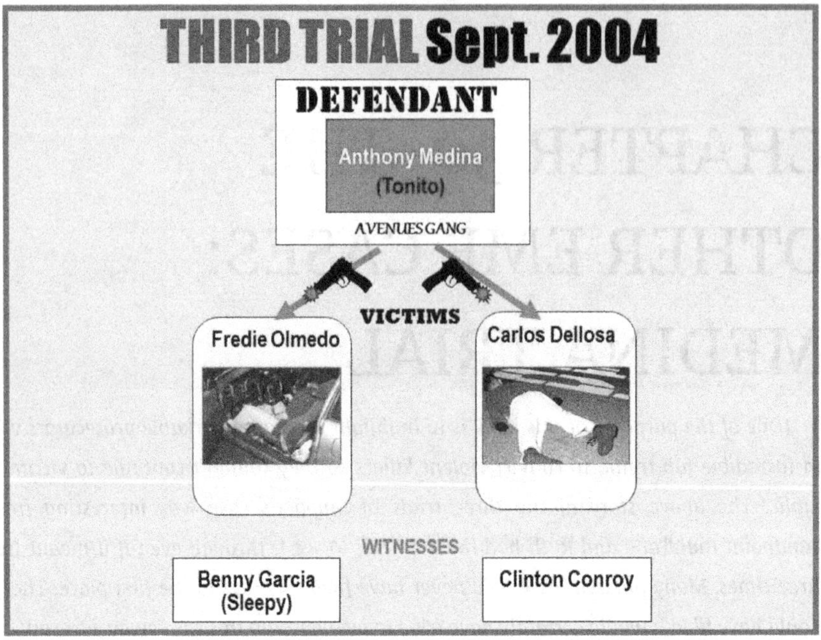
THIRD TRIAL Sept. 2004
DEFENDANT
Anthony Medina
(Tonito)
AVENUES GANG
VICTIMS
Fredie Olmedo
Carlos Dellosa
WITNESSES
Benny Garcia
(Sleepy)
Clinton Conroy

The Anthony 'Tonito' Medina case involved the Avenues Gang having to enforce the EME rules about paying taxes on their sales of drugs. Occasionally, some Asian gangsters would cross over into the Avenues territory and sell without paying EME taxes. Eventually, EME issued a blanket Green Light on any Asian gangster. Anthony Medina took it upon himself to look for such poachers.

Chinatown was only a short distance from the Avenues' territory, so it was understandable how some Asians would slip over the borders to initiate a sale or make a delivery of drugs. However, if the Hispanic gangs let this go on it could have devastating consequences. First of all, it created too much competition. Since the Asians didn't have to pay the EME taxes, they could undercut the prices charged by the Hispanic sellers. As a result, the profitability of the drug business was diminished. The second consequence was that EME wasn't receiving their 10% in business taxes.

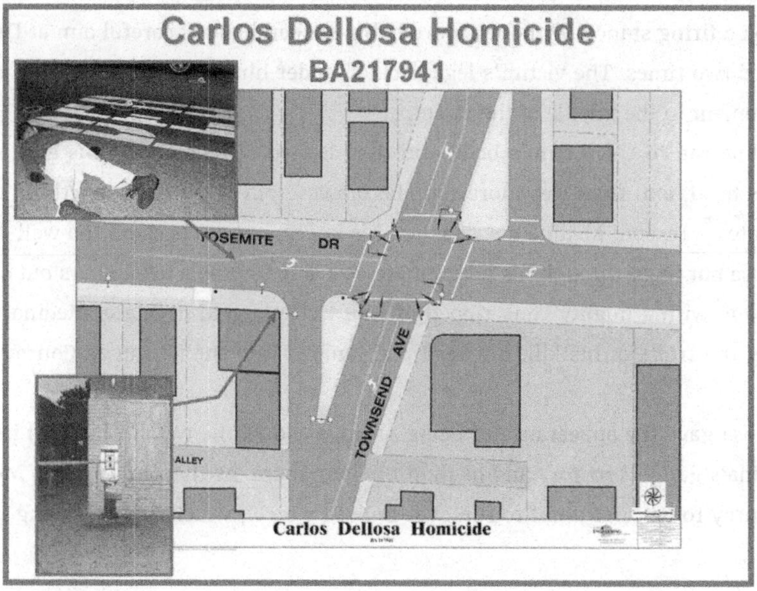

Since the main players in EME were in jail or prison, they had to rely on the EME soldiers who were in the local gangs to put a stop to the encroachment of the Asian gangs. Anthony "Tonito" Medina was a low-level EME soldier who took it upon himself to drive around in the Hispanic gang territory looking for violators. Medina got together with a friend, Clinton Conroy, who was not into gangs but liked to hang out with the Avenues' gangsters.

On November 12, 1995, Medina and Conroy were driving around in a spiffy new Nissan 300 ZX sports car. Medina's friend 'Sleepy' Garcia had loaned it to him to drive around until it was scheduled to be reported stolen. At the time, Conroy was doing the driving as Medina was in the passenger seat acting as a lookout. It was approaching midnight and there weren't many people on the streets. There was a red signal and they stopped at the intersection and waited. They noticed on the other side of the street there was a young man standing on the street corner next to a pay phone. Since the man appeared to be Asian, Conroy stopped the car and Medina got out and went to check out this guy. As Medina was approaching him with a gun in his hand, the man, whose name was Carlos Dellosa, seemed to freeze; then, having assessed the situation, he turned and took off running. Medina stopped in his tracks and took a firing stance. Without a word being spoken he took careful aim at Dellosa and fired two times. The victim's legs buckled under him as he fell forward striking the pavement in the middle of the street.

Medina ran to the victim's body and then leaned over, pointing his gun at the victim's head, and fired two more rounds, blowing out some of the victim's teeth. For whatever reason, Medina got down on his knees, not to check on the well-being of Dellosa but to go through his pockets. He was able to grab a few dollars out of one pocket and with a mighty yank ripped off the victim's gold necklace. Medina, after deriving the fruits of his kill, ran back and jumped into the Nissan as Conroy sped away.

Dellosa gave the appearance of being Asian, although he wasn't, but still he was in Medina's gang's territory and he didn't belong there. As they drove away, Medina told Conroy to be careful not to run over Dellosa's body, which was still lying in the street.

In the excitement of the shooting, Medina had dropped the carrying case of his pager. Fearing that the police would recover it and obtain his fingerprints, they returned to the scene. When they drove back, they saw that a police car had just responded to the location. It was impossible to retrieve his pager case without causing suspicion. He told Conroy to just keep driving and forget the retrieval of the pager's case.

Although the police did find the pager's case, they weren't able to obtain any latent prints off of it. However, this pager case did play an important role in the trial since it provided corroboration to the key witness in the case.

The photo board below shows the various items of evidence that were recovered. Items 1, 2, 3, and 5 were expended shell cases. This provided corroboration that Medina shot his gun four times. Item 4 was a photo of the pager carrying case that Medina had dropped.

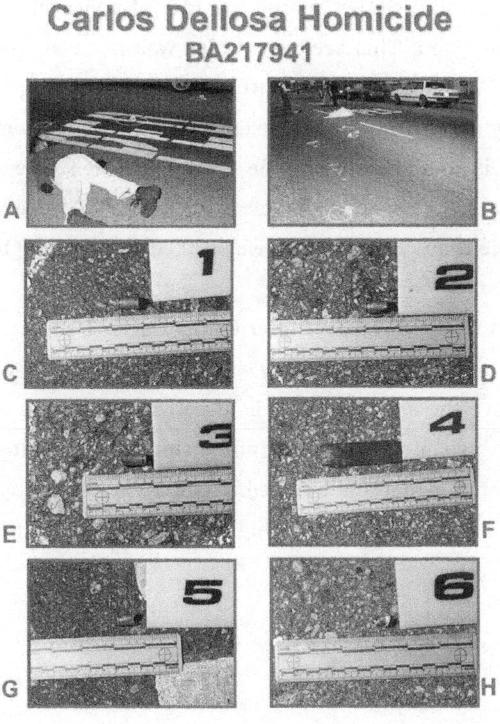

Medina didn't waive his rights and talk to the investigators, nor did he testify on his own behalf at trial. So it was never known the true reason why he killed Dellosa. It could have been just the usual gang-banging when someone encroaches into another gang's territory. Still, the fact that the victim's money was missing indicated that the motive possibly may have been a robbery.

On the other hand, Dellosa might have been mistaken as an Asian gang member (Dellosa was a Filipino) who could have been seen as encroaching on the Hispanic drug-dealing territory without paying their taxes to the Mexican Mafia. The manner in which he was shot in the back of the head would seem to have been meant to send a loud and clear message to others: "Pay your taxes or this is the way you will end up."

The Medina case also included another murder of a victim, Ferdie Olmedo, who also appeared to be Asian. This second murder was not committed to carry out a robbery. It had the earmarkings of a murder to send a message to potential Asian drug dealers to stay out or pay up your taxes. The Asian gangs dominated the area in Chinatown, which is to the north of the downtown area. The Avenues' territory started above Chinatown. There was no clear demarcation between the two areas. It was understandable how common it was for drug dealers to cross over the boundaries.

On November 15, 1995, three days after killing Carlos Dellosa, Medina saw Ferdie Olmedo driving in the Avenues territory near York Boulevard. and Aldama Street. Although Ferdie gave the appearance of being an Asian, he too was really Filipino. Ferdie was driving his car with his wife and sister accompanying him in the front seat. He came to a red signal and stopped. Medina's car came up alongside and he started shooting at Ferdie as he was waiting for the signal to change.

Below is the visual that was used during the trial to illustrate where the shooting took place and where the car came to rest.

Of all four trials of the Mexican Mafia, the Medina case was the only one that involved a single defendant. Medina didn't have the help of anyone when he killed Olmedo. When the victim realized he was being shot at, he leaned his body over to protect his sister and wife. It appeared that the victim was shot from the left side, which was consistent with him driving alongside the shooter. The victim was shot 12 times and there were 11 casings recovered at the crime scene. He was actually struck five times in the head and back. All of the gunshot wounds to the head were fatal. The victim's wife and sister were struck by some of the bullets but were not killed in the attack.

At trial, the wife and sister were able to testify that there was no provocation or words exchanged before the shooting. There was no attempt to rob them. All they remember was a car pulling up alongside them and the driver held a gun in his hand

and shot through the open window. Because the incident happened so quickly, they weren't able to get a good look at the shooter so they were unable to identify Medina as the shooter.

The key witness to the Olmedo shooting was Benny "Sleepy" Garcia, who had testified in some of the other trials. Garcia knew Medina since he was one of the workers of his drug team. Garcia testified that he supplied guns to Medina which were used in the Olmedo and Dellosa killings. He stated that he gave guns to Medina for his protection when he was dealing drugs. He said that Medina didn't have permission to gang-bang with his guns.

Medina was tried for both the killing of Carlos Dellosa and Ferdie Olmedo in one trial. The main witness in the Carlos Dellosa murder case was Clinton Conroy. Tony had granted immunity to get Clinton Conroy to testify to the facts of that shooting. The Defense to both shootings was orchestrated by his Defense attorney, who mainly attacked the prosecution's witnesses. He argued that Conroy couldn't be believed since he was an accomplice (he was the driver). As to Benny Garcia, he shouldn't be believed since he had been a drug dealer at the time of the shooting. The jury listened to both attorneys Arguments and then went out to deliberate. Within three hours the jury came back with two First Degree Murder convictions with Special Circumstances to be true, finding there were Multiple Murders and a robbery in the Dellosa case.

CHAPTER 31 TRIAL FOUR WITH LIL PEE WEE

(As stated in the beginning of the last chapter, the only reason I, the author, have included these additional EME cases is to illustrate the unbelievable challenges that Tony and Ruth faced in their five-year campaign of trying the biggest and longest EME cases of all times.)

The facts in the Lil Pee Wee case was a nightmare of a case to try since it involved three separate shooting/murders. Two of the shootings involved the killing of informants and the third one involved a dope dealer not paying his EME taxes.

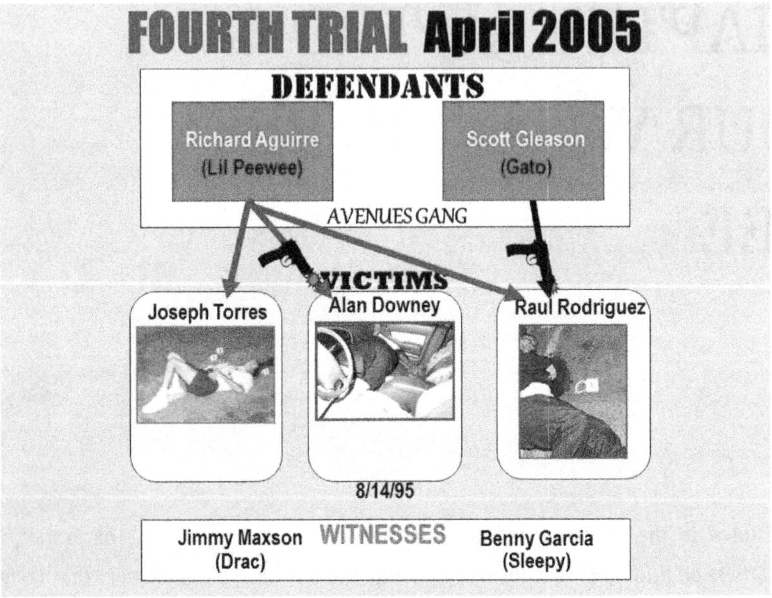

One of the associate members of EME had seen a police report that indicated that **Raul Rodriguez** had told the police that a fellow gang member had been involved in a crime.

"Little Pee Wee" Aguirre ordered Raul Rodriguez to be murdered. He recruited Scotty "Gato" Gleason to do the actual killing. They lured Raul Rodriguez to come to the Montecito Heights Community Center. When he arrived, they got him between two cars in the parking lot. "Little Pee Wee" gave "Gato" a gun and he walked up to Rodriguez and shot him several times in the head.

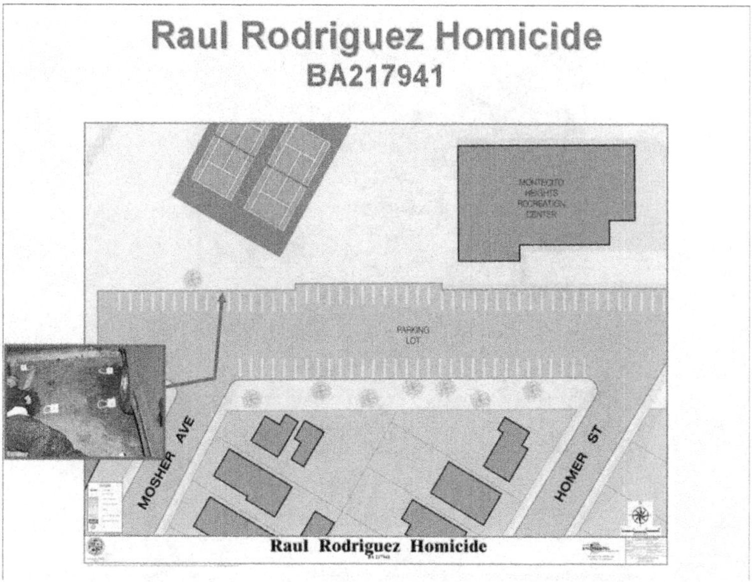

Like in many of the other "Doing Business" killings, Rodriguez's body was left for all to see so people would know what happens to anyone who would consider snitching off a fellow gang member to the police.

An automatic weapon was used to kill **Joseph Torres** since several shell casings were found next to the body. The Coroner testified that the victim was shot in the head. This type of gunshot wound was used in cases in which EME believes that the victim had been a snitch to the police.

The area where Torres was shot was high up on a hillside. From this location, there was a spectacular view of the city of Los Angeles. The crime scene was covered with numerous shell casings, indicating that an automatic weapon was used. His killers left his body to be seen by other gang members in the area. The killers weren't interested in killing Torres in a remote area where others wouldn't get the message that snitching on an EME member resulted in a sentence of death.

Again, Tony had to decide if it would be beneficial in this case to have the jury consider the Conspiracy charge. He was concerned that this would complicate the case for the jury. On the other hand, it provided the jury with the possibility to convict "Lil Pee Wee" of the Conspiracy even if they had difficulty with finding him guilty of the murder charge. Some jurors might find that "Lil Pee Wee" didn't play that much of a role in the actual Murder since he remained in the car when "Gangster" Marquez got out and did the shooting of Torres.

The Coroner testified that the victim, Torres, had been shot in the back of the head as commonly called "Execution Style." The rest of his body was shot numerous times, including his hands and legs. More than one of the bullet wounds would have been fatal. All the wounds appeared to come from the same weapon.

The third shooting involved Alan Downey. The facts of his case have already been discussed. He was killed as he was driving back to the motel he was staying at. As you may remember, he was shot because he didn't know who to pay the EME taxes to.

This trial was lengthy since it required so many witnesses from various crime scenes. Basically, the prosecution relied on Jimmy Drac Maxson and Benny Sleepy Garcia to tell the jury the facts of each shooting. These witnesses had testified numerous times, so they were experienced witnesses. The Defense attorney during his cross-examination wasn't able to make any inroads into the witnesses' testimony. It only took the jury two days of deliberation to convict both defendants. Scott Gato Gleason was only found guilty of shooting Rodriguez.

However, Lil Pee Wee was found guilty of all three murders even though he only pulled the trigger in the Alan Downey shooting. What was strange about his conviction was the fact that five years earlier a younger Lil Pee Wee was given the opportunity to plead guilty to a manslaughter conviction, which meant he would be out in six years. He agreed to the sweetheart deal, which would later melt away.

That was when Detective Andy Teague went looking for another prosecutor who would take a tougher stand in the Lil Pee Wee case. Det. Teague decided to walk through the halls of Major Crimes Division looking for some hotdog prosecutor he had heard about. What was ironic for Lil Pee Wee and all of the EME defendants was that if Tony Manzella hadn't been in that day, none of this would have happened. Also, if Tony hadn't been willing to drive over to LAPD Northeast Division to review these 17 unsolved homicides lying on the homicide detectives' desks, they would most likely still be sitting there. Forlorn Lil Pee Wee and all the other gangsters will never know how their fate was sealed when Tony sat down in a back office in the police station and reviewed all those Murder Books and figured out the key to convicting them all.

CHAPTER 32 THE FINAL TRIAL

This endless series of trials reminds the opera lovers of Richard Wagner's immortal Der Ring Cycle. The Wagnerian operas were so long they never seemed to end. That was just like all the EME trials. However, it came time for the 'fat lady' to sing (Nowadays it would be the 'heavyset woman.') You almost could hear the Valkyries practicing their parts in the dank recesses of the Criminal Courts Building.

In May of 2006, the last of the four core prosecutions came to trial. Defendant

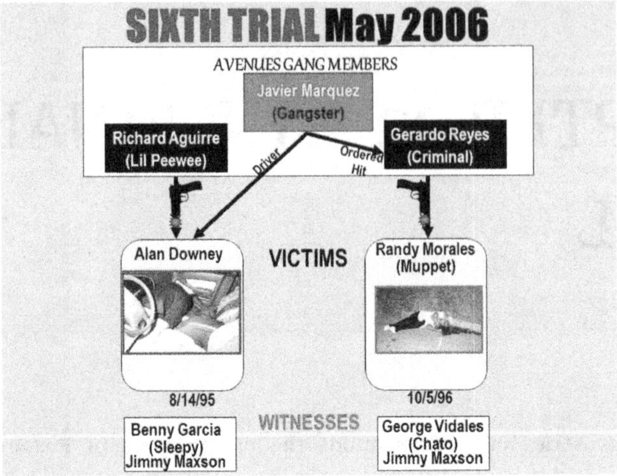

Javier 'Gangster' Marquez had already been convicted of other murders and was looking at spending the rest of his life in prison. Tony and the DA administration believed that Marquez was someone who had earned the Death Penalty from all the years of violence he committed throughout the barrio.

Marquez's Defense attorney claimed that a jail guard had confiscated some documents and diagrams he had in his cell. The attorney argued that those documents were central for his Defense and without them he couldn't get a fair trial. He also made a motion to suppress the statements Muppet had made to the police about Marquez killing several Highland Park men.

Tony successfully argued to defeat both Defense motions; consequently, the trial continued. The trial was basically the same drill since the prosecution had already had to prove up in other trials the killing of Alan Downey and Muppet Morales. Tony explained to the jury that he would be calling Benny (Sleepy) Garcia, who would tell them that defendant Marquez was the driver when Lil Pee Wee shot Alan Downey as he was driving on Eaglerock Boulevard. Also, Tony said that he had an eyewitness who would identify Marquez as being the driver of a car that came back to the crime scene in which a person got out and continued to shoot Downey.

As to the shooting of Muppet, Tony explained that Jimmy 'Drac' Maxson would testify that the defendant admitted to him that he had ordered the killing of Muppet for being a snitch against him. Also, he related that Chato Vidales would testify how Muppet was killed as well as how Marquez was the person who ordered the killing.

For the prosecution, it was like the repeat of 'groundhog' day. All the witnesses testified just like before, and the Defense attorney tried to show how the prosecution witnesses were testifying to get a deal for themselves. However, the elephant in the room was the fact that Marquez had his attorney subpoena for his trial a dozen or so high officials in EME. The State Prison, California Department of Corrections, is required to transport all the prisoners who have been subpoenaed for court. These become big events for the members of EME. This becomes like old home week as the members are brought back to county jail for the reunion.

The courts, the jail, and prison authorities recognized what EME members were up to but the law requires any subpoenaed prison gang member to be transported to the court. Many of the EME members are housed in the Pelican Bay Maximum prison facility, which is way over 500 miles up North. The transportation of so many extremely dangerous prisoners is an awesome task.

Tony couldn't prevent the Defense from subpoenaing all these hardcore killers to court. Nonetheless, Judge Fidler outsmarted the EME members. The judge ordered these prisoners not to be brought to the County Jail but transported to a state prison facility in Lancaster, which is in the northern part of Los Angeles County. In this way the EME prisoners didn't get to visit with their old homies in the County Jail.

Before trial, the Defense argued that all these witnesses were necessary for their Defense. They claimed that they were being called to testify that Marquez was not a member of EME. However, during the entire trial none of these witnesses were ever called as witnesses. The Defense excuse was that the witnesses refused to testify. As a result, many of the EME members were able to have a vacation from their old cell at Pelican Bay. In the process, they may have had an opportunity to socialize with some of their old colleagues.

At the end of trial, both sides gave vigorous Arguments. The jurors listened to both sides and soon the case was in their hands. After a short deliberation, the jury came back with guilty verdicts as to the murders of Alan Downey and Muppet Morales by defendant Javier 'Gangster' Marquez.

The real issue in this case was the question of the appropriate sentence. The prosecution believed that there was more than sufficient evidence that the

Aggravating evidence outweighed the Mitigating evidence. Tony prepared the below chart to show the jurors that Marquez had a long record of violence.

MARQUEZ TIMELINE

March 1994	Use of force against inmate at California Institute for Men, Chino
November 1994	Use of force against staff at RJ Donovan Correction Facility, San Diego
August 1995	Murders of the Sanchez brothers
August 1995	Murders of one person; and attempted murders of two other persons
August 1995	Murder of Alan Downey
January 1996	Use of force against staff at North Kern State Prison
March 1996	Use of force against staff at North Kern State Prison
October 1996	Murder of Randy Morales
November 2000	Use of force against inmate at Los Angeles County Jail
October 2001	Possession of shank at Los Angeles County Jail
April 2006	Possession of shank at Los Angeles County Jail

The jurors listened attentively and went out and deliberated for two hours and came back with a verdict of Life Without Parole. In other words, Tony's hard work of pursuing the Death Penalty was all for naught. Tony sat in his chair at the counsel table as he listened to the court clerk read the verdict. Tony had a slight smile come over his face. He was retiring and this was his last verdict he would ever take. Whether defendant Marquez received the Death Penalty or LWOP didn't matter to Tony. Tony's long distinguished career had come to a close. It was as if the Fat Lady had finally sung the swan song for TONY MANZELLA.

CHAPTER 33
CONCLUSION OF EME TRIALS

The Tony and Ruth story is worth telling. They are two unique individuals who did a public service for the community for neither recognition nor praise. They did what they did for the mere personal satisfaction of doing it better than anyone else. In past times, Tony and Ruth would have been revered for their unselfish devotion for upholding the THIN BLUE LINE. (This is the symbol of the relationship of law enforcement in the community as the protectors of fellow civilians from the criminal elements.)

These days the concept has become highly controversial by certain groups who dislike the so-called 'establishment.' This book is not meant to defend or attack the criminal justice system. But the fact is that there are people like Tony and Ruth who hold society together by not being afraid of taking on EVIL wherever it appears.

Tony gained nothing by taking on EME. Tony said, "The Mexican Mafia is right now where La Costa Nostra was 50 years ago. We've got a shot at keeping it from growing into what La Costa Nostra became." He had a perspective that few others have. For Tony, the filing and prosecuting of so many EME members wasn't a personal vendetta against the group. He made it clear that he wasn't personally out to get anyone in particular. He was merely using the cracks in their organization against them. The fact that EME Green Lighted so many people gave the prosecution the tool to use against EME. The result was that EME had to reevaluate their Green Light killing machine.

Some people reading this book may say that all the people Green Lighted were mainly vile gang members who most likely deserved what they got. That argument has some merit, but does society want to give the EME Carnales the power and right to decide who lives or dies? Most people would agree that a lid needs to be placed on EME. Tony and Ruth understood that what they were doing wasn't going to destroy EME. As long as there are prisons there will be Prison Gangs. However, the Tony and Ruth team had a major impact on the containment of a Mexican Mafia. Their TENCIOUS STRUGGLE AGAINST EVIL truly has made a difference. (For more insight into EME and more details about all these cases prosecuted by Tony Manzella I would suggest the 2007 book ***THE MEXICAN MAFIA*** by Tony Rafael.)

After reviewing the Gomez and Grajeda case plus the Mexican Mafia cases, we can unequivocally agree that TONY MANZELLA should definitely be included in the Best of the Best DAs.

PROSECUTOR HOON CHUN

Gangster McGhee, the Monster of Atwater Village

CHAPTER 34 TAGGING ON FRIDAY NIGHT

On Friday evening, October 10, 1997, many Angelinos were trying to decide whether to go to the movies to see ***Boogie Nights, Most Wanted***, or ***Rocket Man***. Those stuck at home could watch ***20/20, Nash Bridges***, or ***Dateline***. For those who didn't find their way to the movies and were bored with the TV options, they might visit friends. For the younger generation in northeast LA, it was just another Friday night, which meant cruising down Glendale Boulevard on their bikes looking for some mischief they could do without getting caught.

This area of Los Angeles is known as Atwater Village, which is sandwiched between giant Griffith Park on the west side and the City of Glendale on the east side. This community is made up of modest Spanish tile roof houses that indicate pride of ownership while others show their age with deferred maintenance. The population is primarily Hispanic, and many of the residents can trace their ancestors back to Guadalajara, Mexico. Atwater Village is well known for the three gangs that call this area their home turf. To the north is the Toonerville Rifa Gang, the middle section is made up of the Thee Rascals Gang, and on the South is the Frogtown Gang.

The infamous Avenues Street Gang is directly to the east and is separated by the railroad tracks that run along San Fernando Road. The Atwater Village gangs tolerate and respect the Avenues Gang and leave them alone. However, there is a fierce rivalry among the three Atwater Village gangs.

Map of Gang Territory

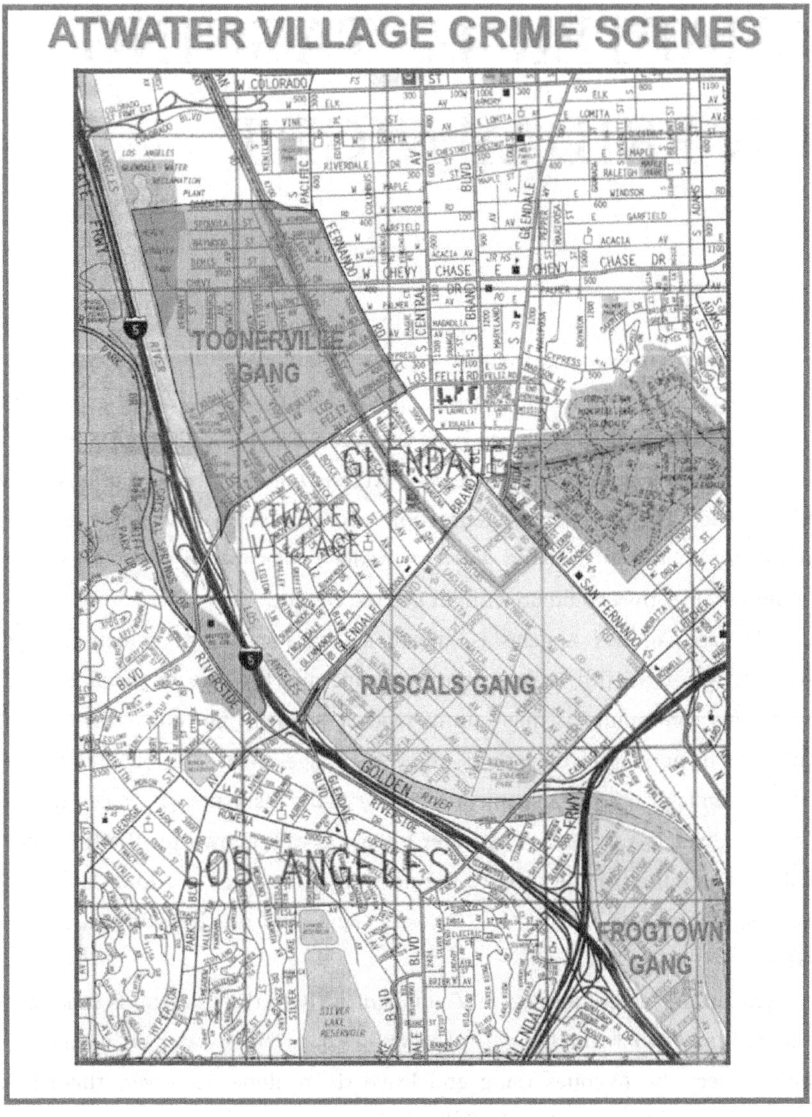

It was about 10:30 p.m. when six or eight members of Thee Rascals Gang were riding their bikes along Glendale Boulevard. As they came to each intersection, the group would separate to the four corners and climb up the street sign posts. When there were no vehicles approaching, they used markers to write their gang's name over the name of the street. For these young Rascal gang members, it was exhilarating to do tagging and not get caught. But most of all, they were telling all their rival gangsters that this is Rascal territory. Glendale Boulevard is considered the gang's demarcation line. The Rascals were in their considered territory as long as they stayed on the south side of Glendale Boulevard. If one crosses to the north side they would be considered in the so called 'no man's land.' This was made up of a four-block area considered a neutral territory that no gang laid claim to.

Some of the Rascals had spray cans, which didn't seem to work as well on the street signs but worked well on the street sign posts. The weather conditions were cooling down and the Rascals felt elated in that the tagging was going well. Several of the Rascals darted across to the north side of Glendale Boulevard and started tagging the street signs in the so-called neutral territory. By 10:30 p.m. Glendale Boulevard still had some traffic but all the businesses on the street had closed their doors and turned off their signs.

The Rascals were having the time of their life. No one was challenging them, and they were becoming consumed by the feeling of being invincible. Suddenly a light-colored Honda slowed and pulled over to the curb. A muscular male in his mid-20s wearing a dark sweater with a beanie on his head exited the passenger side. He stood tall and raised his hand, revealing a large semi-automatic weapon. Not a word was spoken, just the loud roar of the gun. The Rascals were shocked to see this man standing expressionless firing his large gun at them.

The Rascals weren't armed except for their spray cans and Marks-A-Lot markers. They quickly realized that they were in no condition to fight back. The most basic instincts kicked in, which were FIGHT or FLIGHT. Since the first option was unavailable, they had no choice but to RUN. Those who were on their bikes jumped off and two of the guys, Juan C. and Pedro S., started to run. The immediate question for them was where to hide? The man stood next to this car pointing the gun in their direction just deliberately firing at them.

Juan C. and Pedro S. had learned that if they were confronted by the police they were to scatter in different directions, making it more difficult for the police to catch all of them. Juan's reaction was to run into the street while Pedro headed in the other direction for a gas station. This split-and-run technique was working. Yet Juan quickly realized that running into the street gave him no cover from the shooter. He leaned down to make himself a smaller target. In so doing he felt a sharp intense pain in his back. In less than a second, he was lying flat on the asphalt scraping his elbows, and he tried to move his feet but they weren't responding. As he lay in the middle of the street, this shooter continued to shoot at him. Like a colossal stomach punch, he felt as though he couldn't breathe as he gasped for air.

He resigned himself to the fact that he couldn't move out of the way of gunfire. He felt that his life was over and there was nothing he could do about it. At that moment his immediate attention was on the fact that he was in the middle of Glendale Boulevard and there was traffic still traveling east and west bound. The drivers were focused on the man standing shooting the gun and not paying attention to unlucky Juan lying helplessly in the middle of the street.

Juan knew his chance of survival was minimal. The immediate question was whether he was going die from a gunshot or from traffic running over him. Unexpectedly, the shooter's attention was drawn to the other runner and he no longer was looking in Juan's direction. The shooter started pursuing Pedro, who was running for his life going eastbound on Glendale Blvd. Then the shooter started on a foot pursuit of Pedro while holding his gun in front of him. Pedro, who never excelled in track and field at school, took off like a sprinter running the 100-meter dash. As Pedro ran he kept turning his head to watch the progress of the shooter and hoping he could find cover.

Most of the businesses on Glendale Boulevard were shuttered up for the night. Pedro's only hope was a Shell service station that was being converted into mini-mart. The lights were on in the office, although he couldn't see any attendant working inside. Pedro was like a homing pigeon that made a straight path for the front door of the station's office.

He went inside the office portion, which had two large glass doors, and could see the shooter gaining on him. Pedro realized that he was a sitting duck if the shooter got inside the mini-mart. Pedro didn't have any weapon and was no match for the shooter, who continued to aim his gun and fire at Pedro. What should Pedro do in order to survive? There was no way he could lock the two glass doors. Pedro knew that his only hope was to hold the two glass doors closed so the shooter couldn't get inside.

Pedro could see that the glass doors weren't much of a shield to protect him. Pedro used both of his hands to hold the two glass doors from being opened by the shooter. Since the attacker had a gun in his one hand, he had only one hand to try to pull the doors open. Pedro and the shooter were standing nose to nose separated only by a glass door.

It appeared that Pedro's perseverance in holding the doors shut had worked. The man with the gun stepped back and pointed the gun at Pedro on the other side of the glass door. The shooter pulled the trigger and a shot rang out. Pedro spun around as the entire glass door shattered into thousands of pieces. The noise was deafening.

Pedro was left holding the door handle in his hand with no door or anything between him and the shooter. The next thing that Pedro felt was his body falling to the floor after being hit once in the back. Pedro was covered with shards of glass as he lay on the floor. At that point, Pedro thought he was a dead man.

All he could see was the figure of the shooter pointing the gun down at him. Pedro could hear more shards of broken glass continuing to fall on the concrete floor. He heard the faint sound of a police siren. The man with the gun spun around and started to run for the Honda car that had pulled in front of the Shell service station. The man jumped into the Honda as it accelerated in the direction of Toonerville territory.

The irony of the situation was that the police unit was dispatched to investigate a tagging situation and had nothing to do with the shots fired. The police were there to catch the young taggers, which were Juan and Pedro and their tagging crew.

As the officers were driving in search of the taggers, they heard the sound of gunfire and headed in the direction of the sound. The officers saw an injured Juan being pulled out of the street. They instantly pulled their car over to check him out and discovered that he had been shot several times. Fortunately, the paramedics arrived at almost the same time. Juan was taken to the hospital, where it was determined that the bullet had damaged his spinal cord, which meant he would be paralyzed for the rest of his life from the waist down.

The officers were directed by those at the scene to the Shell service station just to the east. With guns in their hands, the officers ran toward the mini-market portion of the Shell station. As they approached the front of the store, they saw two men huddled on the floor where a glass front door had been. They saw the one man still clutching the handle to the front door and another man was trying to give aid to Pedro S.

The perplexed officers didn't know what they had come across. Were these men on the floor victims or suspects? Before they could be asked whether they were okay they noticed blood seeping all over the one man's shirt. The officer asked the paramedics for an assessment of the extent of the injuries. Soon it was determined that Pedro had been shot in the back, but the injury didn't appear to be life threatening.

More questions were asked whether they could identify the shooters. Much later Juan C. was shown a six-pack photo identification. He picked the #2 photo and said that looked like the person who shot him. That was a photo of Timothy McGhee, the shot caller for the Toonerville Street Gang. Later the detectives asked Pedro if he could identify his shooter and he refused to identify anyone. When they asked him about McGhee, Pedro said, "See, you guys already know who it is." The parties considered this a gang dispute which they would resolve on their own.

The police recognized what they were up against. The wounded parties were gang members who would handle this matter on their own. The detectives knew that they would have to rely on other evidence such as forensics if they were to ever have enough evidence to file criminal charges against the shooters. The CSI team arrived after the shooting and spent an extensive amount of time collecting the various shell casings and slugs spread out over a city block. The items that were found were taken to the Crime Lab and examined. The firearms expert was able to determine that there were three guns used at the crime scene. One was .22 caliber, another was .30 caliber, and the main gun was a .40 caliber handgun.

CHAPTER 35 OVERKILL IN FROGTOWN

Then four days later on October 14, 1997, at 12:05 a.m., there was another shooting in the Atwater Village area. It was further to the south and was in an area known by its gang name Frogtown. Its rivals are Thee Rascals Gang directly north of them and Toonerville Gang further to the north. Some Toonerville gangsters from the north were driving around looking for Frogtown members. The purpose was to retaliate for what had happened earlier in the day when one of the Toonerville members had been shot at.

The City of Los Angeles had spent large sums of money to create recreation centers where young people could go to have safe fun. There were all types of sports and recreation activities to keep the young people off the streets. The purpose of the recreation center was to discourage young people from becoming involved in gangs. It was a few minutes after midnight when these Toonerville guys were driving around and saw a young male near the entrance to the Elysian Valley Recreation Park.

That person was Ronald Martin, whose moniker was Cloudy. These gangsters pulled up alongside Cloudy and shouted out, "Where are you from?" The young man looked at the guys in the car and said with a slight smile, "I'm from nowhere." Those words are generally sufficient to give a person a free pass. Ronald Martin didn't want to be confrontational. He kept on walking, hoping other cars would come along and spook whoever these guys were. They asked again, and Ronald casually said that he wasn't into gangbanging.

Ronald felt trapped as he walked along a chain-link fence next to the entrance to the Rec Center. The car kept following him, and the big guy inside the car ordered him to pull up his sweatshirt and show his chest. He didn't dare pull up his shirt since he had a large tattoo of his gang's name, FROGTOWN, emblazoned across his chest. He hesitated in pulling up his sweatshirt. Then guns came out and he figured that he had no option so he pulled it up quickly hoping that they wouldn't be able to read the tat in the dark.

At that moment, Ronald couldn't help remembering his mother's warning not to get such a massive tattoo since that would make him a marked man. They could see the bottom of the word FROGTOWN. Ronald thought maybe they would shout some insults toward his gang and then they would drive off. Maybe he could talk his way out of this bad situation. He started talking and pleading for his life. He begged them not to shoot him. The only reply he got back from the big guy in the car was, "Shut up and die like a man! Not like a bitch." After that, the gangsters got out of the car. Ronald tried to back up hoping to get away. He had no place to run for cover as the guns started blazing. He stumbled backward as bullet after bullet flew through his riddled body. By the time the guns were silent he had been shot 26 times. Without a doubt this was a case of overkill.

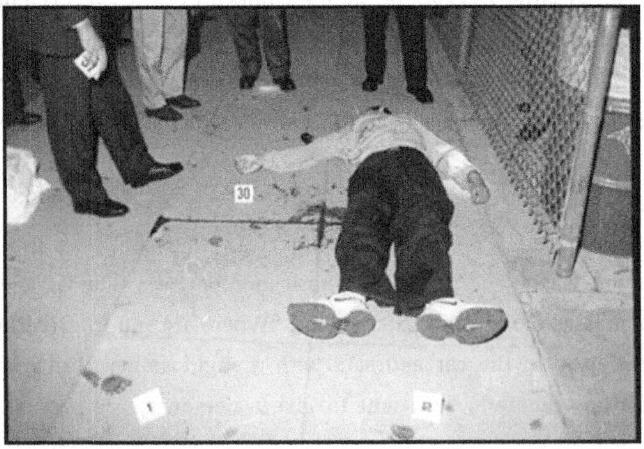

What type of message were these northern gangsters trying to communicate to the Frogtown members? Anyone who was thinking of disrespecting the Toonerville gang would end up the same way as Ronald, looking like a piece of Swiss cheese.

When the police responded to the Rec Center, they found Ronald Martin's body flat on his back with blood seeping out all parts of his body. Since it was after midnight, there were no eyewitnesses who could provide useful information as to who did the shooting. This time the CSI crew had their work cut out for them. There were shell casings and slugs all over the entrance to the Recreation Center. Initially, they could see .40 caliber and .45 caliber semi-automatic shell casings. All the ballistics evidence was taken to the Crime Lab to be later examined. The firearms expert said that the .40 caliber semi-automatic shell had been fired from the same gun that fired .40 caliber shells at Juan C. and Pedro S. four days earlier. Needless to say, after such a savage overkill gangland shooting, no one was anxious to come forward to name the shooters.

CHAPTER 36 THE SHOT CALLER FOR TOONERVILLE

International Terrorism is one of the things that everyone can agree can't be tolerated in a civilized society. It is the notion that someone or some group can strike without warning, creating death and destruction. The result is constant fear as to when and where the terrorists will strike again. The unique part of terrorism is that it takes very few people to hold hostage millions of people who live in the community. Even the largest military with the most sophisticated equipment is powerless against the terrorist. Governments spend billions of dollars to combat international terrorism; however, at times it appears that all the resources thrown at it still can't defeat it.

Urban terrorism comes in many forms. The most common is the hardcore urban gangs who terrorize their communities. Citizens are in fear of going out of their houses because they might be caught in the crossfire of gang violence. Law-abiding members of the community don't want to do anything that will cause the gangsters to retaliate against them. We may not think of gang members as urban terrorists, but they do fit the definition in that they will strike when and where they please. The gang may consist of only a few members, but they are able to intimidate thousands of hard-working people in their neighborhood.

There were several gangs that operated north of downtown Los Angeles just on the southern border of the City of Glendale. As already stated, the Atwater Village area was made up of several gangs: the Frogtown Gang to the South, Thee Rascals Gang in the middle, and the Toonerville Gang in the north. The latter would seem to be a strange name for a gang, but the members were proud of the gang's name. No one would dare make fun of this gang, with a cartoon name, if they wanted to stay alive.

Those who are cartoon buffs may remember the ***Toonerville Folks*** comic strip, which started back in 1908 and continued into the 1950s. It was about a mythical suburban community in which a rickety little trolley called the Toonerville Trolley met every train from the big city and slowly transported the riders to their cozy suburban homes.

In the real world of the 1940s, there was a trolley line that ran from downtown Los Angeles to Atwater Village. The locals gave that streetcar line the name Toonerville Trolley since it met the trains at Union Station (Los Angeles' main railroad station) and crept its way to the suburban area of Atwater Village.

In the 1940s the predominant Hispanic gang in this area was called the 'Latin Souls.' For some unexplained reason the gang changed its name to 'Toonerville.' Such a name doesn't have any Hispanic flavor to it and certainly didn't evoke any macho overtones. By the 1990s the Toonerville Rifa gang gained the reputation of being one of the deadliest gangs in all of Los Angeles. Some wonder whether the fact that the gang has a cartoon name may be the reason its members feel so strongly that they have to continually prove to others how tough they are.

WHO WAS TIMOTHY MCGHEE?

Right in the middle of the Toonerville gang territory was where Timothy Joseph McGhee lived. He was born in 1973; his father was Scottish and his mother was of Mexican descent. Somehow his father left the family when Timothy was young and he grew up with his mother in the Atwater Village community. With a name like McGhee, one would picture a choir boy at the local Catholic Church. However, Timothy Joseph McGhee was no choir boy by any definition. His moniker was 'Huero,' which was slang for the Spanish word Guero, translated as a light-skinned Mexican. Instead, he was the notorious leader (shot caller) of the Toonerville Gang. When the name McGhee is linked to the word Toonerville, one has a toxic mixture of the one person who was most feared in the entire Los Angeles area.

There was a good reason why so many people feared him. His muscular six-foot frame with a shaved head sporting a goatee projected the appearance of a tough guy who could take care of any problem. What made him a unique human being was that he enjoyed 'killing human beings.' He explained to others the incredible thrill he got when hunting down people to kill. He would take other Toonerville gang members with him as he cruised other gang territory hoping to see a rival gang member so he could shoot at them like doing target practice. Leader McGhee knew that it took skill to snare his rivals when they least expected to be attacked. He understood the concept of having overwhelming firepower to quickly silence his prey before they could run for cover or fire back.

When McGhee went on these hunts, he and his gangsters used several high-caliber weapons and often used assault weapons that he used to spray his rivals. Whenever that was done, the bullets went flying and often ended up hitting unintended targets. He and his gangsters had a total disregard for the fact that every time they went out hunting and shot at someone there was likelihood that innocent people such as children might be hit. His attitude was that if an innocent child were hit, "Oh well, that person shouldn't have been there."

McGhee would be the first to admit that it was often difficult to know who was a member of a rival gang. His feeling was that any young male who dressed in baggy jeans wearing a white T-shirt and was walking in rival gang territory was fair game. McGhee tried to be careful in selecting his targets. He enjoyed the satisfaction of causing intense pain on his rivals. He didn't gain any respect or create any fear if he accidentally killed a non-gang person.

McGhee's reputation was so well ingrained in the gang folklore that he was the shot caller for one of the most violent street gangs in all of Los Angeles. Everyone in the community was scared to death of him. To prevent anyone from ratting on him, he was willing to kill anyone who would be an informant or a witness against him. Basically, the police found that McGhee could do whatever he liked and there were no witnesses who would be willing to come forward to testify against him. It wasn't long before McGhee operated his little gang of hooligans with complete immunity from the police and the criminal justice system.

CHAPTER 37 HOMICIDE AVALANCHE CRASHING ON NORTHEAST STATION

The LAPD Northeast Division was experiencing one homicide after another, with the numbers adding up. The detectives would get the word on the street that McGhee was involved, but when it came to finding witnesses it was as though they had vanished. Some of the best LAPD homicide detectives were finding that there was no way of making a case that would stand up in court against McGhee. If there were any witnesses to a homicide, they never made it to court. McGhee had no fear that the police would ever be able to make a case against him. He continued to kill more and more people whenever he felt like it.

He became so untouchable that he became elevated to the level of a "Godfather" that no one would cross.

The LAPD established a task force made up of their very top investigators to see if there was some way of ending or at least reducing the number of murders. When homicide detectives can't find witnesses to the actual crimes, they try to find someone the killer may have bragged to about the murder. This route utilizes the so-called informant who is willing to testify in exchange for favorable treatment for some case that they may have against them. Usually, these are Jailhouse Informants who keep their ears open to try to get some type of incriminating statement from one of their fellow inmates. After McGhee was in custody, there was a jailhouse informant who claimed that McGhee had told him that he was involved in four different shootings which resulted in the deaths of seven victims.

There was incredible pressure to get McGhee. Everyone knew he was a killer, but he seemed to be coated in Teflon and nothing was going to stick to him. This jailhouse informant was just what everyone had been waiting for—a person who wasn't afraid to testify in court as to all the incriminating facts that McGhee had told him. The police and the politicians were thankful that the homicide rate was greatly reduced after McGhee was taken into custody.

The DA's Office started the lengthy prosecution of McGhee. Because of the importance of the case, it was given to the most senior trial litigator in the DA's Office. He worked closely with investigating officers. He started to check out some of the facts that the jailhouse informant had related, such as he hadn't had much contact with McGhee in the past. Then it was learned that the informant and McGhee were arch enemies who had tried to kill each other. As a matter of fact, the informant had tried to kill McGhee countless times and McGhee had tried to kill this informant at least on one occasion.

The prosecutor realized that the informant's credibility was at stake. The last straw was when a smuggled copy of the police report of one of the shootings was found in the informant's cell. At that point, the prosecutor became suspicious of all the stories that the informant had told the police. The DA's Office was so concerned that it completely dropped the informant from the case against McGhee. This completely gutted the prosecution's case. The DA's Office realized the importance of keeping McGhee off the streets, but it couldn't do it with questionable testimony from this informant.

There was a meeting with the lead detectives to see what evidence still could be developed in order to prosecute McGhee. The case was given to Detective Andy Teague and his partner. They were very tenacious and willing to follow up on any lead to develop evidence against McGhee. After months of investigation, these two detectives had worked tirelessly and had gotten to the point they had talked to enough people that they were building a solid case piece by piece. The DA's Office was breathing much easier.

The Senior Prosecutor on the case was pleased with the progress of the case. These detectives had developed a rapport with certain key people who were willing to talk only to them. Some of these people were helping the detectives locate the crucial witnesses that the prosecution would have to bring to court to build the case against McGhee. The detectives had to spend time trying to relocate some people so McGhee couldn't find them.

CHAPTER 38 ONLY ONE HUERO

The gang violence subsided during the year 1998 and part of 1999. It wasn't that everyone in the gangs decided to live in Peace and Harmony, but definitely there was less violence between the gangs. The real reason was that McGhee was no longer on the streets of Atwater Village, since he was in state prison. However, not all good things last forever. By June 3, 2000, McGhee was out of prison and back leading his Toonerville gang.

He wanted everyone to know that McGhee was back and in control of the community. He knew that he needed to reassert himself so he would be feared and respected. McGhee was proud of his moniker "Huero," which meant light-skinned Mexican. When he returned, McGhee learned that someone in Thee Rascal Gang had decided to use the moniker "Huero." This fact infuriated McGhee since that was a sign of ultimate disrespect of him. The Rascal who claimed the name was Ryan Gonzales, who was merely 16 years old and had no of idea the hornets' nest he had disturbed.

In the earlier morning hours, McGhee and his fellow gang members were driving around looking for someone to shoot. They were slowly cruising in a dark pickup truck. They knew that many of Thee Rascal Gang members were attending a party in the heart of Rascal territory. It was 1:50 a.m. and Ryan Gonzales was walking home alone. McGhee saw Gonzales and told the driver to pull over so he could get out and confront him. McGhee jumped out with his gun in his hand.

It was unknown if McGhee knew that this was the person who was using the "Huero" moniker. McGhee walked up to Ryan Gonzales and a few words were exchanged. Whether the words spoken were the word "Rascals" or "Huero," the result was instantaneous death. McGhee fired a 9mm semi-automatic at Gonzales. If the first round didn't hit him the barrage of gunfire did hit its mark and Gonzales's feet buckled as his body spun around coming to rest on the asphalt of the street. As Gonzales lay moaning in the gutter, McGhee came up to stand over the body and he continued to shoot at the victim for a total of eight times.

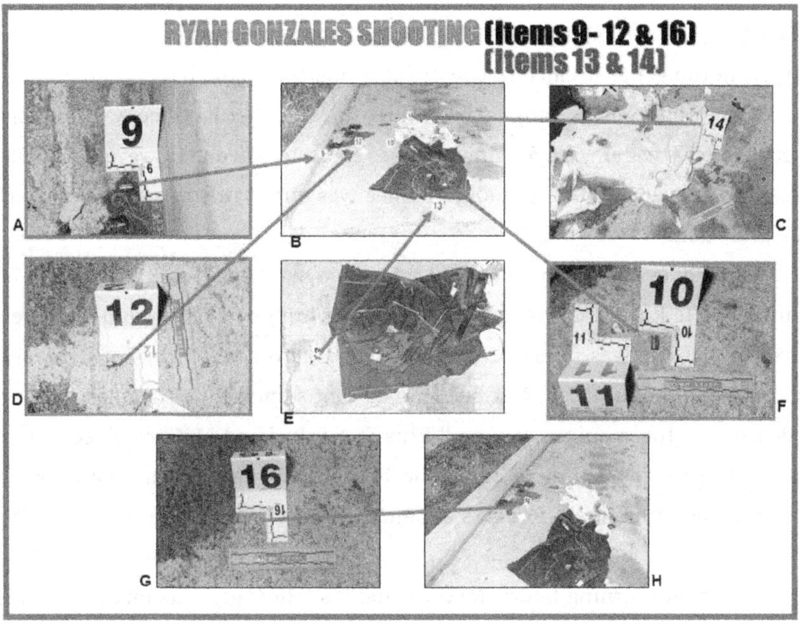

Afterwards, McGhee bragged to his associates, "Fuck Huero, I fucking killed that mother fucker... I'm the real Huero from Toonerville. They know I'm the Huero in Atwater Village." McGhee was back in town and he wanted everyone to know he was back in control of the Atwater Village community. McGhee ran his gang like a paramilitary group. Many gangs have no one person in charge. Often gangs are run by a group of senior members. However, in the Toonerville Gang there was no doubt as to who was in charge.

McGhee is a hands-on leader who actively directed the gang members in doing calisthenics and other times took them for target practice. He wanted his members to be fit and ready for any situation. McGhee demanded absolute loyalty from his members. He demonstrated paranoia for his turf and was afraid that Rascals and Frogtown gangsters would encroach into the Toonerville territory. To prevent any poaching of his area he had members who acted as armed sentries equipped with cellphones or walkie talkies to watch for rivals.

With the sound from the eight shots fired at Gonzales, the neighbors on Silverlake Boulevard quickly called the police and officers responded to see Gonzales lying in a pool of blood. The paramedics weren't far behind and quickly were cutting off the clothes of this 16-year-old in order to try to resuscitate the victim. After several futile attempts, they decided to transport the victim to a hospital to see if someone could bring the victim back to life.

When the homicide detectives arrived, they instructed the CSI crew to locate all the shell casings, which seemed to be spread over a large area of the street and sidewalk. Next, the detectives went door to door to see if anyone saw anything. Since it occurred after 1:30 p.m., none of the residents were awake at the time. The detectives inferred that the shooting was gang related since there were no signs of a robbery or barroom fight. The detectives only hope was the possibility of ballistics connecting this shooting to a certain firearm that may be recovered in the future.

After the autopsy reports were completed by the Coroner's Office, a green three-ring binder was prepared and it joined the stack of other gang homicides which cluttered the homicide squad's desks.

CHAPTER 39 PURSUIT ENDING IN SHOOT-OUT

One month had elapsed since Ryan Gonzales was shot and nothing magic had occurred to solve the case. It was July 4, 2000, and everyone was looking forward to the fireworks shows. Most people enjoy this time of the year when families get together and have parties outdoors. Independence Day is commonly associated with parades, barbecues, carnivals, fairs, picnics, concerts, baseball games, and especially family gatherings.

This special day is topped off by colorful fireworks displays that leave the spectators in awe. Young children look skyward with their mouths open and eyes staring in wonderment while the family dog tries to find a safe haven from all the loud whistling sounds.

On this July fourth holiday, few Americans think of the real reason for celebrating this day. Even fewer know why this day is so meaningful to true patriots. Someone might say that it was the beginning of the United States of America. That might be a partial answer. Others will say that was the day that the Constitution was signed by a group of men in Philadelphia, Pennsylvania. That answer would be wrong since that's a different document signed on another date.

July fourth was meant to celebrate the legal separation of the Thirteen Colonies from Great Britain. That was when the Second Continental Congress voted to approve a resolution of independence. All of this occurred on July Second, 1776, not the Fourth. The story goes that after they had voted for Independence some guy by the name of Thomas Jefferson was given the task to prepare a document explaining the representatives' decision. That document was called the ***Declaration of Independence***. Jefferson had to round up all the representatives to sign the document. It wasn't until July Fourth that everyone had signed. (However, historians have now learned that not everyone signed the Declaration by July Fourth. It wasn't until August the Second, 1776, that all members had signed the document.)

Jefferson had to make one of those executive decisions as to what date to put on the top of the document. To be more accurate, he should have dated the document July 2, 1776, when the representatives decided to declare their independence from Great Britain. However, Jefferson thought the crucial date should be when everyone had signed. That was why he wrote at the very top of the Declaration of Independence these words:

IN CONGRESS, JULY 4, 1776

THE UNANIMOUS DECLARATION of the thirteen united STATES OF AMERICA.

After this new nation survived the Revolutionary War, the citizens wanted to celebrate the birth of their nation. Years later the leaders wanted to find a date they could use for a national holiday. The easy answer was they looked at the Declaration of Independence and saw the date July 4, 1776, on the top and decided to use that date for the national holiday.

That is the long and short of how July Fourth became a revered holiday in America. It is unknown how Timothy McGhee felt about July Fourth, but we know that he spent the early morning hours listening to the police scanners so he would know when the police were entering the Toonerville Gang territory. He took special notice when he heard a LAPD dispatcher mention a 211 (Robbery) in Thee Rascals Gang territory. Moments later they heard over the scanner an officer giving a description of a four-door brown Honda Accord. The officers continued to give their location as they followed the Honda with its three occupants. The description of the Honda matched that of a car that one of the Toonerville members drove.

As more information was transmitted, McGhee and the other gang members realized that the Honda was headed in their direction to the Toonerville territory. "We've got to do something," said McGhee to the others. They grabbed their guns and devised a plan to ambush the police car as it drove through their area. When McGhee and his crew went outside, they noticed an old washing machine near the curb ready for the morning trash pickup. Two of the guys got behind it and pushed it into the street in order to force the police to slow down when they approached it.

AERIAL OF BRUNSWICK & BEMIS

McGhee and the others could hear the siren of the police car growing louder as it got closer. They could see the headlights of the Honda coming up Brunswick Street. Not far behind was the police car with its red lights and siren. The Honda made a hard-right turn on Bemis Street and continued down by the school and park. McGhee was standing in the shadow of several parked cars just waiting for the ambush. His partner threw a bicycle in the street to force the police car to brake hard in order to maneuver around it.

Mc Ghee fired his 9mm semiautomatic at the driver's side of the police unit. One of the bullets went through the Los Angeles City seal, which is in the center of the door. This bullet struck the officer who was driving in his pant leg but didn't injure him. Other shots fired by McGhee struck the trunk and rear window. Fortunately, none of the bullets hit either officer.

The police car continued through the hail of gun fire and followed behind the Honda. While they were slowing down someone in the Honda threw out onto the sidewalk an assault weapon. After the police car crashed into the back of the Honda, several people saw McGhee take off running. One of the occupants in the Honda exited the car and took a stance firing a Tec 10 at the officers. The occupant in the back seat fired at the officers through the Honda's broken-out rear window. One of the assault weapons jammed and was thrown out. In and around the two cars were dozens of rounds that were fired from the occupants of the Honda and fired by the officers once they got out of their police car.

It took the CSI crew hours to collect all the shell casings and the slugs. Again, the items were taken to the Crime Lab for ballistic examination. It was learned that some of the 9mm shell casings matched the same shell casings found at Ryan Gonzales's crime scene. The same gun that was used to kill Gonzales was fired at the officers as part of an ambush. This was an interesting fact, but what did it all mean?

The bottom line was that both officers survived and the three guys in the Honda were eventually captured. With so many rounds fired, everyone was lucky that no one was killed. The three men in the Honda were prosecuted in a separate trial and they all received life sentences. However, McGhee and his cohorts involved in the ambush were not arrested or prosecuted in the original case.

The Los Angeles River makes up the westside boundary of the Toonerville gang territory. McGhee didn't have to spend time guarding the westside to prevent rival gang members from passing through Toonerville territory. Those who weren't familiar with the Los Angeles River may think it was a raging navigable waterway cutting through the heart of the second largest metropolitan city in the USA. Nonetheless, for the native Angelinos it is a giant concrete culvert that seldom has a trickle of $H^{2}O$.

During the early history of the city of Los Angeles, heavy rainstorms would cause massive flooding as the river weaved its way to the Pacific Ocean near Long Beach. Not until the catastrophic 1938 Flood did the city fathers act to do something to control these floods. The Army Corp of Engineers was brought in to begin an ambitious project of completely encasing the river's bed and banks in concrete. For over 70 years there hasn't been a flooding along the banks of the LA River. One would think this record of success would be lauded. However, only in Los Angeles could there be a group who want to tear out the concrete canal and allow the LA River to flow more naturally as when the native Indians occupied the riverbanks several hundreds of years ago.

Strangely enough, this group has been successful in having trees and bushes grow in the bed of the river. The result is that the portion of the LA River next to the Atwater Village is used by some die-hards to kayak for several miles on the bottom of the LA River. Most of the time there is no natural water that flows down the river. What the kayakers are paddling through is reclaimed sewage water from the Tillman Water Reclamation Plant, which collects the sewage from the 800,000 homes in the San Fernando Valley.

However, what the city fathers don't understand is that the concrete banks of the LA River serve another vital purpose for the gangs. Constantly, the gangs are tagging the concrete banks by spray-painting their gang name in gigantic graffiti letters for all to see.

On September 14, 2000, Gregory Roybal, a 17-year-old young man was leisurely sitting on the side of the LA River making sketches of the landscape. It was a relatively peaceful place since this is an area where there is still a ribbon of concrete of the LA River with the backdrop of the scenic hills of the Griffith Park. There was nothing provocative about his sketches or offensive about Gregory's conduct. Out of nowhere McGhee appeared and for no explainable reason he started shooting at the young artist. Within seconds Gregory Roybal was dying from his gunshot wounds.

Off to the side was a homeless man who was observing what was happening. He did nothing to involve himself in the shooting. Shortly thereafter McGhee went over to the homeless man and pointed his gun at him. Without a word being spoken, McGhee squeezed the trigger, thereby assuring there would be no witnesses as to the original shooting. This killing seemed so unnecessary since this homeless man was no threat to anyone. His only ambition was to find some soda or beer cans that he could redeem for cash.

It was late in the year 2000; McGhee was still on parole and was definitely in violation of the terms of his parole. As a result, the level of gang violence diminished considerably when McGhee was returned to state prison. Unfortunately, when McGhee was released criminal activity became rampant with a vengeance.

On June 11, 2001, McGhee, shortly after his release, was cruising along Los Feliz Blvd. on the west side of Atwater Village. He was the passenger in the front seat and was all eyes trying to catch up with everything that took place while he was gone. He and his friend came up parallel to another vehicle and he glanced at the other driver and thought he recognized him. As they continued to drive he realized that the driver was a member of Thee Rascals Gang. His name was Manuel Apodaca (21) and he was driving with his pregnant girlfriend.

Apodaca and his girlfriend weren't doing anything threatening or disrespectful to McGhee's gang. McGhee's immediate response was to pull his handgun out of his waistband. He raised it and held it slightly above the window ledge. Without a word being spoken, he gently pressed the trigger and bullets began to fly into Apodaca's car. McGhee was an accurate marksman in that Apodaca was fatally hit and his girlfriend was struck in the head, causing extensive brain damage. Amazingly, the fetus was successfully delivered. Nevertheless, the child's future wasn't all that bright since the father was dead and the mother was severely incapacitated.

Two months later on August 8, 2001, a neighbor of McGhee's sister reported to police that drug dealing was being conducted at McGhee's sister's home. It was unclear why this neighbor, Cheri Wisotsky, reported the activity to the police.

McGhee didn't take kindly to the fact that Wisotsky had blown the whistle on his sister. Wisotsky didn't like the intimidation from McGhee and stood up to him. For McGhee this was a 'no brainer'; he had to settle their dispute the way he settled all disputes, which was to kill the other person. However, the killing of Wisotsky had a domino effect in that there were several witnesses who saw the killing. That was how a minor dispute over selling drugs escalated into what was later called the 'Wisotsky massacre.' One of the lessons that McGhee had learned well was 'Leave No Witnesses.' That was why he also thought it was necessary to shoot Wisotsky's mother and Bryham Robinson. (It was never clear whether the Mexican Mafia had approved McGhee's killing of these two women and the man)

CHAPTER 40 KILL THE MITSUBISHI

Over the next year, there were numerous shootings in the Atwater Village area. McGhee was still on the streets, and the level of violence in this part of Los Angeles continued to escalate. The area patrolled by the Northeast LAPD was having a wave of crime that was unprecedented for this working-class community. As the list of shootings continued to rise, there were no witnesses who were willing to testify against McGhee and his Toonerville gangsters.

Exactly three months after the Wisotsky Massacre on November 8, 2001, there was a shooting in which a Toonerville gang member was shot and killed. McGhee felt this blatant act required swift retaliation from the Toonerville Gang. McGhee with another Toonerville gangster went out looking for someone to kill in Rascal territory. It was just past midnight and McGhee spotted a Mitsubishi car with three people in it. McGhee followed the car driving almost bumper to bumper.

The driver of the big Mitsubishi SUV was Duane N. His common-law wife Marjorie Mendoza was in the front passenger seat. She was a mother with two young children. There was a female in the backseat who was a friend of the couple. Duane was a member of the Atwater Pinoy Real gang (this was a splinter gang associated with Thee Rascals). Duane hadn't been involved in the shooting of the Toonerville gang member and wasn't doing any gang banging. When he saw the car following on his tail, he pulled over to the right so that car could go around him. He was almost at a stop when suddenly the other car pulled in front of his car and abruptly obstructed them. Two males exited their vehicle and started firing at them with semiautomatic weapons. The front of the Mitsubishi was riddled with bullets.

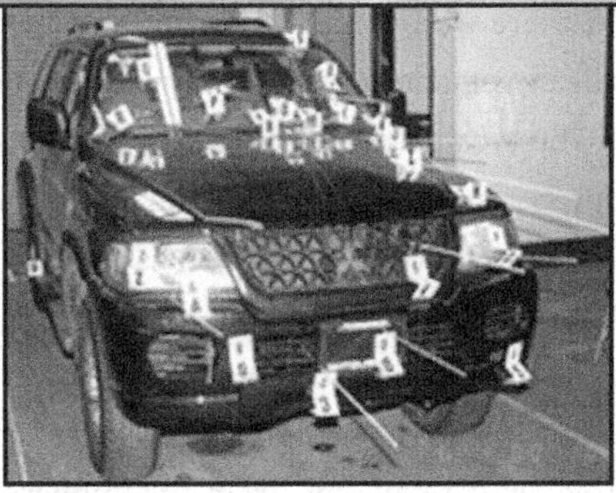

Duane ducked down and made himself as low as possible. He could see that Marjorie his wife was bleeding profusely and not breathing. The noise from the shooting and the shattering of glass were the only sounds. Duane didn't know how to react. He had his foot jammed on the brake to prevent the car from moving further into the line of fire. Should he accelerate to hit the shooters in front of them? Or should he put the SUV in reverse and try getting away? Suddenly he was able to move the gear shift into reverse and moved his foot over to the accelerator. The result was that the car shot backward like a bullet. After traveling several car lengths, he could feel his car scraping along several parked cars. The sound of the gun fire seemed to subside.

When his SUV came to a stop, Duane heard the other car drive off. He raised his head slightly hoping there was no one waiting to blow his head off. Then he felt a severe pain in his right hand. He looked at Marjorie and could see part of the left side of her head had been blown away. Their friend Erica, who was in the back started screaming, although she appeared to be alright. Duane's only thought was to take his wife to the hospital to see what they could do for her. He accelerated forward and tried to think where the closest emergency room was located. He ended up going to Glendale hospital, where Marjorie was pronounced dead from her severe gunshot injuries.

This shooting became McGhee's Achilles Heel and it all happened in a mysterious way. A lady by the name of Monica had a house in the area of the shooting. She had been watching her children when she heard all the shooting occurring outside her house, so she opened her front door slightly to see what was happening. The lighting from the streetlights enabled her to see two persons holding guns firing in the direction of a big black SUV. She was captivated by what she saw, and as abruptly as it started both cars drove off in different directions.

She returned to her house and called 9-1-1 and reported what had occurred. Since the cars were gone, the police were having difficulty knowing where this gun battle happened. Shortly thereafter, Monica went back outside and this time she saw a female who she later identified as Christina Duran. This woman appeared to be looking for something. Monica asked her as to what she was doing. Christina said that she had lost something. She gave several other explanations as to what she was doing there. When Monica had stepped away from Christina, she overheard her say in an excited voice "we got 'em."

This was one of the pivotal points of this case. Monica, for some reason, thought something was wrong with this picture. It moved her to take action. She could have returned to her house thinking this isn't my problem. Yet something didn't seem right to her and she took the initiative to walk over to one of the police officers and said that she thought something was suspicious about this woman who came back to look for something. The next remarkable occurrence was that the officer listened to

Monica and acted immediately. He instructed another police unit to pursue the car that this other woman, (later learned to be Christina) was driving. This all happened within a span of a very short time.

The other police unit was able to catch up with Christina's car seven blocks later as Christina turned onto Glendale Boulevard. As the police turned on its red lights behind Christina's car, she pulled over to the curb. The officers didn't know what they had or what they were supposed to do. They used caution and found a male in the back seat of Christina's car with a blanket covering him. This fact might seem suspicious to some, but what did it all mean? The officers had to make a split-second decision without knowing the gravity of the situation.

The officers received word from the other officers that the woman driver, Christina, seemed suspicious and might have been involved in a shooting. The officers set up a Field Identification and transported Monica to see if she could identify the SUV and also the woman who had been pulled over and stopped by the police. When Monica saw the black SUV she said that looked like the SUV involved in the shooting. She also identified the woman as the one she saw looking for something where the shooting had occurred. (This witness had mixed up the two SUVs and thought Christina Duran's Toyota 4 Runner was the Mitsubishi Montero driven by Duane that had been the one involved in the shooting.)

Graphic of Mitsubishi and Toyota 4 Runner

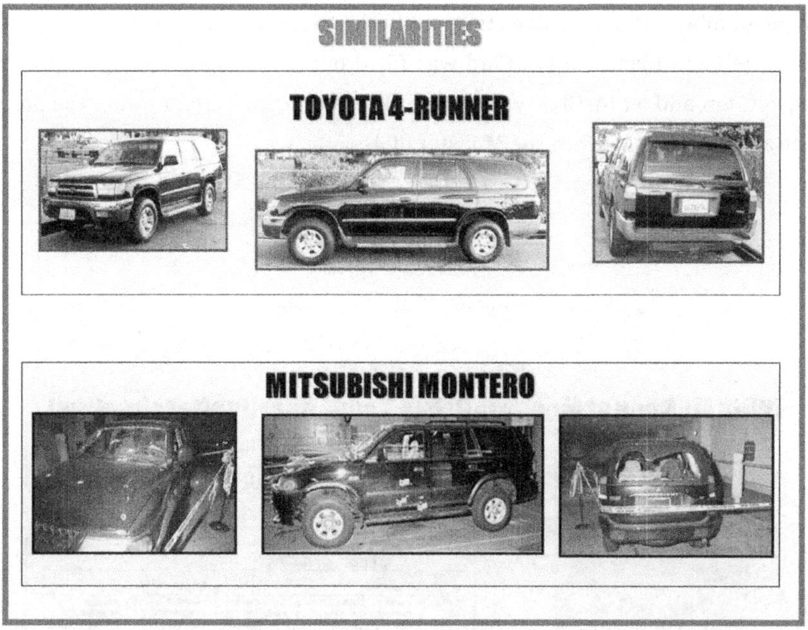

Again the officers had to make another important decision. What should they do with Christina, the lady driving the Toyota 4Runner SUV? Patrol officers are always getting yelled at by the detectives for not detaining crucial parties at at a crime scene. Out of an abundance of caution one officer told the other officer to transport Christina Duran to the station so the detectives could question her. (The officer didn't realize that decision would have life-and-death consequences for the lady as well as lead to the capture of one of the FBI's 15 most-wanted persons.)

The next question was what the officers should do with this guy who was under a blanket in the backseat? The officers reflected on all the training that they had had at the academy. What grounds did they have to detain someone in the backseat of a car when there was no mention of such a person by the officers who were at the scene of the shooting?

The detaining officers proceeded to do what they thought was a good compromise, and that was to fill out an "FI" Card on the subject in the back seat. If this person later turned out to be important, they would have his name, address and telephone number, which the detectives could use to contact him later.

After the Field Identification Card was filled out, the officers apologized for the short detention and let McGhee walk away. (Those officers weren't aware the person was better known as 'McGhee the Monster of Atwater')

Graphic of Field Identification of McGhee

The police officers then transported Christina to the station, where she must have become traumatized by the situation. Could the police think she was involved, and if so could she be considered an 'accessory after the fact' for looking for the cellphone? Didn't she know whether to talk to the detectives or remain tight-lipped? The detectives wanted to test her hands for gunshot residue (GSR). She realized that she was in serious trouble and she knew she hadn't fired or even touched any gun.

Christina must have thought, why not be cooperative then she could walk away from this incident? She was willing to admit that she was asked by an old friend, Timothy McGhee, to help him look for a cellphone he had dropped. Since she hadn't been at the crime scene at the time of the shooting, she couldn't say for certain who started it or who actually did the shooting.

Christina went on to explain that she only went back to the crime scene to look for a cellphone. She said that McGhee was afraid that someone might be able to recognize him so that was why he remained covered with a blanket in her backseat. When the police realized that they had actually detained McGhee only to release him, they were shocked and perplexed. In Christina's mind she wasn't 'ratting' on McGhee but only explaining why she was trying to help him.

CHAPTER 41 CHRISTINA HAD TO GO

The detectives were furious that the patrol officers had let McGhee slip through their fingers. The detectives were convinced that Christina wanted to be helpful to the police. They used her information to file a criminal complaint against McGhee as well as obtain an arrest warrant for him. Somehow the word went out that McGhee was wanted. McGhee believed that it must have been Christina who had 'ratted' on him. One might think that McGhee's number one priority should be to get out of town or out of state or even out of the country. However, McGhee's main concern was to get Christina for snitching on him.

Under the Mexican Mafia rules, he couldn't kill her without getting permission from the leadership of the EME. In short order, he was able to expedite the EME procedure in order to get an immediate Green Light to kill Christina. McGhee had people contact her boyfriend and set up a birthday party for her. The party occurred in Baldwin Park with a number of guests being invited. McGhee was one of the guests and everyone had a good time.

Around 2:30 a.m. Christina and her boyfriend left the party. At some point when driving away the boyfriend had been told to pull to the curb and get out of her Toyota 4Runner. He did as he was told and parked the car, leaving Christina all alone inside. McGhee approached from the rear with his gun in his hand. Christina may have seen McGhee coming and all of sudden realized what was about to go down. In desperation, she tried to push down all the door locks inside the car so McGhee couldn't get to her

As she was leaning back to push down the back door lock, McGhee pulled the trigger and blew out the backseat window. Christina's body fell into the back seat. McGhee then held the gun with both hands and slowly aimed at Christina's head. With execution-style precision, he pulled the trigger, shooting Christina several times in the back of the head. (It was only two days before that McGhee was hiding under a blanket in the same back seat.)

McGhee's cold-blooded killing of the woman who was so willing to help him out to find his cellphone was a message to everyone. Don't snitch on McGhee no matter who you are. If you do, you will end up the same way that Christina did, with a bullet hole through your skull. That type of intimidation would make it next to impossible for the police to find witnesses who would be willing to testify against McGhee. The prosecution had a major problem since they had already filed murder charges against McGhee. Since the prosecution's key witness was dead and unable to testify, how could McGhee ever be successfully prosecuted?

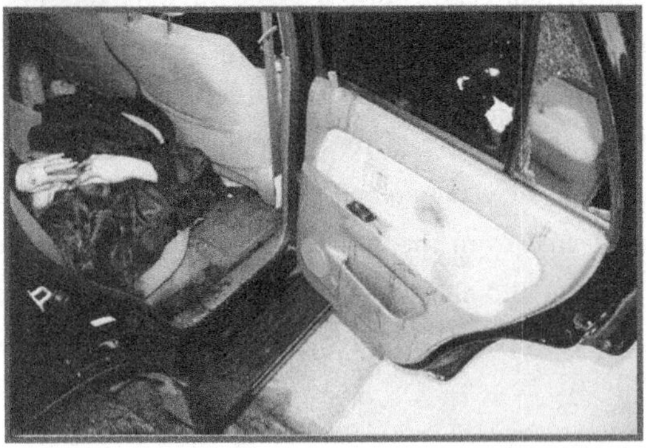

CHAPTER 42 MCGHEE ON THE RUN

McGhee was like a cat with Nine Lives. He could intimidate or kill anyone who could be a witness against him. However, the dropping of the cellphone during the Marjorie Mendoza shooting changed the dynamics for him. That cellphone had been found by the CSI team and they were able to trace it back to McGhee. No matter how much intimidation he could exert, the Cellphone and Telephone Companies' records weren't going to cower in fear of Timothy McGhee.

McGhee's mother hadn't raised any fool for a son. Even macho McGhee was the first to recognize that it was time to 'Get Out Of Dodge.' At the time there was only one warrant for his arrest, although law enforcement had named him in over a dozen homicides. When it became apparent that McGhee was still running the Toonerville Gang from out of the state, the US Marshals Service became involved.

The Los Angeles City Council issued a $50,000 reward for information that would lead to McGhee's arrest and conviction. Even with the tidy reward sum, no one came forth with information on McGhee. One had to wonder if any amount of money would convince someone to blow the whistle on him. It appeared that no amount of reward money was going to lead to the capture of McGhee.

McGhee had relocated to Bullhead City, and he needed a place to live. This desert community was never big into street gangs. It was a big adjustment for McGhee to accept the slow pace of life in the desert community. McGhee wanted to fit in with the locals, so he went to the one place where everyone congregated. That place was the "Losers' Lounge." McGhee had the good fortunate to meet a young damsel by the name Dawn B. Although she was not into gangs, she and McGhee hit it off. It wasn't long before they began living together as a happy couple in a dilapidated apartment.

Graphic of Losers' Lounge

McGhee took on the name Joe Montiel and tried hard to blend in with the locals. It was interesting that he was partially accurate in the story he told Dawn. He explained to her that he had been involved in some type of gang shit and he had dropped his girlfriend's phone. He told Dawn that he went back to get the phone and the car he was in was pulled over. The police took the woman to the police station and released him. He felt that the woman gave incriminating information to the police about him. However, he stressed to Dawn that he wasn't worried anymore about her since she was no longer alive.

Since the Reward for information about McGhee wasn't paying off, the next tactic was to use the TV program ***America's Most Wanted*** to run a segment about McGhee. This method had been highly successful in catching some of the most notorious fugitives. The LA DA's Office had been forever grateful to ***America's Most Wanted*** in the capture of Kathleen Soliah, the SLA fugitive who became a resident in Minneapolis and was able to escape justice for over 20 years.

In McGhee's case, he had only been on the run for a little over one year. In some circles, he had reached the pinnacle of success when he was placed on the top 15 WANTED criminals in the country. Few criminals are elevated to such a high distinction, such as Billy the Kid, Jesse James, and the legendary duo Bonnie Parker and Clyde Barrow. McGhee might have felt it was an honor to join such infamous characters of American history.

What made McGhee distinctive were his many tattoos. However, he could grow his hair out and wear long sleeve shirts to cover them up. McGhee's prison photos were not old and gave a good likeness of what he most likely still looked like. Then the *Mojave Desert News* published a photo of McGhee and indicated that he was wanted for murder. It isn't known why this little hick newspaper carried that story. Most likely the editor needed to cover several inches on the front page and the McGhee story was the perfect filler.

The following day a reader of the *Mojave Desert News* glanced at the newspaper and saw the photo of McGhee. Apparently, the reader had nothing better to do but stare at McGhee's photo. Maybe things were slow in town since the rattlesnake races had been canceled or the jumping-over-the-cactus contest was scratched. The reader contacted law enforcement and said that he had seen that guy go to an apartment in Bullhead City. The task force didn't know how much credence to give to this reader in the desert who might have been in the sun too long.

Nevertheless, one of the task force members indicated that McGhee's father had a business in Bullhead City. With that corroboration, the task force headed to Bullhead City where they met with the reader, who took them over to Ramar Street where he had seen the person go in and out of that dilapidated apartment building. The task force set up surveillance of the apartment.

The next day they saw a stocky muscular male leave and walk a short distance to a ramshackle building. The surveillance crew stayed there and waited. After several hours, McGhee came out and got into a vehicle driven by a woman. They waited for the vehicle to pull away, and when it was safe, they made a traffic stop. The car was surrounded by over 25 officers from LAPD, US Marshal's Service, and of course the Bullhead City police. McGhee sat motionless in the passenger seat.

After a number of commands, McGhee stepped out of the car and his eyes glanced back and forth assessing the situation. With so many shotguns and rifles pointing at his head, he slowly lay down on the hot dirty asphalt street. One of the officers moved cautiously behind him and cuffed his hands. At last the moment had arrived. McGhee was no longer a threat to the general public, and his name could be removed from the US Marshal's Most Wanted list.

However, no one could anticipate the reign of terror that Timothy McGhee would create in the future for the prison guards and fellow inmates.

When the police executed a search warrant on the apartment where McGhee was living, they seized a notebook which contained McGhee's handwritten rap poetry. This notebook was purposely labeled fiction. However, it portrayed McGhee's mindset as to his killing of others.

Other items found in his apartment were two T-shirts. One said *Run, Jump. Throw Donut* and the other T-shirt titled *Fugitive Can't See Me.* What type of fugitive would brag how clever he was? McGhee was without a doubt one of a kind.

CHAPTER 43 PROBLEMS WITH PROSECUTION

Det. Andy Teague highlighted the facts that the news media was obsessed with the Charley Manson case, in which a mere five people were killed. However, Timothy McGhee was responsible for more than a dozen killings, yet the news media was barely interested in covering this as a story. The news media seems fickle at times as to what stories they should cover. One possibility may be that the media places a different value on each person's life. A gang member's life is not worth as much as a Hollywood celebrity's. What it points out is that certain types of killings the media and the public don't care about. Gang violence has been relegated to an acceptable nuisance that society tolerates. A killer like McGhee, whose crime is killing of a dozen gangsters, isn't worthy of news coverage. Some might say that such a killer should be commended for his service of eliminating gang riff-raff from the community.

As previously stated in this book, prosecutor Tony Manzella had taken on the prosecution of the Northeast massive number of gang homicides. The vast majority of those cases involved the Avenues Gangs with their connections to the Mexican Mafia (EME). Still, Toonerville gang with McGhee was even more prolific in that he was connected to 12 homicides, including nine individuals killed in less than three months.

It's no wonder why all of the McGhee cases were assigned to Tony Manzella. The plan was that Tony would finish up the Avenues cases before starting on the McGhee cases. That theory seemed to be working out since McGhee had become a fugitive and there was no need for a speedy trial. However, the surprise capture of McGhee on February 12, 2003, upset the apple cart. Tony's trial calendar was full since he was about to start the first trial involving the informant Muppet who was shot on the side of the road while urinating with his homies. Tony was scheduled for the next three years prosecuting the Mexican Mafia (EME) cases.

The Los Angeles District Attorney's Office had to select another prosecutor to take over all the cases involving McGhee. Pat Dixon, the head deputy of Major Crimes Division, was given the task to find a trial prosecutor who could handle so many difficult gang cases. No prosecutor wanted to be known for losing such an important case and letting such a monstrous person such as McGhee be released back on the streets. Pat knew that he had the authority to order anyone of his Major Crimes attorneys to take over the McGhee cases. He knew that prosecuting McGhee would require an attorney who was tenacious and who was willing to take on the challenges of the McGhee cases. If the prosecutor wasn't sufficiently energized, he or she wouldn't be able to handle the myriad of witnesses and forensic problems. Pat had some very talented attorneys assigned to his Division, but he knew that they didn't mind tough cases as long as they were winnable cases. No one wanted to be handed a potential loser like the McGhee case.

Pat went down his roster of attorneys and came to the name of Hoon Chun. He remembered that he had given Hoon the *Maxfield case* and the *Angel Cruz case*, which were two of the toughest cases to prosecute. In neither case did Hoon complain about having to take over such difficult cases. Hoon had worked extraordinarily hard preparing both cases even though they both had the word "loser" written all over them. Pat recalled that all of the cases that he had given to Hoon involved hardcore gangsters. Then Pat recollected that prior to being transferred to Major Crimes Division, Hoon had been assigned to the Hardcore Gang Division. Pat contacted Hoon and told him that he was thinking of assigning the McGhee cases to him. Hoon thought of the McGhee case as an oversized gang case, which was his specialty. Hoon was pleased that Pat, his boss, had such confidence in him as to give him such an important case to try. Hoon may not have been totally aware of the innumerable problems that had befallen the case.

There was no question that Hoon had the academic qualifications for such a case. He graduated from Harvard Law School. He was not naïve in believing that the McGhee cases would merely be a piece of cake.

Hoon quickly learned that a jailhouse informant who had come forth with supposedly incriminating statements by McGhee later turned out to be untrustworthy. Within days Hoon met with the detectives who were assigned the McGhee cases. Hoon asked them what crimes could be proved without using the jailhouse informant. He went over every murder and attempted murder case and asked what evidence was available to connect McGhee to the crimes. It became apparent to everyone in the room that there wasn't much evidence in any of the crimes to prove McGhee did it. The few eyewitnesses who had been relied on originally now were changing their stories and claimed that they couldn't identify Mc Ghee as being involved.

It became apparent that most of the murders were going to be dismissed since the evidence was so thin without the testimony of the jailhouse informant and the changing eyewitnesses. What Hoon was able to glean out of all the facts was that one murder and one attempted murder were connected by a .40 caliber gun. Then as to another murder and another attempted murder they were connected by a 9mm gun at their crime scenes. Then there was another murder and an attempted murder that McGhee was connected to by way of a cellphone which was found near the shoot-out.

In a nutshell, that was all that was left that could be used to prosecute McGhee. Hoon told the detectives that there were only five shooting situations that had any chance of being prosecuted. He wanted to examine every piece of evidence on those five shootings to see if there was anything that could be further done to provide more evidence. He started reviewing them in the chronological order in which they occurred.

CHAPTER 44 DEVASTATING TRAFFIC ACCIDENT

The DA's Office had totally relied on two detectives, Det. Andy Teague and Det. Abiel Barron, to line up the evidence that could be used in court against McGhee. Both detectives were sharp and had a wealth of experience working on homicide cases. Both had a dogged determination to solve cases and could be depended on to get the witnesses to court to testify. The prosecutors completely relied on the two of them.

On June 25, 2003, the phone call came to the DA's Office from LAPD that forever changed the McGhee case. That was when the DA's Office received the word that the two detectives were involved in a fatal automobile accident. The one detective was killed and the other detective was in a coma with critical injuries. The first reaction was this couldn't be true. These two detectives were invincible. The first reaction was to check the names because this must be a mistake. Then reality set in that it was the two homicide detectives from Northeast station.

Then the question was, what happened? The LAPD representative explained that the detectives were driving through the desert in the Antelope Valley on their way to check on the relocation of a witness. The detectives were traveling eastbound on Highway 138 when the driver of a pickup truck that was traveling westbound behind a slow-moving big rig decided to pass it on this two-lane road. The pickup driver pulled out and as he was passing the pickup crashed head-on into the detectives' vehicle. The driver was Det. Abiel Barron, who was pronounced dead at the scene of the accident. His partner, Det. Andy Teague, who was the passenger, was airlifted to Loma Linda Medical Center with major injuries. The detective's vehicle was crumpled back to the windshield and the pickup had withstood major front-end damage. The driver of the pickup was charged with Manslaughter with gross negligence.

Graphics of Highway 138 One of the Deadliest Highways in California

It took several days before anyone at the DA's Office could grasp the extent of what had happened. One of the prosecutors went to the hospital to visit Andy Teague. They, as a team, had grown particularly close since they had worked together for over a year. The prosecutor described Teague as a fearless cop and a gentleman. He said, "He's one of the finest investigators my assistant and I have ever worked with."

What they learned was shocking. Apparently, Andy's head must have struck some part of the car with such force that his brain was severely injured.

The bad news was that the one detective lost his life but the good news was that the other detective was still alive. As the days and weeks passed, the good news was that Detective Teague eventually recovered, but the bad news was that he had totally lost his memory. When the DA's Office was able to talk to him about the cases, it became apparent that he couldn't remember anything about the McGhee case. As hard as the detective tried, he couldn't recall who he and his partner had been talking to regarding the case.

I, the author, was very concerned about the McGhee case, especially after the traffic accident. Over the years I had gotten to know Det. Andy Teague on various homicide cases. He was an unforgettable character who you couldn't help but like. He was a hard charger and you quickly learned that he was the type who wore the white hats. I worked with him on early stages of the McGhee case when Tony Manzella was in charge of the prosecution. Teague was always helpful in supplying photos or documents when I was preparing the exhibits for the case He was like a walking encyclopedia and could give chapter and verse as to where to find things in the Murder Books.

When I heard about the traffic accident, I was shocked but relieved when I learned Andy Teague survived. When Tony Manzella told me that Andy was seriously injured, I figured it was just a matter of time before everything would be okay. I waited several months before I made any further inquiries. I knew Tony was preoccupied with the Mexican Mafia case, but one day I asked Tony when Andy would be coming by so I could ask him some questions.

Tony stopped and with a curt reply said, "Ron, Andy won't be coming back anymore." That was a strange answer, especially since I knew that Det. Teague had survived the crash. I tried one more time asking Tony to have Andy stop by my office the next time he was in. That was when Tony looked me in the eye and said, "Andy has lost his memory and doesn't remember anything about the McGhee case."

That just couldn't be happening. All homicide cases had two detectives assigned to them. If something happened to one of the detectives, the other one would step in, making any change seem seamless. In my entire 40-year career I was never faced with a homicide without one of the two original detectives. Now in this extremely difficult McGhee case, one of the detectives was dead and the other, Andy Teague, had lost his memory. For all practical purposes, Det. Teague no longer was able to help in the prosecution of McGhee in that he couldn't remember any of the facts of the McGhee case.

It now appeared that the McGhee case was over. Several new detectives were brought in to see what could be salvaged. So much information about the cases had been in the minds of the two detectives. True, there were thousands of pages of police reports, but someone needed to connect the dots. If it wasn't quickly figured out, McGhee was going to be a free man. The clock was ticking for the preliminary hearing. The DA's Office didn't want the Defense to realize how fragile the prosecution's case had become without the two detectives.

Hoon had the new detectives meet in his office to chart a course of what could be proven and what evidence was still available. They started with the first gang-violence case, which was the shooting of the Rascal taggers Juan C. & Pedro S. This shooting occurred almost ten years earlier, and at that time Juan tentatively identified McGhee from a photo line-up. He claimed that photo number 2, which was of McGhee, looked like the person who shot him.

As to Pedro S., he knew McGhee quite well since they had gone to school together. Pedro got a close look at McGhee since he was holding the glass door closed while McGhee was shooting at him only feet away. However, Pedro didn't want to identify him out of fear. Later, when the detectives were asking him if he knew a Timothy McGhee, he said, "See, you already know it."

Even though the Juan and Pedro shootings weren't overly strong, when they were combined with the Ronald Martin shooting it was strengthened because in both shootings a .40 caliber firearm was used. Although there was no eyewitness to the shooting, at least McGhee had bragged to others that "I smoked this guy and there were over 40 shots fired." This described the Martin shooting since it was the only one where there were 40 shots fired.

The police told the prosecutor that McGhee was involved in a shooting at a recording studio when a guard was killed. The original detectives had information about this shooting, but now, since the traffic accident, no one knew who the key witnesses to this incident were; therefore it was dropped as a possible charge.

The new detectives reviewed the Ryan Gonzales shooting. They were aware that a Mark G. was willing to testify that he was out with McGhee and they were driving around looking for rival gang members when McGhee yelled at him to stop. He pulled over to the curb and McGhee jumped out of the King Cab pickup truck. He saw McGhee chase after someone and moments later heard shots fired and McGhee ran back and got into the truck. Later he told the guys in the vehicle, "I really blasted that fool." All of this occurred at the location where Ryan Gonzales' body was found shot.

At the Gonzales crime scene, 9mm shell casings were found which matched shell casings found at the pursuit shoot-out. Therefore, the Gonzales and the pursuit cases were connected through ballistics. The Pursuit involved the two LAPD officers who were able to capture the three in the car but they couldn't identify McGhee. Again, this Mark G. was willing to testify that he was with McGhee and they were hanging out with other Toonerville gang members when they heard over their police scanner information about the pursuit. When they realized that the car was headed back to Atwater Village, he said McGhee and some of the others left to see what they could do. McGhee had a gun with him when he left. When he returned, he said, "We really dumped on the cops."

Although connecting McGhee to the pursuit shoot-out was weak, the detectives came up with another witness, John P., who claimed he heard the sirens from the police car and he looked out his apartment window and saw muzzle flashes as the police car turned the corner. Immediately, he saw McGhee walk away from that area and cross the street.

Also, what corroborated McGhee's involvement in the shooting at the police car was the fact that the ballistics experts indicated that a 9mm shell casing matched the shell casings found at the Randy Gonzales crime scene. The prosecutor felt that with all those factors McGhee could be charged with the shooting of the police car.

The next thing that the prosecutor had to consider was whether there was still enough evidence to charge McGhee for the shooting of Marty Gregory Roybal near the LA River. The rumor on the street was that McGhee shot the victim as he was sketching the LA River. Det. Teague had been able to make the connection to McGhee, but after the traffic accident he couldn't remember who supplied the information. There was no forensic evidence to help out, so the prosecutor had to write off this shooting due to a lack of evidence. This was especially difficult since this had ended up a double murder because of the homeless man who had witnessed the shooting was also killed.

Next on the list of homicides that McGhee was suspect of committing was the shooting of a couple driving along Los Feliz Blvd. minding their own business. As McGhee pulled up alongside the victim's vehicle, he began firing at the two. This encounter proved to be deadly for the driver Manuel Apodaca and his girlfriend Nina, who was left with severe brain damage.

Again the prosecution was faced with the reality that it was unknown if the detectives who were in the traffic accident had some witnesses or evidence that would connect McGhee to this tragic homicide. As difficult as it was to accept, no charges could be filed against McGhee as to this shooting.

The next set of homicides was the one that the media called the Wisotsky Massacre and may have been the most appalling of them all. Cheri Wisotsky (46), who lived in the Atwater Village area, was trying to be helpful by letting the police know that narcotics were being sold out of McGhee's sister's house.

McGhee not only killed this lady for being an informant but he then went on to shoot everyone who had witnessed him doing the killing. That included Wisotsky's mother and a neighbor. Three innocent lives snuffed out, for wanting to clean up Atwater Village, was a disheartening situation. But when the new detectives explained that no one was willing to come to court to testify to McGhee's involvement, the prosecutor had no choice but not to file charges.

Everyone in the community wanted the killer to pay for what he had done. Some other DA's Office may have taken the easy way out by filing charges in the Wisotsky shooting, even though they knew there wasn't any evidence. However, the Los Angeles District Attorney's Office just wouldn't file charges unless the witnesses and evidence truly existed.

Since the DA's Office had already filed charges against McGhee in the murder of Marjorie Mendoza, those charges were transferred over to the new case they were bringing against McGhee. The Prosecutor knew that the Mendoza murder would strengthen all the other charges when they were all combined into one criminal complaint. The Mendoza homicide had compelling evidence since the cellphone recovered could be traced back to McGhee.

When the prosecutor got to the conclusion of the homicides, he had to make a tough decision as to what should be done with the execution of Christina Duran. Should that be included in the new case against McGhee? The dilemma was that it was going to be questionable how this shooting would be tied to McGhee. Later witnesses were uncovered and the decision was to use the Christina Duran killing for the Death Penalty phase of the trial.

Graphic image of the charges is as follows:

DECISIONS AS TO CHARGES

CT	CHARGE	DATE	VICTIM	SPEC. FINDING	SPEC. CIRCUM.
1	Att. Murder	10/10/97	Juan C.	Deliberate/Premeditated Benefit Criminal Street Gang	
2	Att. Murder	10/10/97	Pedro S.	Deliberate/Premeditated Benefit Criminal Street Gang	
3	Murder	10/14/97	Ronald Martin	Benefit Criminal Street Gang	Convicted of more than one Murder
4	Murder	6/3/00	Ryan Gonzalez	Benefit Criminal Street Gang	Convicted of more than one Murder Further Criminal Street Gang
5	Att. Murder	7/4/00	Officer T. Baker	On a Peace Officer Benefit Criminal Street Gang	
6	Att. Murder	7/4/00	Officer C. Langarica	On a Peace Officer Benefit Criminal Street Gang	
12	Murder	11/9/01	Margie Mendoza	Benefit Criminal Street Gang	Convicted of more than one Murder Further Criminal Street Gang
13	Att. Murder	11/9/01	Duane N.	Deliberate/Premeditated Benefit Criminal Street Gang	
14	Att. Murder	11/9/01	Erica R.	Deliberate/Premeditated Benefit Criminal Street Gang	

CHAPTER 45 RAP LYRICS TELL A STORY

After the traffic accident and the loss of the two lead detectives, prosecutor Hoon knew he would have to be creative to convince a jury to convict McGhee of the remaining charges he had included in the new complaint. Hoon remembered that when McGhee was arrested a notebook was found in his apartment. The big question was, could any of the material in the notebook be used in court?

On the outside cover of the notebook the following words were written:

EVERYTHING IN THIS BOOK IS FICTION

The following 30 pages consist of a notebook written by McGhee. It isn't clear as to the purpose of the writings. Could it be McGhee's idea of poetry? After one examines the lyrics in this notebook, one might think that it was McGhee's attempt to be a Rap Artist. At that time in history (2003), hip-hop music was popular and many of the singers sprinkled the notion of Hate and Violence in their musical lyrics. Strangely enough, at that time the outlaw motif was fashionable, even including the killing of the police.

Hoon started going through the notebook line by line to see what he could use in court. Certain passages in the notebook could help the prosecution to prove certain elements of the charges and special allegations. Hoon brought an IN LIMINE MOTION to permit the defendant's notebook in court. The prosecution justification was as follows:

1. The defendant committed all of his crimes with the intent to promote or benefit his gang as charged in the Gang Special Allegation.

2. The defendant was an active gang member when he committed the murder of Marjorie Mendoza.

3. The defendant hated, and was motivated to kill, anyone he believed to be a rival gang member.

4. The defendant hated, and was motivated to kill, police officers.

The defendant had knowledge of, and made reference to, the murder warrant against him, and he intended to flee from such charges when he left California.

Needless to say, the Defense objected to the prosecution using any part of the notebook, claiming that it was too highly prejudicial since it showed a propensity for violence. They claimed that the lyrics might be interpreted as reflective of a generally violent attitude, which could be said to substantially outweigh their probative value.

The first thing that the prosecution had to prove was that the notebook was McGhee's and he had written it. To prove this, Hoon indicated to the court that McGhee's girlfriend, who he had been living with, said that she had seen McGhee writing in this notebook. She also said that the notebook was in a big box full of his personal belongings that he had brought to her residence the day before his arrest.

The other factor that Hoon used to show that the notebook was written by McGhee was the fact that it was written in the first person. Even though the front page claimed the writing was FICTION, the main character fit McGhee perfectly. The content of the notebook was self-authenticating in that it accurately made repeated references to McGhee's real-life gang affiliation to Toonerville. The document further describes the tattoo of Toonerville on his back: the actual gang moniker of Eskimo (this was in addition to the 'Huero' moniker) and the bald hairstyle.

On the following graphic pages are some of the relevant passages that Hoon wanted to use in the trial.

Graphic of Notebook

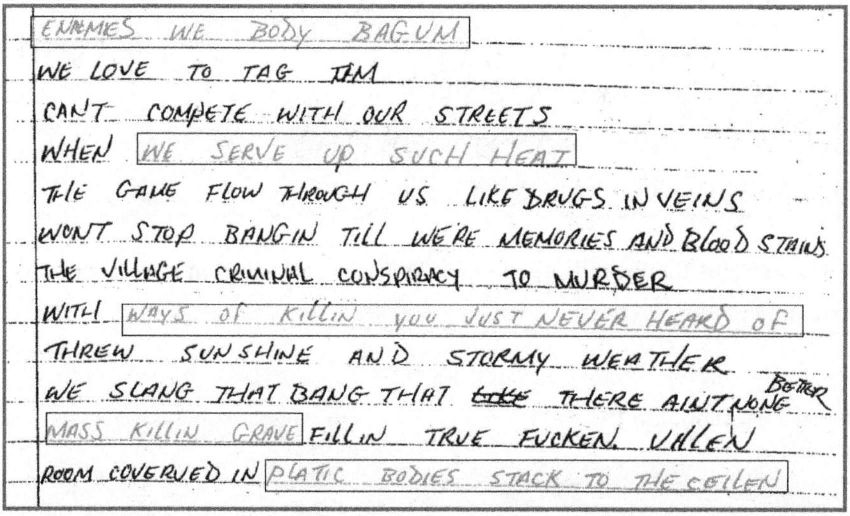

ENEMIES WE BODY BAGUM
WE LOVE TO TAG TEM
CAN'T COMPETE WITH OUR STREETS
WHEN WE SERVE UP SUCH HEAT
THE GAME FLOW THROUGH US LIKE DRUGS IN VEINS
WONT STOP BANGIN TILL WE'RE MEMORIES AND BLOOD STAINS
THE VILLAGE CRIMINAL CONSPIRACY TO MURDER
WITH WAYS OF KILLIN YOU JUST NEVER HEARD OF
THREW SUNSHINE AND STORMY WEATHER
WE SLANG THAT BANG THAT ~~LIKE~~ THERE AINT NONE BETTER
MASS KILLIN GRAVE FILLIN TRUE FUCKEN VILLEN
ROOM COVERED IN PLATIC BODIES STACK TO THE CEILEN

Here McGhee is bragging about killing his rivals (enemies) and having them placed in body bags. He talks about having the firearms to kill people in so many ways. He goes on to reference the mass killings where the victims' bodies are stacked all the way up to the ceiling.

Graphic of Notebook 2

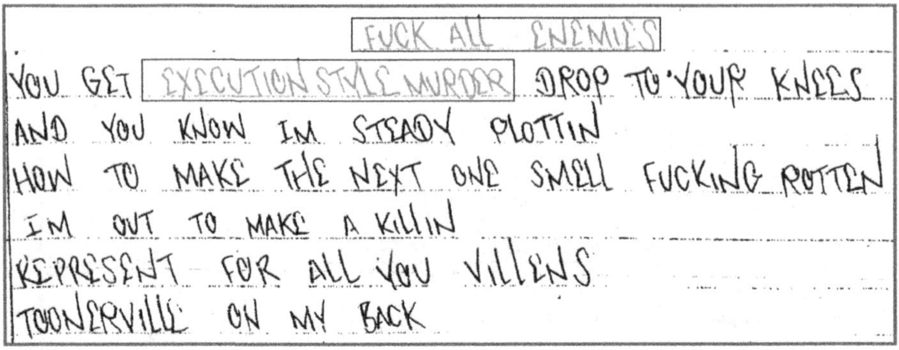
FUCK ALL ENEMIES
YOU GET EXECUTION STYLE MURDER DROP TO YOUR KNEES
AND YOU KNOW IM STEADY PLOTTIN
HOW TO MAKE THE NEXT ONE SMELL FUCKING ROTTEN
IM OUT TO MAKE A KILLIN
REPRESENT FOR ALL YOU VILLENS
TOONERVILLE ON MY BACK

McGhee explains that he kills his enemies by using the execution style. He is out to make another killing.

Graphics Notebook #3

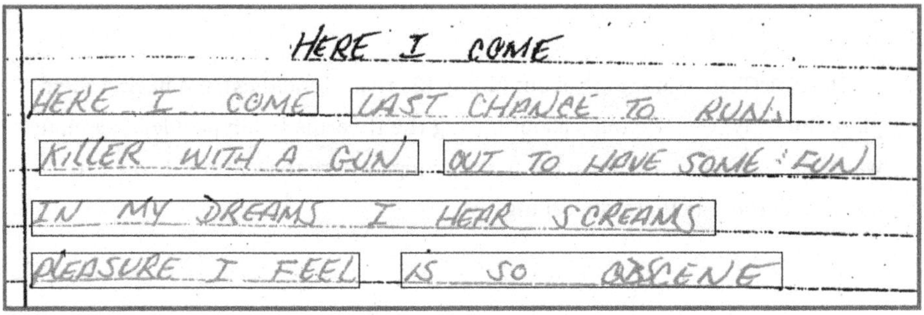
HERE I COME
HERE I COME LAST CHANCE TO RUN
KILLER WITH A GUN OUT TO HAVE SOME FUN
IN MY DREAMS I HEAR SCREAMS
PLEASURE I FEEL IS SO OBSCENE

McGhee wanted people to respect him as he comes running after them just to kill them for the fun of it. He recognized the pleasure he felt was obscene.

Graphic of Notebook #4

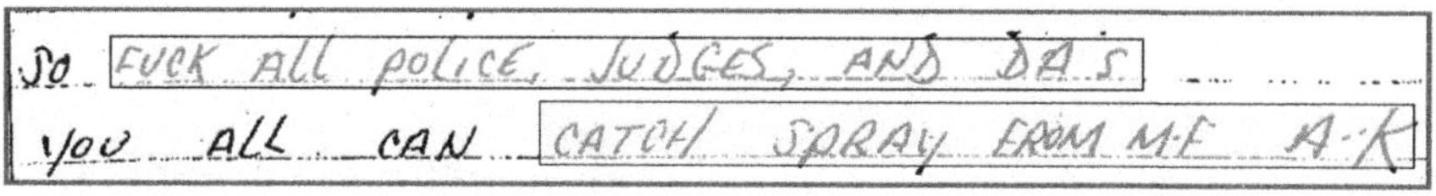
SO FUCK ALL POLICE, JUDGES, AND DA.S
YOU ALL CAN CATCH/ SPRAY FROM M-F A-K

He shows his contempt for the police, judges, and DAs, and he indicates that he would like to kill them with his AK 45.

Graphic of Notebook #5

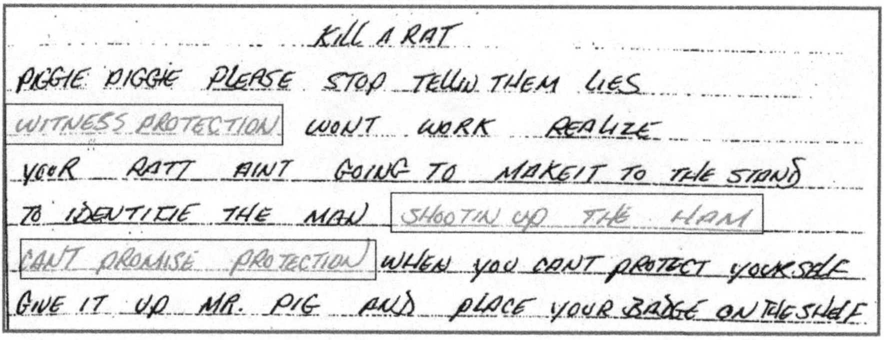
KILL A RAT
PIGGIE PIGGIE PLEASE STOP TELLIN THEM LIES
WITNESS PROTECTION WONT WORK REALIZE
YOUR RATT AINT GOING TO MAKEIT TO THE STAND
TO IDENTIFIE THE MAN SHOOTIN UP THE HAM
CANT PROMISE PROTECTION WHEN YOU CANT PROTECT YOURSELF
GIVE IT UP MR. PIG AND PLACE YOUR BADGE ON THE SHELF

Here McGhee claims that the police can promise witness protection but he will get the informant before they have a chance to testify in court. He suggests that the police can't protect themselves so why don't they give up.

Graphic of Notebook #6

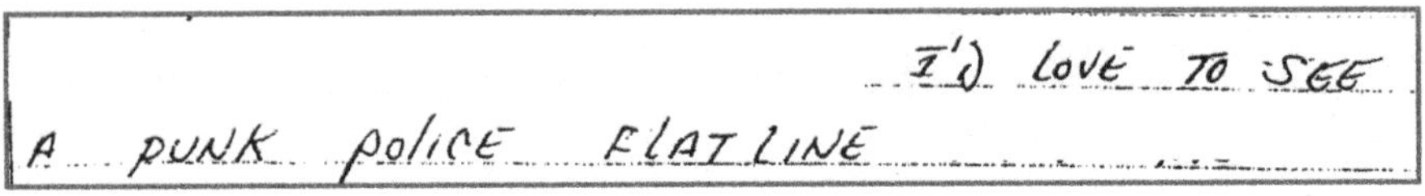
I'D LOVE TO SEE
A PUNK POLICE FLATLINE

McGhee makes no secret of his contempt for the police and loves to see them dead. This supported the facts regarding the shooting of the police car during the pursuit.

Both sides vehemently argued their position, and the judge finally ruled that the above passages could be used as evidence and shown to the jury. This was a critical win for the prosecution and really put McGhee on the defensive.

CHAPTER 46 TIME FOR TRIAL

After four and half years of delays, the McGhee trial began in Judge Perry's court. He would never be described as a warm and fuzzy judge. He had an obsession for not wasting any of the court's time. The bane of a prosecutor is not knowing how long a Defense attorney will spend cross-examining the prosecution witnesses. Therefore, in Judge Perry's court, the prosecutor always keeps witnesses nearby in case they are needed to fill in at the end of a short court day.

Although this is an inconvenience for witnesses, it pays dividends to keep Judge Perry happy and from going into his rant about utilizing every moment of the court's time. The benefit of having a contented judge is that he may look more favorably on prosecution motions.

Judge Perry doesn't like either side to waste time in the selection of the jury. This can be devastating for the prosecution since they have to get all 12 jurors to convict. Sometimes the prosecutor needs a little more information before exercising their peremptory challenge. Judge Perry doesn't want to waste time asking questions to the jurors. However, Hoon wasn't too concerned in this particular case since McGhee wasn't going to gain much sympathy from any type of jurors.

In Perry's court, jury selection is conducted at a record pace and the next thing the prosecutor knows is that it is time for the Opening Statement. Hoon knew that his Opening had to hit the mark, since at that moment the jurors' only impression of McGhee was of him sitting at the counsel table looking like a young executive who was merely climbing up the corporate ladder. McGhee was decked out in a black suit with a blue dress shirt and a blue tie. His hair had grown out and completely covered his tattoo on the back of his head. For years he had been so proud of that tat displaying the Mexican Mafia symbol of an eagle on a prickly pear cactus with a snake in its beak and talons. (This is also displayed on the Mexican National flag.)

Hoon started his Opening Statement like he was slowly and methodically peeling back an onion one layer at a time. He knew that the jurors were all looking at this defendant named Timothy McGhee and wondering how this young man could be mixed up in some type of diabolic killing in which he was charged with three murders and six attempted murders. As he sat there projecting the image that didn't match the charges, Hoon tried to paint a more accurate picture of McGhee.

The prosecutor said this was going to be a case of 'Who done it.' He warned them that not everything was how it seemed. He advised them they were entering another world that they might not be familiar with. They would learn about gangs and how they operate from expert witnesses that would be called to testify. Gang rivalry and retaliation coupled with gang territory would become important in explaining the defendant's behavior.

Hoon wanted the jurors to understand that some of his other witnesses wouldn't have stellar backgrounds. When you are in the gang world, everyone will have some blemishes on their reputation. He wanted the jurors to understand that some of the witnesses would be gangsters, and that even with their tarnished backgrounds they could be believed when their testimony can be corroborated.

Some of that corroboration would be in the form of writings that the defendant had made in a notebook. Hoon gave the jurors a sample of the rap lyrics that supported the prosecution's position. The defendant hated his gang's rivals and especially loathed the police. Hoon very briefly explained some of the basic facts from each of the shootings so the jurors would be familiar with what they would be hearing about for the next several weeks.

After both sides had finished their Opening Statements, it was time to present the evidence portion of the case. The first shooting involved the taggers, Juan and Pedro. The initial witness was Juan C., who came rolling into the courtroom in his wheelchair. He testified that on the night in question he and a group of Rascals were having fun tagging the street signs. They crossed over Glendale Boulevard and started tagging when a vehicle pulled up and two guys jumped out. As he began to run, he was shot and fell into the street. He remembered pulling himself up to see if any cars were coming. He explained to the jury that he was shot in the back and was paralyzed from the waist down.

Then the moment came when Hoon asked him if he could identify who shot him. Even though this had occurred ten years earlier, he obviously didn't want to identify McGhee. Hoon asked him if he had circled a photo of McGhee on a photo lineup card. The best that Hoon was able to get him to admit was that he had indicated that it sort of looked like the photo of the person in the number 2 position. It was strange how this witness didn't want to identify McGhee even though he was the person who was responsible for causing him to be a paraplegic for the rest of his life.

Hoon was hoping that Juan would have been a stronger witness, but he realized that in the gang world you never rat on anyone, even your rivals. Hoon called his next witness, Pedro S., and he related the same facts as Juan except when the shooting started, he headed for the safety of the Shell service station. The jury listened intently as Hoon walked him through the facts of him holding onto the handle of the glass door for his dear life. He was almost nose to nose with the person who shot him twice as the door shattered into thousands of shards of glass.

He told the jurors that all of sudden there was the sound of police sirens and the shooter turned abruptly and ran off to a waiting car. Pedro said he fell to the floor holding the door handle without any door. Hoon then asked the $64,000 question as to who was the shooter. Even though he had grown up and had gone to school with McGhee and knew him well, he wouldn't identify him as the shooter. The most Hoon was able to get out of Pedro was the fact he made a reference to McGhee. When the detectives had asked him about Mc Ghee as the possible shooter, Pedro's response was, "See, you already know who it was." But Pedro, the Rascal gang member, couldn't utter the name "McGhee" as the shooter even though a decade had passed.

Hoon called a witness who testified that a Toonerville member had been shot shortly before the attack on Juan and Pedro. That evidence was presented to show that the motive for the shooting was in retaliation for an earlier shooting. There was an additional witness who testified that two days after the shooting, McGhee came back to Rascal territory and demanded to see Pedro. Although this person didn't say he had been the shooter, the inference was that McGhee wanted to finish off Pedro since he survived the first attack.

A CSI witness was called next to testify that he was called to respond to the crime scene and had recovered a number of .40 caliber expended shell casings. Although this testimony was tedious, it would become important when evidence of the Ronald Martin shooting was presented to the jury.

Since Hoon wanted the jury to become familiar with the rap lyrics spelled out in the notebook, he called Dawn B. She testified that she met McGhee at the Losers Lounge in Bullhead City and they struck up a friendship. Eventually, he moved in with her and he brought a box with him which had the notebook in it. She had seen him earlier write rap lyric in the notebook. At that point Hoon had her look over the notebook and authenticate that it was McGhee's and then he had it introduced into evidence.

Then it was time to present evidence on the first murder, that being of Ronald Martin. Since Hoon didn't have any eyewitness, he had to use circumstantial evidence to prove McGhee's involvement. First he called the police officers who responded the Elysian Valley Park Recreation Center. They set the stage by describing the crime scene in which the victim was lying flat on his back wearing a blood-soaked gray sweatshirt and baggie pants finished off with athletic shoes.

As the dead body lay on the sidewalk, the victim's hands lay at his side not holding any weapon. When the officers examined him, they saw numerous gunshot wounds. The one officer with latex gloves on gently moved his fingers along the side of the victim's neck looking for a pulse. The only movement coming from the victim's body was the continual seeping of blood from his mouth and midsection of the body. Hoon showed the officer photos of the victim's body on the sidewalk. This grabbed the jurors' attention as several leaned forward in their seats to get a better view. For years these jurors had seen dead bodies in movies and on TV; however, seeing the real scene was spellbinding to them. One female juror leaned back in her chair and grimaced at the sight of the bloody victim as she folded her arms in disapproval.

Hoon had definitely gotten the jurors attention by the horrific sight of an individual being shot 28 times. However, the more important task that the prosecutor had was how to connect McGhee to the shooting. Hoon called a Mark G. who knew McGhee well and testified that several days after the shooting of Ronald Martin McGhee said to him, "I really smoked this guy and there were over 40 shots fired."

Another witness testified that McGhee related that he and two other Toonerville gang members were driving through Rascal territory looking to kill someone. The purpose of the shooting was in retaliation for the shooting of a Toonerville member. When they came upon Ronald Martin they asked him where he was from and he said, "Nowhere, I'm not into any gang." They ordered him to lift up his sweatshirt and show them his chest.

They persisted and when he raised the shirt the guys saw the word FROGTOWN in bold, elongated letters inscribed across his chest. At that point, the victim must have felt like the little mouse being played with by a malicious Tomcat. Ronald Martin didn't know how to respond to the dire situation he was in. He couldn't run since his back was against a chain link fence. He had no gun or knife to defend himself. He was just all alone with guys from Toonerville pointing guns at him. The only thing he could think about doing was to start to beg for his life. As he was pleading for mercy, he recognized it wasn't the most macho thing to do. At that moment Ronald Martin wasn't concerned about his self-image. All he wanted to do was to live for another day. That was when McGhee told him to take it like a man and not like a bitch. At that moment, the guns started roaring as a hail of bullets filled Ronald Martin's body. Did he die like a man or a bitch? We will never know.

What we do know is that the medical examiner at the Coroner's Office counted at least 26 bullet entry wounds on the victim's body. A gang expert was later called as a witness and explained the reasoning why gangsters will do an overkill like in Ronald Martin's murder. The purpose is to instill fear in the hearts of their rival gang members.

Hoon again called the CSI technicians to explain how and where they found the expended shell casings. They were able to determine that three separate guns were used, in particular a .40 caliber weapon. A firearms expert was called and testified that the .40 caliber shell casings were identical to the .40 caliber shell casings found at the Juan and Pedro shootings. Now there was a link between the two separate shootings. That meant the same gun was used and one could infer that the same person was involved in both sets of shootings.

The Ronald Martin shooting was certainly a case of overkill, while the Ryan Gonzales shooting was more like big game hunting in an urban setting. In this later case, Hoon used a witness who was present at the crime scene. Mark G. was given 'use immunity' and testified that he was driving around in Rascal territory with McGhee. McGhee was in an upbeat mood and said that he felt 'LUCKY.' As they drove around, McGhee continued to look down alleys and streets for anyone who was out and about. He knew there had been a party at one of the Rascals' houses and he figured the guests would be leaving the party.

As they turned down Silverlake Boulevard they could make out a male walking toward them. McGee told Mark to stop since he wanted to check out this guy walking alone. Mark could see that McGhee had a gun in his hand and he ran further down the street. It was dark out and he was several houses away when he heard gunfire. Mark G. couldn't make out who shot whom, but the next thing he knew was McGhee had jumped back into their vehicle.

Another witness indicated that McGhee said, "I blasted that fool." He explained that McGhee, just like in the Ronald Martin shooting, had asked the victim where he was from. This victim didn't know how to respond so he implored not to be killed. Mc Ghee was on a mission and it was unfortunate that Ryan Gonzales had to be the sacrificial lamb.

McGhee was connected to this shooting by the testimony of these two witnesses. In order to corroborate these witnesses, Hoon called the CSI tech to testify that he found numerous expended shell casings from a 9mm gun. This testimony would become relevant as to the shell casings found at the shooting during the police pursuit.

Then Hoon moved on to the so-called police pursuit which resulted in the attempted murder charges involving the two LAPD officers Baker and Langarica. They responded to a radio call about a robbery in the Rascals' territory. Officer Baker was driving the patrol car and around 3:00 a.m. on July 4, 2000, they received the call of three male suspects committing a 211(Robbery) near Glenhurst and Larga Avenues at the lower end of Atwater Village. The suspect robbers were described as leaving in a gray Honda.

As the police arrived, they saw a gray Honda racing away. Officer Baker made a U-turn and started to follow the Honda. That was the genesis of a wild LAPD pursuit. They traveled westbound on Fletcher and when they got to Riverside Drive they made an abrupt right and raced north, headed to the entrance to Griffith Park. The officers thought possibly the Honda would enter the Park, which could cause major concerns for the police.

Most Angelinos think of Griffith Park as an oasis in the middle of the second largest city in the nation. Everyone has a benevolent opinion of the founder of the park, Griffith J. Griffith. What a wonderful human being to graciously give 3,015 acres to the City as a parkland. However, most people gloss over the part in which old man Griffith was convicted and went to prison for shooting and severely injuring his wife in 1903. When Mr. Griffith got out of prison, he tried to donate more money to the city to build an amphitheater and observatory. However, the city fathers turned him down. It wasn't until after his death that the city was willing to take his money to create the renowned Greek Theater and iconic Griffith Park Observatory, which is often used to depict the great City of the Los Angeles.

Both officers were relieved when the robber's car veered off to the right on Los Felix Boulevard. With their red lights flashing and siren blaring, Officer Largaris used the radio to inform the dispatcher of their every move, hoping another police unit could help them out. Several blocks later the Honda made a hard-left turn onto Brunswick Avenue. By then the officers realized that they had just entered Toonerville turf run by Timothy McGhee. Officer Baker indicated that they were closing in on the pursuing vehicle.

As Officer Baker tried to gain on the Honda he saw an object out in the middle of the street. He tried to maneuver around what looked like a washing machine. Just as he tried to steer around the object, a bicycle without a rider came flying toward the police car. That was a moment of adrenaline overload as he heard and felt bullets come flying through the driver's door of the police car. The bullets were shattering the rear side windows and he felt a bullet tear through his pants leg.

As all this was happening, the Honda had made a hard right onto Bemis Street. As Officer Baker swiftly turned the steering wheel to the right, he could hear a hail of bullets blow out the rear window. By now both officers were leaning down in their seats, barely looking out of the windshield. To their amazement, the Honda seemed to pull over to the right side next to Chevy Chase Park. It seemed that someone in the Honda was firing some type of automatic weapon at them. The officers were sitting ducks as they approached the Honda. Officer Baker pointed the police unit at the Honda and crashed into it.

The police unit plowed into the Honda as the officers abruptly leaped out of their car looking for cover from the car doors and trees along the parkway. Fortunately, other police units converged on the site, and within seconds a volley of gunfire was let loose on the three gangsters in the Honda. As the Honda became riddled with bullets, the occupants surrendered, giving up their assault weapons.

Hoon showed photos of the handguns to Officer Baker and asked if he could identify them, which he did. The Tec-DC9 was found in the Honda and a Cobray M-11 was recovered down the street, where it had been tossed out of the car. Both officers explained that they truly believed that they weren't going to survive such a large number of shots fired at them. When Officer Baker later examined the police car door, he noticed that a bullet had struck the LAPD logo and went all the way through the door. Both officers were lucky to survive this assault. Months later both officers received the prestigious Medal of Valor award from the city for their bravery.

The jurors were listening to the officers' testimony, but up to this point no one mentioned McGhee being involved. The three gangsters who were in the Honda were captured and all separately prosecuted. Hoon at this stage had to make the connection of this shoot-out to McGhee. Again he used Mark G. to testify that he was with McGhee when this all went down. During the early morning hours, these Toonerville members were doing what they do all the time and that was to listen to the police scanners. This witness, Mark G., indicated that when he heard the officers say they were going north on Riverside Drive that was when McGhee grabbed a gun and said let's do something.

Although Mark G. claimed that he didn't participate in the shoot-out, he related to the jury that McGhee shortly after the shooting said, "We really dumped on the cops." However, Hoon was relying on a John Perez to connect McGhee to the ambush. Witness Perez testified that during the early hours of July 4 he heard the police sirens and was curious as to what was going on. He looked out of his bathroom window and could see Bemis Street. He noticed the police car make a wide turn going in the other direction on Bemis Street. At that same moment, he saw muzzle flashes coming from the northwest corner of the intersection. After he heard the crash of the cars and the volley of shots, he noticed someone walk across the street. The streetlight was shining down on the person and that was when he recognized the person to be McGhee, whom he had grown up with. He had lost track of McGhee over the years.

Hoon walked this witness through every step of what he had seen, knowing that McGhee's Defense attorney was waiting to pick apart his testimony. After intense cross-examination, Hoon's next witnesses were the CSI technicians, who had spent hours recovering the myriad of expended shell casings that littered more than a city block. Then the ballistics expert testified that the shell casings from the northeast corner of the intersection were 9mm caliber, which matched the shell casings found at the Ryan Gonzales shooting crime scene.

Hoon recognized that the jury was getting bored with the ballistics testimony. That was when he started to change over to the more interesting shooting of Marjorie Mendoza. Then he called witness Duane N., who related one of the most horrific situations that anyone could ever face. He with his wife Marjorie and their friend Erica had driven to the Sav-on Drug Store to get some change. Duane was driving his new Mitsubishi Montero SUV back home when a light-green compact car started to tailgate his car. He knew he was driving through Rascal territory and he was affiliated with the Pinoy Real gang, but he felt safe to do so. As Duane made a number of turns, so did this car behind him.

Duane didn't want to scare the girls in the car, so he turned the music down and he told the girls that he was going to pull over to let the car go by. He came to a complete stop next to some parked cars. The other car drove around his car and suddenly pulled in front of him at an angle to prevent him from leaving. Duane could see two men get out of the car, one wearing a hoody and he appeared to be raising his hand holding what looked like a gun. Duane realized that a shooting was about to occur.

Without a second thought, Duane ducked for cover. He didn't give any warning to the two girls. In less than three seconds a shower of bullets tore through his new car. Then there was a lull, and he popped his head up to see if it was over; that's when a volley of shots came roaring in from every direction, but most of them struck the passenger door next to his wife. All Duane could think about was how to get out of there. He knew the light-green car was blocking him in front. Within seconds he was able to reach the shifter and forced it into reverse, and at the same time he pressed on the accelerator, causing the car to fly backward. Since he had his head down in the floorboard area, he had no idea where they would end up.

Then there was a sudden jerk as his new car struck a parked car and came to rest. Were the shooters going to come after them? Duane waited for the next round of bullets, and he reached over to see how his wife, Marjorie, was doing. He could feel blood dripping from the side of her head, which shocked him into realizing that she had been severely injured. In panic mode, he tried to think where the closest hospital was located. All he could think of was the Glendale Memorial Hospital, which wasn't far away.

Duane sat up and sped to the hospital emergency room entrance. He jammed on the brakes as the car came to a rest and he jumped out of the car yelling for anyone to come help him. Within seconds a nurse appeared and examined Marjorie. When the nurse looked at her partially disfigured face, all she could do was declare her dead-on arrival. The hospital security contacted the police department and explained that they had a shot-up vehicle at the entrance to the ER.

Since this was the shooting that would be the downfall of McGhee, Hoon wanted to walk the jurors through every step of what happened. Hoon next called Monica M., who explained that on November 8, 2001, around midnight she heard what sounded like gunfire, so she looked out of her house to see what all the commotion could be. She saw several cars, one of which was a large black SUV type, and within seconds both cars raced away. The neighborhood became silent, so she returned to her house to check on her children. Everything was peaceful in her house, so she again stepped outside and this time she walked down Hollydale Drive. She was surprised how quiet everything was until she noticed a car come back driving very slowly. Monica became scared and looked for a place to hide. All she could find was a spot behind a van, so she ducked behind it.

A man got out of the car and was trying to direct a woman to look for something. This man said to her, "I think I dropped it near here." Both were looking under the parked cars that lined both sides of the street. The woman came up next to Monica, at which time Monica asked her what she was looking for. The woman hurriedly said my friend lost something around here. She continued to walk to the side of the parked cars and looked under them. Then Monica saw the man slowly moving by the other side of the cars. What stood out about his appearance was a large tattoo on the back of the man's head. (Later she identified a photo of McGhee as the man she saw looking under the cars.)

Eventually, Monica saw the woman get back in the large black SUV with the man. That woman drove slowly down the street. By that time police officers arrived and Monica approached the nearest officer. She didn't know what to say but pointed to the large vehicle driving away and said to the officer, "I think that car had something to do with the shooting." This officer didn't know much about what had happened except he was told by the dispatcher that there might have been a shooting in the area of Hollydale Drive near Petit Court.

The officer hadn't found any shooting victim, any car, or any weapons at the scene. So this officer felt compelled to listen to Monica, who was saying that one of the vehicles was in the process of leaving. How should this officer react? For whatever reason, he got on his handheld radio and told one of the responding units to stop the large black SUV driving north on Hollydale Drive. One of the units saw the large vehicle and activated his red lights as he pulled behind the vehicle. The officer was surprised how compliant the driver was to pull to the curb and stop. The only unusual thing to occur was the fact that when he was approaching the vehicle, he saw a male cover himself with a blanket in the back seat.

The officer approached the female driver and kept his eye on the person in the back. He engaged the driver, Christina Duran, in conversation as to what she was doing there. Christina was a 28-year-old attractive Latina who didn't look the gangster type. She was caught off guard as to what to say to the officer. Unfortunately for her, she didn't know what McGhee might say if asked questions about being in the area.

Christina started to mix up her stories as to what she was really doing there. Monica had said that this large black vehicle may have been one of the cars involved in the shooting. In order not to release someone who may have been involved in the shooting, the officers decided to have a Field Identification. One of the units took Monica over to where Christina was stopped. The officer asked Monica if that was the SUV she was talking about and if that was the woman she had seen earlier. Her response was that it looked like the car involved in the shooting and that was the woman she had talked to about looking for something.

Trying to sort out what type of shooting had occurred, the officer told the other officer to transfer Christina to the station so the detectives could speak with her. As to the guy in the back seat, they couldn't think of any legal reason to further detain him. The officer tried to draw upon all his training to think of a reason for detaining this guy who just happened to be in the back of the car. He knew he didn't have sufficient probable cause to detain or arrest him so he decided to fill out an FI card on this person. After this was accomplished, McGhee was released and he walked down Hollydale Drive as a free man. Surprisingly, LAPD had the Monster of Atwater in their grasp, only to release him. It would take dozens of law enforcement almost two years to eventually track him down again.

Unfortunately for Christina, she was totally out of her element as she was ushered into one of the interview rooms at Northeast station. She started to weave a web to protect McGhee. One of the detectives started asking tough questions of Christina. Christina wasn't a criminal, and her mind was on her children, who she dearly loved. The detectives made it clear to her that if she didn't start telling the truth she could be held as an aider and abetter and in the process possibly could lose the custody of her children. Christina broke down in tears and started to reveal McGhee's involvement in the shooting. He had asked her to help him find a cellphone that he dropped during the shooting. She explained that she tried to help him but they never found the cellphone, so she was in the process of leaving with him when the police stopped her.

She would tell them what happened, but she would never testify in court as to what she had told the detectives. She was in deadly fear of retaliation from McGhee and his fellow gang members if they found out she talked.

Hoon called as his next witness the officer that found the cellphone. He indicated that he was shining a flashlight under a large white utility van and noticed something shiny. He used a stick and pulled the item toward him, at which point he recognized it as a cellphone. He said he had the item placed in an evidence bag for the detectives and Crime Lab to examine.

The follow-up witness on the cellphone was from the telephone company's records section. That person was able to determine the cellphone's number. From their phone records, this witness was able to indicate that the registered owner was Lisa M., who was McGhee's girlfriend back in 2001, and the address listed on the phone records was the place where McGhee lived in Pomona, CA. Hoon was pleased that the phone record was a strong piece of circumstantial evidence to buttress the eyewitness account of Monica M.

CHAPTER 47 TIME FOR ARGUMENT

After Hoon had finished presenting all his witnesses and had his evidence received by the court, it was the Defense's turned to call witnesses and present their evidence. The Defense attorney had a few witnesses to counter the prosecution's case. However, everyone was waiting to see if the rough and tough Monster of Atwater would take the witness stand and tell his side of the story.

Throughout the entire trial, the jurors had a view of a self-assured, almost arrogant McGhee, who was the fearless leader of the Toonerville gang. Every day McGhee was decked out in his Sunday best, projecting the image of a young up-and-coming professional. He certainly didn't evoke the image of the type of person who would commit such atrocious crimes. When the moment arrived for McGhee to take the witness stand, he resisted the temptation. McGhee was one smart dude. He realized that there were so many questions he couldn't answer without looking like a cold-hearted killer. As much as Hoon was hoping to cross-examine McGhee, he wasn't going to have that pleasure.

Hoon knew if he were to win this case against McGhee it would have to be through his Argument. He needed to paint a more accurate picture of the real Timothy Joseph McGhee. Since this case involved so many separate crimes spanning so many years, Hoon was concerned that the individual jurors might get lost in the 'weeds.' As a prosecutor who had tried some of the most challenging cases in the DA's Office, he understood the importance of using visual aids to communicate with the jurors.

He used a poster-size chart which was called the EVIDENCE AGAINST MCGHEE. Basically, this was a way for Hoon to summarize all the evidence of the case on one board. Why he used it was for the jurors to understand how all the various pieces fit together from all the dozens of witnesses they had heard from over the several weeks of the trial.

Graphic Page of the Summary of the Case

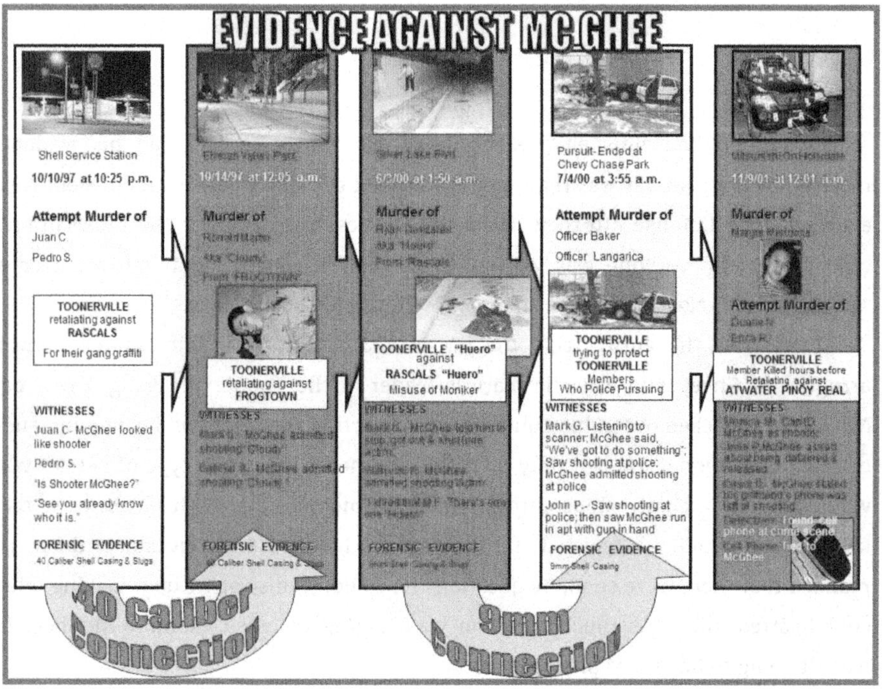

Graphic Page about the Ballistic Connecting

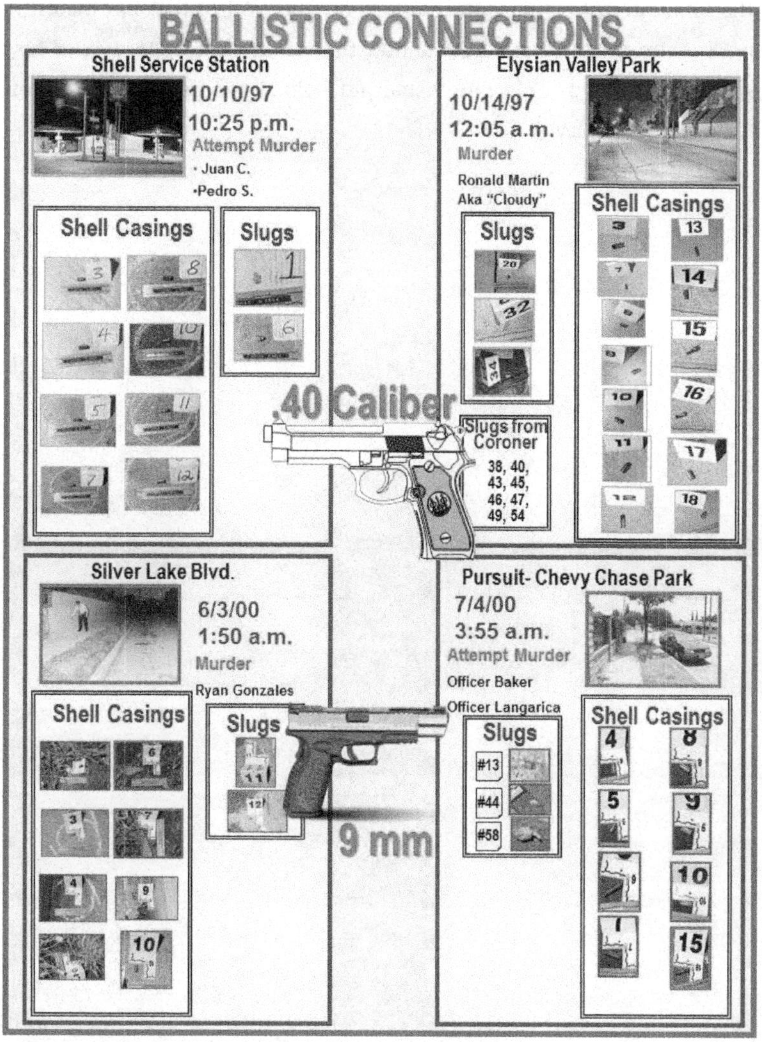

Hoon realized he needed forensic evidence to connect McGhee to the crimes. He used the below visual aid to show that the .40 caliber gun was used in the shooting of Juan and Pedro as well as used in the shooting of Ronald Martin. Next he wanted to show how the 9mm was connected to the shooting of Ryan Gonzales and the shooting during the Police Pursuit. Hoon had invested so much of the trial time building the foundation for this connection to McGhee. All of that hard work would be useless if the jurors didn't understand how the ballistic evidence showed how the shootings were connected. This one visual aid helped the prosecutor explain the ballistic evidence to the jury.

After Hoon had given the jurors the big picture, he was ready to walk the jurors through the detailed evidence of each of the crimes and how McGhee was connected to these crimes. First, he discussed the Juan C. and Pedro S. shooting near the Shell Station on Glendale Boulevard. Even though this shooting occurred almost a decade before, Hoon wanted the jurors to see how McGhee was so callous as to shoot Pedro S. through a glass door even though the two had grown up together.

The below graphic shows where the expended shell casings were found in front of the Shell Station.

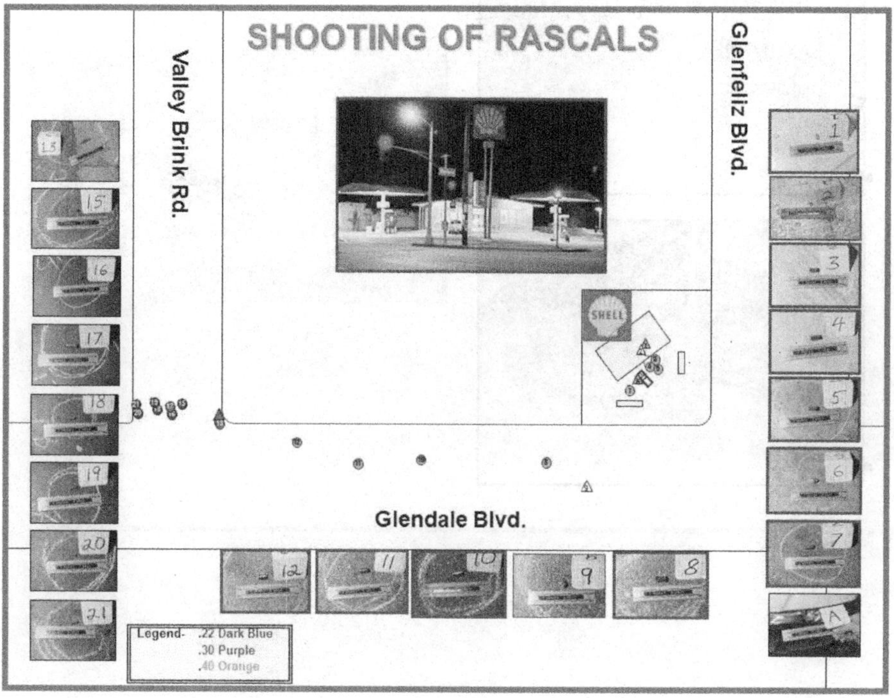

The below graphic shows where the victims dropped their bikes and took off running for their lives. When Juan C. was shot, he fell down on the street. His friends pulled him to safety so the cars traveling on Glendale Boulevard didn't run over him. When the police arrived, he was on the sidewalk

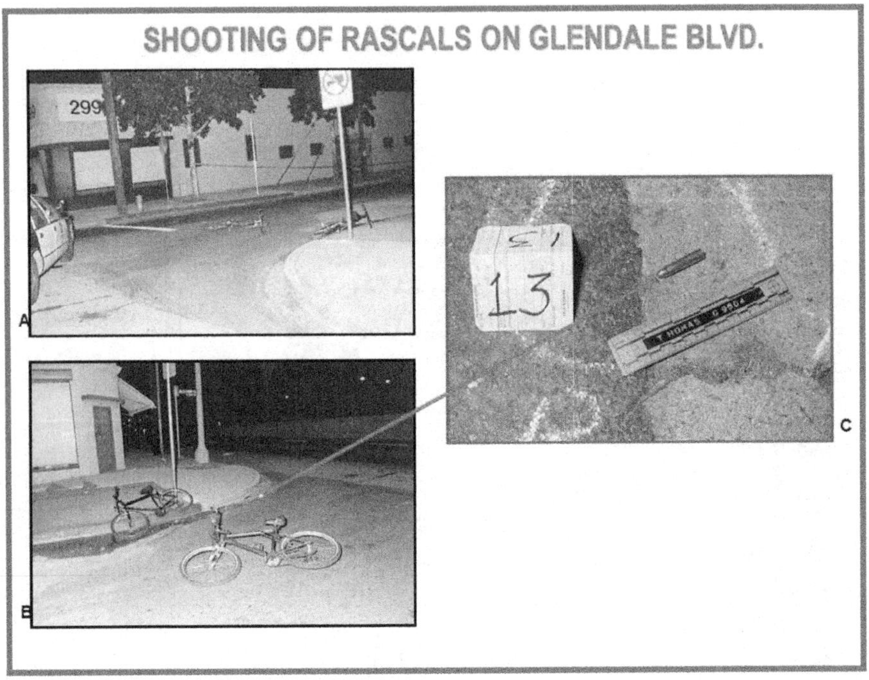

Hoon recognized that Juan C. and Pedro S. identification of McGhee as the shooter was weak; however, Hoon believed that his evidence in the Ronald Martin case was stronger. When Hoon started to discuss the facts of the Martin shooting, he used the below graphic to show clearly that it occurred near the entrance to the Elysian Recreation Center, which was set up by the city as a safe place for the young people to congregate without encountering gang violence.

Hoon wanted the jury to understand how many times Ronald Martin was shot. This graphic was used by Hoon to illustrate how much of an overkill this shooting was. The ballistic experts indicated that at least three guns were used against Ronald Martin. One of them was a .40 caliber handgun, which was fired eight times into the victim's body.

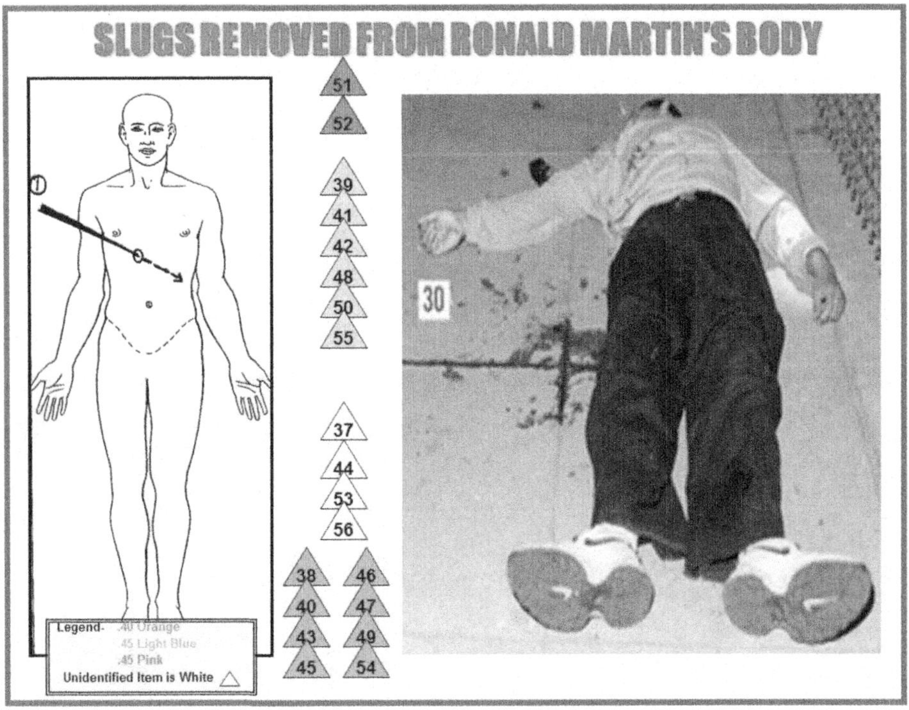

Hoon didn't want the jurors to become confused between the Martin and Gonzales shootings, so he used a completely different visual aid to depict the Ryan Gonzales crime scene. The below visual explained to the jurors where Gonzales was shot numerous times as he was walking home alone from a late-night Rascals' party. This was where McGhee got out of the vehicle and asked Gonzales, "Where are you from?" Not receiving the answer he wanted, McGhee shot him several times. The victim had been transported to the hospital, where he succumbed to his gunshot wounds.

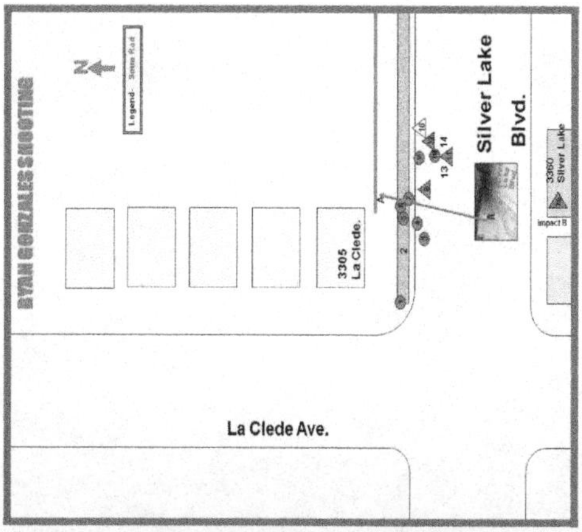

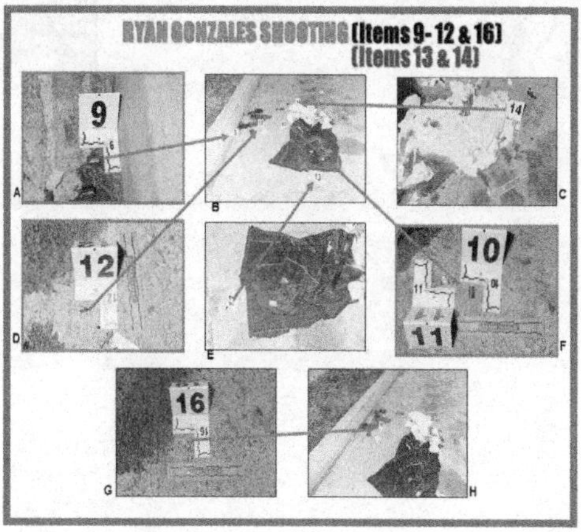

Hoon knew that the jurors would have difficulty understanding all the facts of the pursuit shooting. Since it covered several miles, he wanted the jurors to focus on the facts near the end of the pursuit. He used the visual aid below to show the exact route the robbers and pursuing officers took. It started in the southern portion of Atwater Village and ended up at the north end, which was the Toonerville territory.

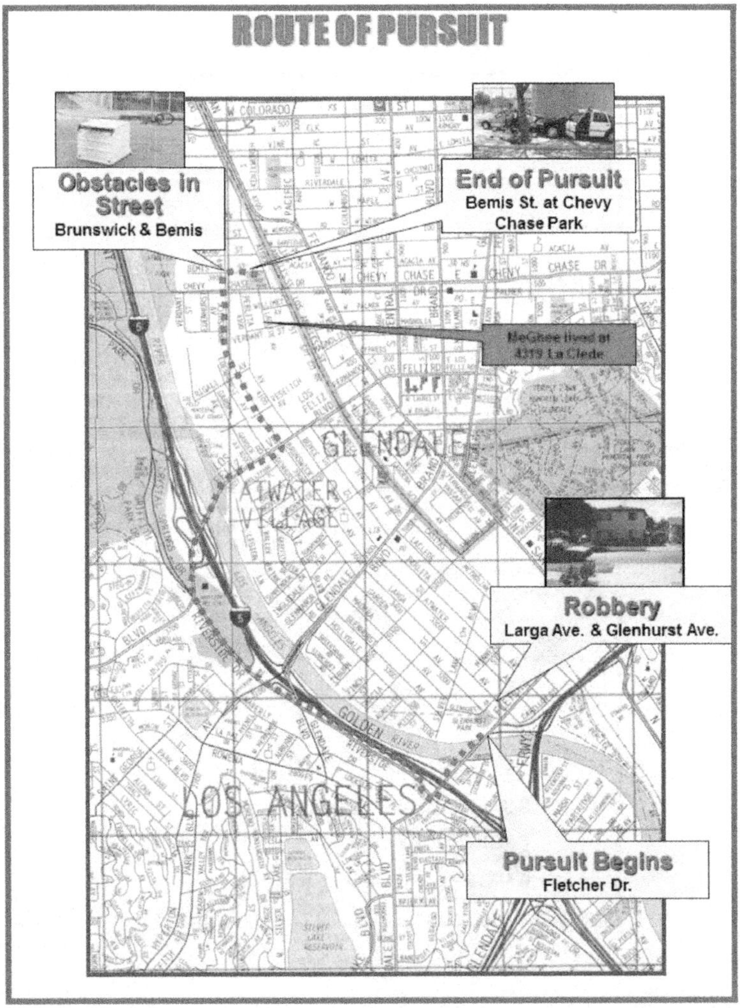

Hoon wanted the jurors to focus on when the police car turned from Brunswick Avenue onto Bemis Street. That was the point where McGhee fired his 9mm at the police car as it made the turn. The other visual showed where the pursuit ended next to the handball courts at Chevy Chase Park.

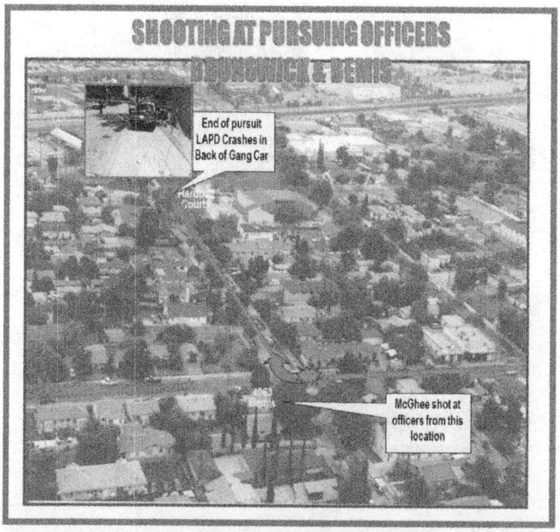

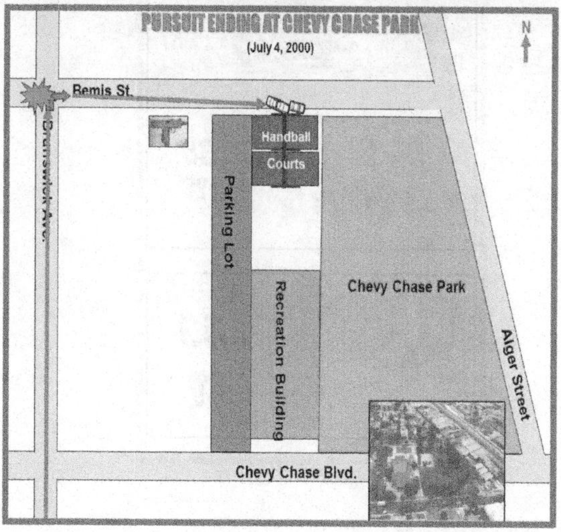

The below visuals show where the police car came to rest against the Honda. The CSI technicians had to collect and document where every shell casing was found. The 9mm shell casings matched the 9mm shell casing from the Ryan Gonzales shooting. There were shell casings and projectiles found all over the street, sidewalk, and park.

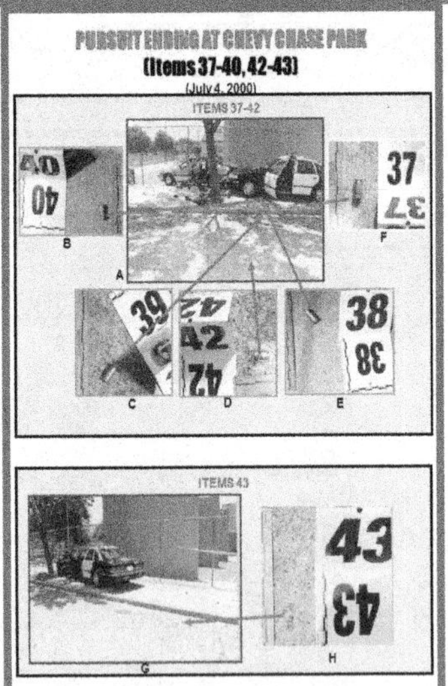

Hoon wanted the jurors to see the firepower the gangster had was greater than what the officers had. The Tec-DC9 was used to shoot at the pursuing officers and it was found in the Honda after it crashed. The Cobray M-11had fortunately jammed, and the gangsters threw it out just before they crashed.

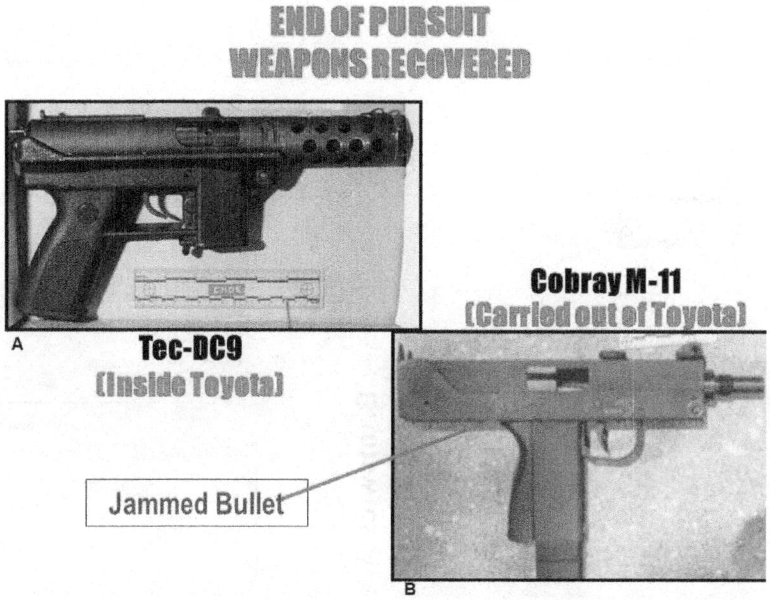

Hoon used this diagram to show exactly where the 9mm shell casings were found near a truck parked on the North West portion of the intersection. This was where McGhee fired the 9mm at the police car as it turned to go east on Bemis Street. These 9mm shell casings matched the shell casing found at the Ryan Gonzales shooting.

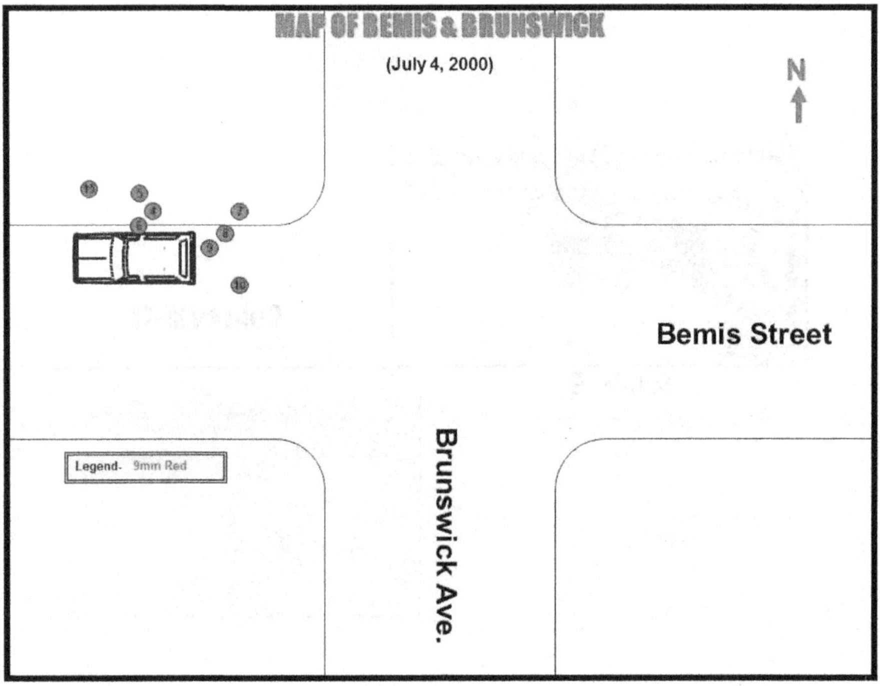

The Mendoza shooting was the one that Hoon was most confident that the jurors would understand because he had such a stellar witness, Monica M. She heard the firing of weapons and looked outside to see two men standing near a Ford Focus firing at a black SUV. Later she saw Christina Duran looking for something under the cars. When the police arrived, she pointed to a black SUV and told the one officer that was the vehicle involved in the shooting. The police stopped the SUV, which was being driven by Christina Duran. Monica was able to identify Christina and later able to identify McGhee. Hoon used this graphic to show all shell casings recovered at this crime scene.

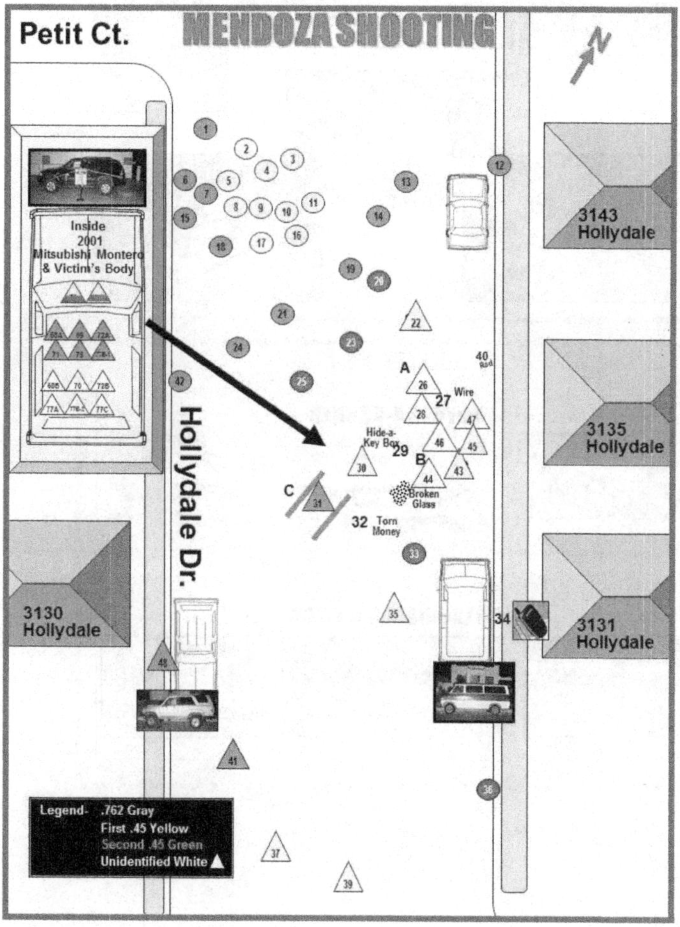

Hoon used the top graphic to show how many times the black SUV was shot and the trajectory of the bullets. The bottom graphic was used to illustrate the similarity between the Mitsubishi Montero and the Toyota 4-Runner. This was to explain why Monica M. mixed up the Toyota 4-Runner driven by Christina Duran with the Mitsubishi Montero that Marjorie Mendoza was a passenger in when she was shot.

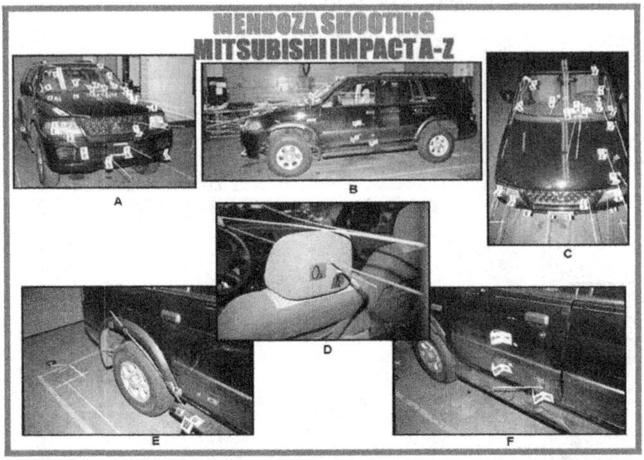

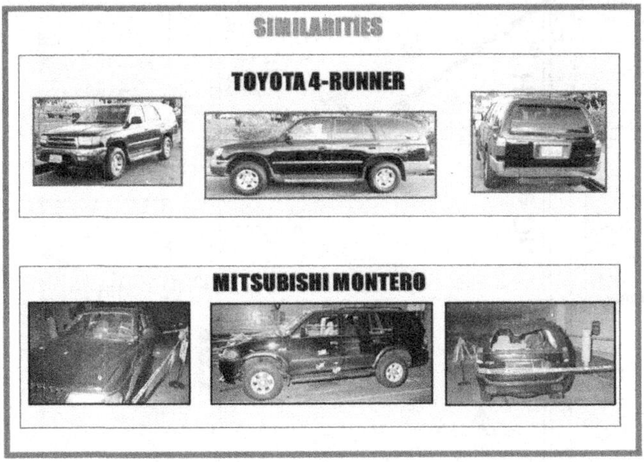

Hoon needed the jurors to fully comprehend the fact that McGhee was present at the crime scene moments after the shooting of Marjorie. That was proven by the FI (Field Identification) Card. The officer detained Christina Duran and McGhee long enough to do a field identification. Afterwards, they took Christina to the station to be interviewed by the detectives. However, the officers couldn't determine any reason to further detain McGhee, so they let him leave after they had filled out an FI Card. Below is the FI Card on McGhee, which proved that McGhee was at the scene of the shooting of Marjorie Mendoza.

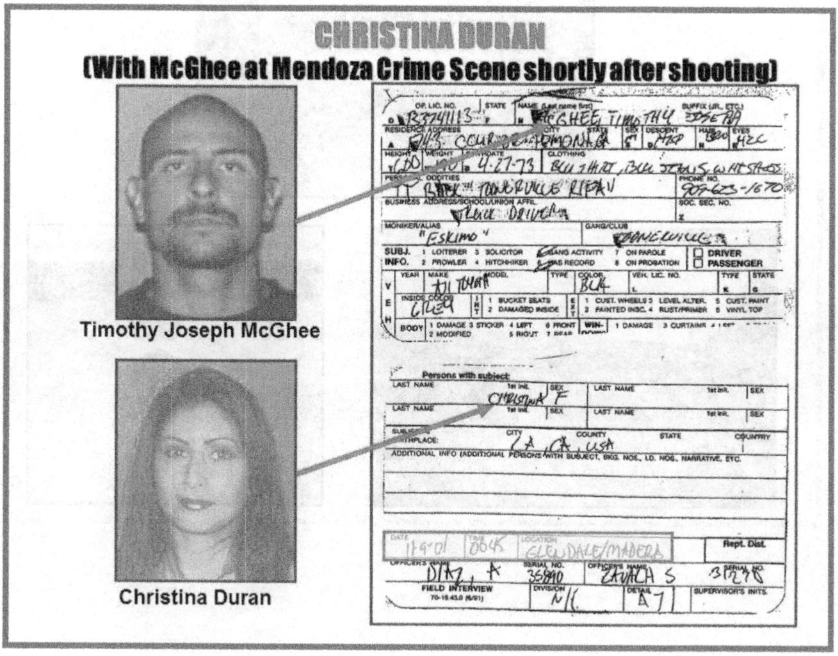

The key piece of evidence that connected McGhee to the shooting of Marjorie was the cellphone he dropped during the shooting. Even though Christina and McGhee couldn't find the cellphone, one of the officers found it under a van parked along the curb.

The cellphone was such a crucial piece of evidence. It was so important that the jury understand that this was McGhee's cellphone even though the number was registered in the name of Lisa M., his girlfriend in 2001. Hoon needed the jurors to see that the address on the cellphone records was the address McGhee had given the DMV as his address. Although the below visual aid may appear to be busy, it contained all the information the jurors needed to know in order to come to the conclusion that the cellphone found under the van was McGhee's. Hoon used this visual to slowly and methodically walk the jurors through every step of the ownership of the cellphone.

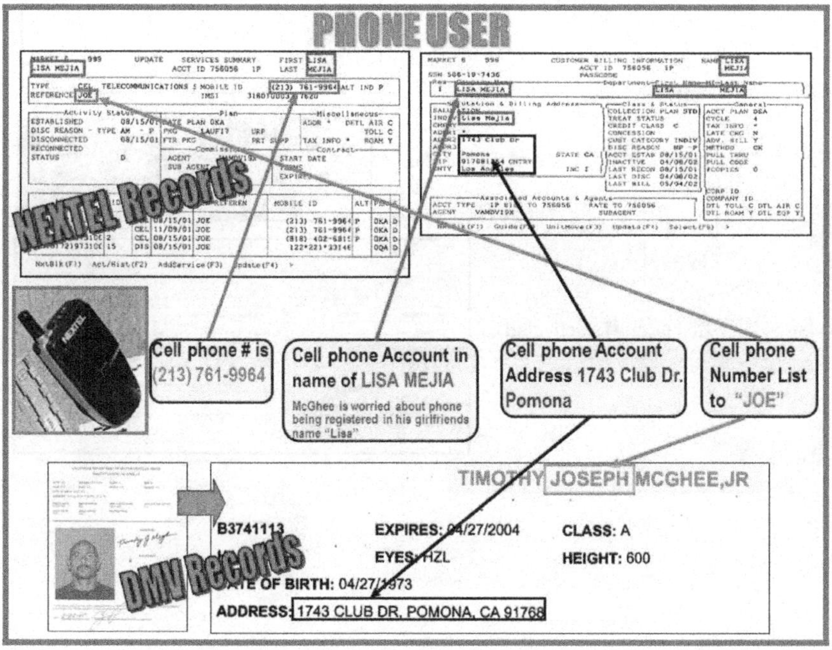

The other issue involving the cellphone was for the jury to understand when the cellphone was last used and when it was deactivated shortly after the shooting. The contact person was listed as a "Joe," which is McGhee's middle name: Joseph. This below graphic easily showed the most recent activity of the cellphone.

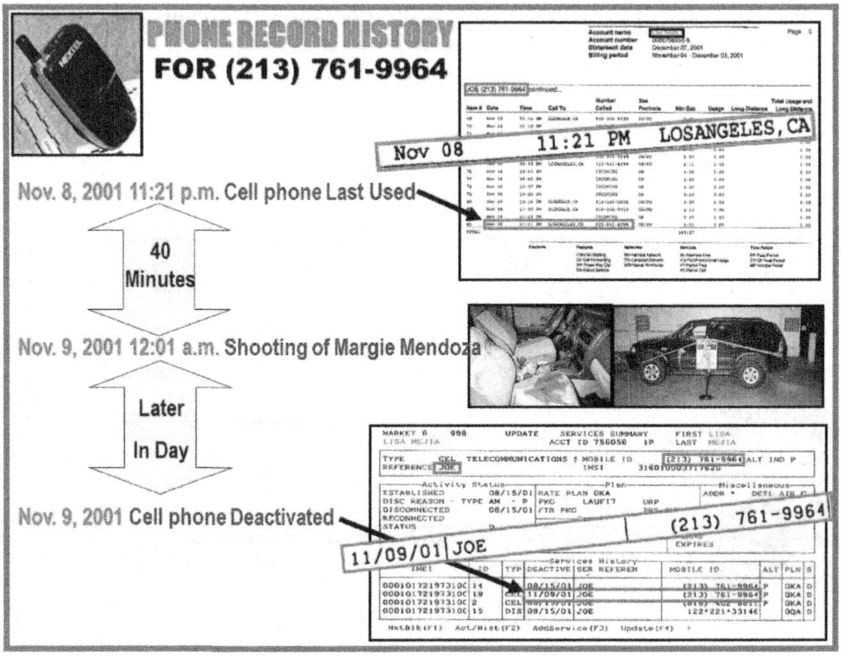

Hoon spent the rest of his Argument discussing the jury instructions that the judge would give the jurors as to the elements of murder and attempted murder. One of the instructions discussed was FLIGHT AFTER CRIME. Hoon wanted the jurors to consider the fact that McGhee was on the run as a fugitive for almost two years. This fact may be considered by the jury in the light of all other facts as to the defendant's GUILT. Hoon could use the fact that McGhee had become one of the top fugitives in the USA.

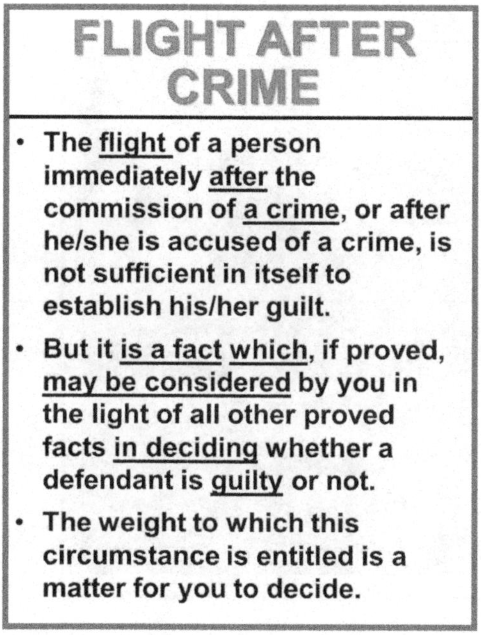

The prosecution had alleged that these murders and attempt murders were done in furtherance of the Toonerville Gang. In order to prove this allegation, Hoon wanted to show the jury that McGhee was a gang member as proved by all his gang tattoos. Needless to say, the Defense objected, claiming that the jury would be adversely prejudiced if they saw his gang tats. The judge ruled that the tats were relevant since he was charged with the gang allegation. All the work by the Defense attorney to dress McGhee as a choir boy in his oversized suits seemed a waste since the below visual aid showed the defendant for what he was, which was the proud leader of the Toonerville Gang.

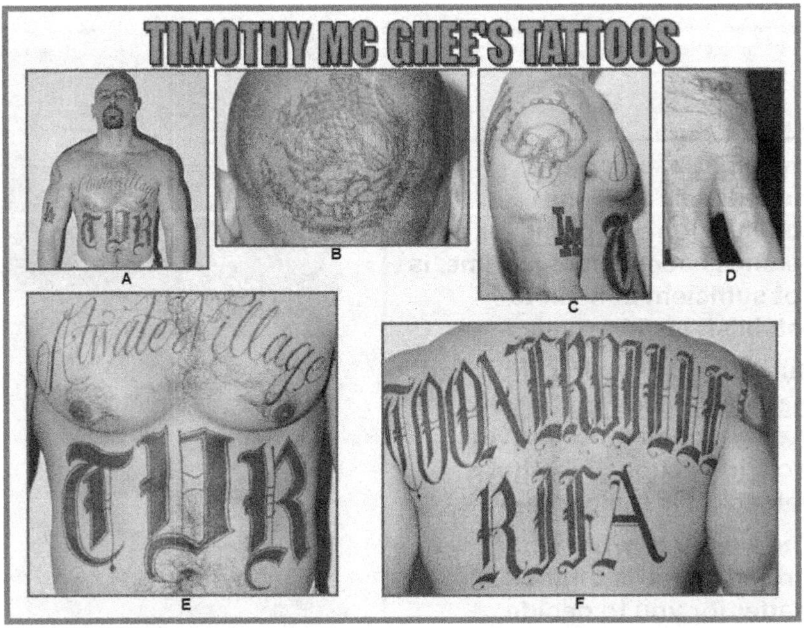

After the prosecutions Argument, McGhee's attorney went on the attack claiming that McGhee was being set up by other rival gangs. The attorney spent considerable time trying to undercut those gangsters who testified against McGhee. Many of the gang members who testified against McGhee had what might be considered a questionable past and questionable motives for testifying. Hoon had tried to explain in his Argument that when you are in hell there are NOT going to be many angels or saints to be called as witnesses.

During the prosecution's Rebuttal Argument, Hoon showed how he could supply corroboration for every crime charged and special allegation. Then Judge Perry gave the final jury instructions and the jurors were ushered into their deliberation room.

Then the long wait began to see if the prosecution was able to convince all 12 jurors that the defendant was guilty beyond a reasonable doubt. The days rolled by without a verdict, then out of the blue the buzzer rang indicating that they had reached a verdict on all the charges. Within an hour, Judge Perry's courtroom was packed with LAPD officers and administrators. Attorneys from all over the Criminal Courts Building had funneled into the courtroom. Even other judges from the ninth floor were squeezing into the standing-room-only court to hear the verdicts.

Hoon sat ramrod straight with a serious look on his face. Then the foreperson passed the verdict forms to the bailiff, who carried them over and handed them to Judge Perry. The judge, without showing any expression, shuffled through all the forms and arranged them in some type of order. Next the courtroom clerk stood up and started reading the verdicts. She started with the attempted murder charge involving Juan C., saying "In the above-entitled action the jury finds the defendant Timothy McGhee NOT GUILTY of attempted murder of Juan C." This was quickly followed by another NOT GUILTY as to Pedro S.

Hoon's face turned a pale white. Could it be that this jury had totally rejected the prosecution evidence and had been more impressed with the Defense's Argument? Or did the jurors just not like the fact that the prosecution used some informant witnesses? Every prosecutor and law enforcement officer in the courtroom was contemplating the unthinkable: that McGhee might be walking the streets that night as a free man.

Finally, the courtroom clerk continued on with Ronald Martin's murder and Ryan Gonzales' murder, and the air in the courtroom was refreshed by hearing the word GUILTY. By this time Hoon's ashen face gained some color as a large smile crossed over his face. He quickly caught himself and wiped the inappropriate smile off his face. From then on there was nothing but high five GUILTY verdicts.

At the end of the verdicts, the judge, who didn't like to waste one minute of court time, explained that the court would be adjourned for the rest of the day and would start the Penalty Phase first thing the next day. Hoon didn't have time to savor the moment of victory but needed to immediately reach his DA witnesses coordinator to get the Death Penalty witnesses to court for the next day.

CHAPTER 48 DEATH PENALTY

America is split almost down the middle as to whether cold-blooded murders should be executed or not for their killings. Your author has written a book titled ***Death Penalty Designee***, which showed how the Los Angeles District Attorney's Office handled Death Penalty cases. No question most of the public have strong beliefs as to the appropriateness of the Death Penalty. The purpose of that book wasn't to debate the merits of the Death Penalty but only explain how the procedure was handled in this McGhee case.

For those readers who are opposed to the Death Penalty, the McGhee case may be harder to justify the sentence of Life in Prison Without the Possibility of Parole. McGhee doesn't fit in the category of being mentally ill; having a poor abusive childhood; the killing was isolated behavior; possibly the defendant may be innocent; or that he will not continue to be a danger if locked up in custody for the rest of his life. McGhee could be the 'poster child' for justifying the Death Penalty.

Since the state of California has the Death Penalty, the DA's Office has the discretion to seek the ultimate punishment if they believe it is appropriate. In the case of Timothy McGhee, the DA's Office believed the Death Penalty was warranted. It was Hoon's job to present the evidence to the jury so they could decide on the proper sentence.

Hoon had handled other Death Penalty cases and knew how difficult it is for jurors to understand the law and procedure they must follow. So Hoon used his

Opening Statement as the time to explain to the jurors what they needed to consider in determining the appropriate sentence.

He used the below chart to show how the jurors are to consider whether the Aggravating circumstances substantially outweigh the Mitigating circumstances.

DEATH PENALTY v. LIFE WITHOUT PAROLE

You determine which penalty is justified and appropriate:

- **By considering the totality of the aggravating circumstances**
- **With the totality of the mitigating circumstances.**
- **To return a judgment of death,**

you must be persuaded
that the aggravating circumstances are so substantial
in comparison with the mitigating circumstances
that it warrants death instead of life without parole.

Next, Hoon showed the jurors the list of factors they could consider in determining whether there were Aggravating or Mitigating circumstances.

FACTORS TO CONSIDER DURING PENALTY

a) Circumstances of crime and any special circumstances found true

b) Presence or absence of criminal activity involving violence

c) Presence or absence of felony convictions

d) Was Def. acting under influence of extreme mental or emotional disturbance

e) Did victim participated in or consented to Def.'s homicidal conduct

f) Did Def. reasonably believe offense to be morally justified or extenuated

g) Did Def. act under extreme duress or domination of another

h) Was Def. unable to appreciate criminality of conduct or conform conduct to requirements of law due to mental disease or effects of intoxication

i) Age of Def. at time of crime

j) Was Def. an accomplice and was Def's participation relatively minor

k) Any circumstance which extenuates gravity of offense or any sympathetic or other aspect of Def.'s character

After explaining the Penalty Phase procedure, Hoon touched on the Aggravating factors he would be presenting to them. The most hotly debated was whether the jury could hear evidence about Christina Duran's cold-blooded slaughter. The below graphic spells out the timeline of the events leading up to the killing of Christina Duran.

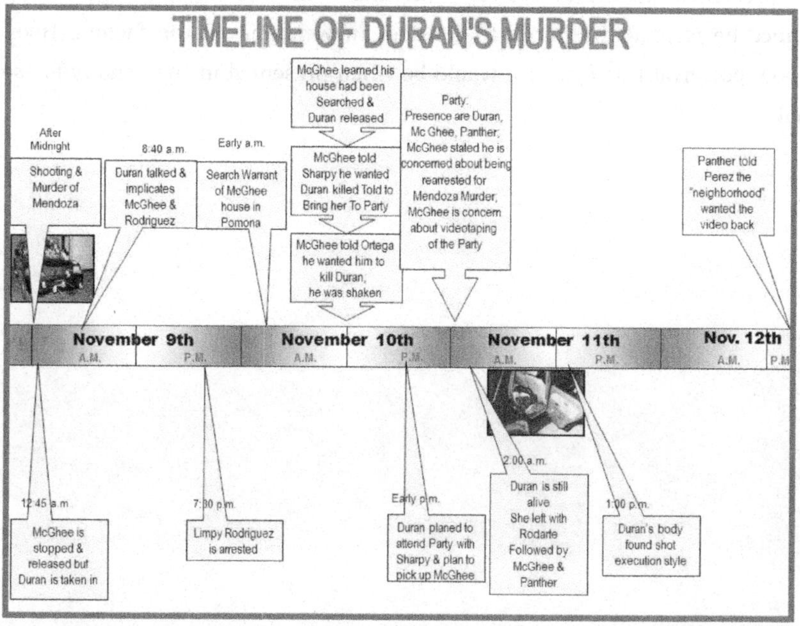

What seems so aggravating about this killing was the fact that Christina Duran was willing to stick her neck out to help McGhee look for the cellphone so he wouldn't be connected to the Marjorie Mendoza murder. For her actions, Christina could have been prosecuted for Accessory After the Fact. It would seem that McGhee should be forever indebted to her for what she did for him.

Within 24 hours McGhee was planning a 'Kiss and Die' party for Christina. He arranged for her to celebrate her 29th Birthday with a party in West Covina. After the party had ended, she left with her boyfriend in her black Toyota SUV. McGhee with one of the guests left immediately after Christina. He followed her and when she got to an isolated area her boyfriend, the driver of her car, stopped and got out. McGhee approached the back of her car with a gun in his hand. At that moment in time, Christina realized that she had been set up. For self-protection, she scrambled around inside the car trying to lock all the car doors. As she crawled into the back seat, a barrage of bullets tore into the right side of her face. Her last act was to raise her hand to block the bullets. As her outstretched hand was blown back, her body slumped to the floor of the back seat.

Hoon presented the evidence of Christina's murder as an Aggravating circumstance he wanted the jurors to consider in weighing all the factors. Hoon realized how powerful this evidence would be when presented in the Penalty Phase of the trial.

Below are the photos of Christina's 4-Runner with her body lying on the backseat floor.

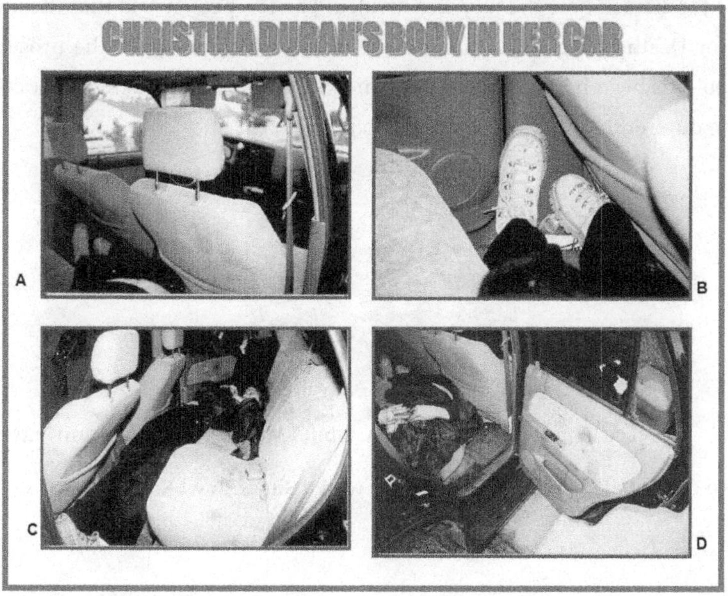

Hoon presented additional Aggravating evidence about McGhee being involved in various acts of violence while in custody. After all the guards were finished testifying, Hoon had the victims' families testify how the death of their loved one had impacted their lives. The Defense didn't have much in the way of mitigating evidence. After several days of testimony, both sides gave passionate Arguments for what they believed was the appropriate punishment. Then the judge sent the jurors out to deliberate.

The jury continued to deliberate on the appropriate penalty for several days. This was strange, since this jury had taken only one day to decide McGhee's guilt. How could this jury splinter into various groups? Judge Perry certainly didn't want to have the court spend precious court time retrying the Penalty Phase of the McGhee case. He encouraged the jurors to try harder to find a way of reaching a unanimous verdict as to the appropriate sentence. The judge had to be careful not to appear to be dissuading jurors from giving up their individual opinions.

But after several tries the jury returned to court claiming that they were hopelessly deadlocked. With much regret, Judge Perry found that there was a hung jury and declared a mistrial. After the mistrial was declared by the judge, the judge asked the foreperson how the jury was divided. The foreperson said that the jury was split 10 for Death and two for Life. This was a crushing blow for the prosecution. Hoon shook his head in disbelief and felt an extreme disappointment. What could he have done differently to persuade those two jurors?

Hoon's sad face showed his dejection while McGhee's smile from ear to ear seemed so delighted, as though he had just won a Super Bowl Ring.

CHAPTER 49 TRY IT AGAIN

Several months later, Hoon was back in court retrying the Penalty Phase of the McGhee case. Unfortunately for the witnesses, they all had to reappear to testify again. The second jury didn't have to consider whether McGhee was guilty of the Ronald Martin, Ryan Gonzales, Marjorie Mendoza murders or any of the attempted murders of the officers during the pursuit, or Duane and Erica. The prosecution didn't have to reprove the guilt; however, realistically the new jurors needed to be convinced in their own mind that the defendant was guilty of the crimes. So basically, Hoon knew he had to call all the witnesses so the new jury wouldn't have a lingering doubt about the defendant's guilt.

Again, the prosecution had to present all the prior acts of violence, which included a number of jail and prison guards to explain the acts of violence McGhee had been involved in. The relatives of the victims again had to testify to the impact they had experienced as a result of the victim's death.

Hoon knew that the judge wouldn't permit him to retry McGhee a third time, so he had to go all out to convince the jurors that McGhee clearly deserved the Death Penalty. This time Hoon tried to convey to the jury that McGhee was a DANGER IN AND OUT OF CUSTODY. In other words, giving McGhee Life Without the Possibility of Parole (LWOP) would mean that prison guards and other inmates would be subject to McGhee's wrath and acts of violence. If McGhee were executed, he could no longer be a danger to anyone. In other words, McGhee would never be able to harm another human being.

The following graphic timeline MCGHEE IS A DANGER IN & OUT OF PRISON allowed Hoon to argue that when McGhee was on the streets he committed crimes against others and when he was in custody he committed violent acts against the guards.

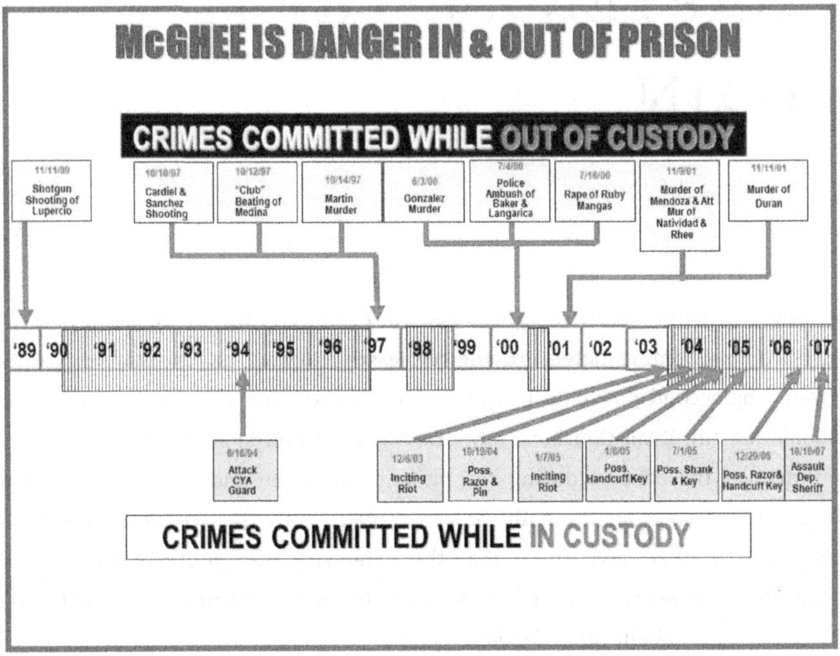

Apparently, this second Argument hit the right chord with this second jury. They recommended the Death Penalty.

At the time of sentencing, Judge Robert Perry made the observation that McGhee seemed to think killing was some kind of perverse sport, as if he were hunting human game. The judge gave McGhee the Death Penalty and shipped him off to San Quentin to join over 700 inmates on Death Row who have been waiting years to have their execution carried out. The final chapter of Timothy McGhee's story may take years to be concluded.

CHAPTER 50 HOON'S COMMITMENT

This book was written to illustrate to the public that there are certain people who make our Criminal Justice System work. I marvel at all the institutions in our country in which government employees do their jobs. Since I, the writer, worked for the Los Angeles DA's Office for 43 years, I came across a number of amazing people.

I am not suggesting that Hoon is the so-called perfect prosecutor. Nor should he receive some type of reward or bonus for a job well done. However, he did a remarkable job in the McGhee case. When it was determined that the informant that had supplied so much evidence against McGhee wasn't being candid, Hoon could have used that as an excuse to dump the McGhee case since it was fraught with so many problems.

Again, when the homicide detectives were in the deadly traffic accident, Hoon could have punted the case because there was no way of knowing where all the evidence and witnesses were for trial. On top of all those problems, Hoon could have said that he had to come in as a substitute prosecutor when the original prosecutor, Tony Manzella, was unable to try the McGhee case.

Attorneys are competitive people who like to win—or, one could say, they don't like to lose. The McGhee case had the word LOSER written all over it. But Hoon wasn't deterred by the fact that most of the witnesses didn't want to be involved. As to the safety aspect for Hoon and his family, Hoon doesn't dwell on the fear factor, but it is real and is always in the back of your mind.

Hoon isn't deterred by problems with a case. He looks at problems as something to overcome. To him it is the search for a solution that makes it all worthwhile. How do you describe such a person? The following words may describe Hoon Chun:

Dedicated

Tenacious

Stubborn

Dogged

Grit

Steadfast

Persevering

However, Hoon is something more than any of the above words can describe. He definitely should be included as one of the Best of the Best Prosecutors. Thank God there are people who do great jobs not for the money or the prestige. They are just incredible people who are dedicated to making our communities a safer place to live in. THANKS TO HOON FOR A JOB WELL DONE.

PROSECUTOR HOON CHUN

ANGEL CRUZ CASE

CHAPTER 51 TGIF PARTY TIME

It was a hectic Friday afternoon in the City of the Angels. To the hard-working people of this metropolis, it was time to unwind from all the stress and struggles of the long week. It was no wonder that the term 'Thank God It Is Friday," better known as TGIF, was coined. For the college students, this period of time just before the final exams can be even more than nerve-racking. They have to attend all their classes while trying to be a human sponge memorizing all the esoteric facts that they have to recite back at exam time. For students, the beginning of the weekend is a double delight.

Los Angeles is blessed in having two great world-renowned universities within its city limits. UCLA is located on the Westside of Los Angeles and borders Bel Air and Beverly Hills, where it is surrounded by the homes of the rich and famous. The UCLA campus projects an academic grandeur, with stately Ivy League brick buildings like Royce Hall. Its campus is scattered over rolling hills of well-landscaped grounds, giving the appearance of being a fine institution of higher learning.

Students are mere steps from the entrance to Westwood Village, where they can enjoy a piece of pizza or catch a Hollywood premier at one of the classic movie theaters—either the BRUIN or the FOX. UCLA is a state university run by the Regents of California. Originally, it was founded as a tuition-free school, although through the years the student fees have unfortunately continued to rise. It is ranked as one of the top universities in the country. Because of its high ranking and its lower tuition, it is inundated with applicants. In order to be considered for admission, a high school graduate would have to have a straight "A" average and proof of completion of various college prep classes. However, there is a less academic reason why high school students are clamoring to attend UCLA, and that is the fact that it is just a hop, skip, and a jump from the sunny beaches of Santa Monica.

Your author has to show his bias since he and his fraternity brother Lon Clearwaters attended this fine institution and we have many wonderful Bruin memories.

The other major university in Los Angeles is USC, and it truly has many pluses but also has some minuses. First, the USC campus is not in the best of locations. To be politically correct, one would say that it is in an area in 'transition.' Originally when it was founded it was in a prestigious residential area. But the neighborhood has changed over time, and it would be fair to say it is in a blighted area of Los Angeles. The trustees of USC had to make a decision whether to move out or stay and create a fortified island in the center of HELL. Since the university had invested so much in buildings and research facilities, the trustees decided to stay and try to isolate the campus from the surrounding afflicted areas. The USC campus is attached to the rest of the city by the Harbor Freeway (I-110), which is the artery that permits the students safe access to the campus.

With such an unfortunate deprived location, one would think that USC wouldn't be a place any parent would want to send their precious darlings. Besides the location problem, the other negative factor is the real fact that USC's tuition is extremely expensive. It would be twice as expensive to attend USC compared to its cross-town rival UCLA. One would therefore think that USC would have few new student applicants. What is surprising is that USC has more applicants than it can accommodate. The entrance academic standards are almost as high as UCLA's. However, the difference is that USC has an incredible reputation. Part of that may be due to the fact that USC has received endless publicity from its myriad of football championships over the years.

The author has to confess that after graduating from UCLA I did the unthinkable thing of crossing town to attend USC Law School, where I received my Juris Doctorate degree.

However, what makes USC one of the most recognized universities is the fact that it has an incredible alumni association that other universities can only envy. Loyalty and Tradition are the hallmarks of the USC alumni, which provide the necessary contacts to assist any graduate to enter into the various professions as well as the business world. Possibly the high tuition and the fortified conditions of the campus cause the graduates to feel proud of the fact that they were able to survive the challenges of attending USC. For many families, it is well worth the few hardships to have one of their children graduate from USC.

The Hazlett family lived in Hawaii and was proud of the life style they enjoyed on the islands. But when it came to college the family thought it would be better for their son, Maxwell, to have the university experience on the mainland.

Maxwell Hazlett

Maxwell Hazlett had grown up in the relaxed Hawaiian environment. After high school he was trying to find himself and to figure out what he wanted to do with his life. Maxwell Hazlett submitted his application to attend USC. He and his family were elated when he was accepted by USC. This was the perfect school for Maxwell, and it didn't take long for him to adapt to Trojan life. As a result of being raised in Hawaii, he was used to the openness and the diversity of the student body. Maxwell grew up as an avid surfer and had a love for Asian music. It was only natural he would gravitate to other students having his same interests. He quickly made staunch friendships with a group of Asian students who he could identify with. He was majoring in Chinese cultures and language, which was an ambitious attempt for him but he found it fascinating.

During his freshman year, he lived on campus and enjoyed the active social life. The experience of living in the center of all this excitement of football games and endless social exchanges can be overwhelming for a kid from the little island of Oahu. After Maxwell received his freshman grades, the reality set in that he needed to scale back on the social distractions that had occupied so much of his time.

Looking for a way of improving his grades, Maxwell learned that some of the students had found that moving off campus was a way to avoid the temptations of all the fun things available on campus. Maxwell heard that the Promenade Apartments in the Los Angeles downtown civic center was a good substitute.

The apartment was several miles from campus, but he could take a "DASH" bus that would provide him easy access to the USC campus. Maxwell realized that he couldn't afford such an apartment on his own but he could afford the rents if he shared it with a roommate. He teamed up with Marc M. and the two of them shared the apartment. Although this off-campus living had its challenges, Maxwell soon realized that his studies and grades were benefiting from this new living arrangement.

Marc and Maxwell enjoyed each other's company and hung out together. Yet this buddy relationship suddenly changed when Marc met a certain young lady. Marc started spending more time with her than his old roommate Maxwell. Even the weekends changed as Marc decided to spend more time over at his girlfriend's place. Maxwell didn't resent Marc's new girlfriend entering the picture, but it meant he had to find others to socialize with on weekends.

This Friday Marc had already decided to go over to his girlfriend's place to spend the evening. That meant that Maxwell was on his own to find something exciting to do. Late in the afternoon, Maxwell received a phone call from Jonathan P., his old-time friend from Hawaii. Jonathan telephoned Maxwell to see what he had lined up for the weekend. He related that some of the other USC students were going to the Ivar Nightclub in Hollywood. Since Maxwell didn't have anything to do, he jumped at this opportunity to get out of the apartment. When he heard the word 'Hollywood,' Maxwell thought that this might be a good place to meet some girls. Like all male college students, the possibility of finding new female companions seemed like a worthwhile endeavor to expand one's dating pool.

CHAPTER 52 HEADING TO HOLLYWOOD

For the older crowd in town, 10:00 p.m. was the time to say Good Night to the World and go to bed. However, this was just the time the young people are heading out to their favorite watering holes. Maxwell's friend, Jonathan P., pulled into the driveway in front of the Promenade Apartments and picked him up a little after 10:00 p.m. They drove down Figueroa Street toward the USC campus to meet the rest of the group. They breezed by the Staple Center, since the game was still going on and the crowd hadn't emptied out thus causing a traffic jam. As they approached the campus on Figueroa Street, all one could see were fast food restaurants for several city blocks. Their blinding neon signs might seem an unsightly glow except for the hungry students. As they drove down the street, they couldn't help but smell the aroma of greasy burgers and fries, not to mention the grilled onions.

When they saw the giant Felix the Cat sign on top of the local Chevrolet dealership, they knew it was time to turn right and maneuver over to where their friend Fred (pseudonym) lived. Much to their surprise, they learned that Fred had a newer Mercedes. It didn't take long for the boys to realize that the Mercedes would be a classier way to drive to Hollywood. It was agreed that they would park Jonathan's car and everyone would pile into the larger Mercedes.

Fred and his girlfriend, Debbie, were in the front seat while Maxwell and Jonathan occupied the rear seat. After a short drive they picked up another coed, and then they made a beeline for the Ivar Club in Hollywood. Everyone was in a jovial mood and wanted to forget about classes and term papers.

The Ivar Nightclub had a reputation of being a jumping place, especially on Friday night. It had a typical trendy chic look with a long bar and a fancy dance floor. When they arrived, they split up, with the couples heading for the dance floor.

Maxwell and Jonathan were more interested in roaming the nightclub rooms and sizing up the female clientele. They spotted some hot chicks that looked worth checking out. However, the guys needed to determine which of the gals were taken and which were truly available. All young men their age have experimented with 'pick-up' lines. One had to adapt the greeting depending on the type of woman involved. Some of the young ladies were secretary/receptionist types looking for a future husband, and the others were college students more interested in finding someone who knew how to have a good time. Also, women in groups had to be approached completely differently from single ladies.

The guys wanted to appear 'cool' or 'hip' and didn't want to appear desperate for female companionship. Maxwell, being from Hawaii, relied on what had worked for him back home. He attempted to play the lost surfer approach in which he relied on 'beach talk.' This approach only caused several of the young ladies to raise their eyebrows and with disinterest say, "Whatever." Maxwell could see he wasn't impressing any of the young women. He motioned to Jonathan to head over to the bar to get another drink. Both assessed the situation and decided that they each needed several more drinks to make themselves appear to be a smoother operator. The alcohol can build a young man's confidence; however, too much alcohol can make a guy look like an inept buffoon.

Maxwell was well aware of the fact that he and booze weren't under control. His lack of success with women caused him to drink to excess. It became a downward spiral when he slurred his speech to the point where he didn't impress anyone. However, the alcohol had a side effect in that it made the homely girls look like a worthwhile catch.

Eventually, Maxwell came to the realization that "Miss Perfect" wasn't there to be found. He chose to give up on women and reverted to smoking and drinking. Just for curiosity, he decided to call his roommate, Marc, on his cellphone. To his delight, his roommate answered and indicated that he was having fun with his new girlfriend at her place. For Maxwell, this made him feel even worse. While he was trying to impress some lassies only to be rejected, his roommate sounded like he was scoring big time with his girlfriend.

Since Maxwell had lost contact with his buddy, Jonathan, he used his cellphone to locate him in the jam-packed Ivar Nightclub. Jonathan was working on some Asian girls in the corner, but they weren't that impressed with his small talk. They weren't looking for a mere student but someone who had a job and at least had a new BMW. Jonathan could sense that Maxwell had had enough. He had to accept the fact that he too was striking out with the girls. The two of them tracked down the couples they had come with and indicated they wanted to leave.

By 1:00 a.m. everyone was ready to call it a night. All six of the USC students agreed to congregate at Fred's Mercedes and head back to campus. Maxwell was the most discouraged with the lack of success in meeting any girls. He felt like a total loser in that he hadn't got even one phone number. All he could think of was spending the rest of the night alone in his apartment. He got the idea that some beer drinking would perk him up and mellow the evening out.

So he asked Fred to stop somewhere along the way back to campus so he could go in and buy some beer. They saw a convenience store in a mini-mall, and Fred pulled in and found a parking space. Maxwell jumped out of the backseat and walked into the store. Near the back he found a refrigerated container packed full of Budweiser and Coors. Without any hesitation, he grabbed a six-pack of Bud and went over to the sales counter. The clerk took one look at Maxwell and immediately asked for his ID. Maxwell automatically reached into his pocket and pulled out his wallet. When he started to remove his ID, he noticed that it was gone.

He shook his head in frustration when he realized he forgot to pick up his ID from the Ivar Nightclub when they were leaving. Maxwell was getting a sinking feeling that everything was going wrong. His immediate concern wasn't the beer but getting back his ID, so he asked Fred if they could return to the Ivar. Fortunately, they weren't too far from the night club, so Fred made a big Uee and they drove back toward club. It took several minutes to track down his ID, but soon they were on their way back to USC. Maxwell recognized that he had inconvenienced everyone, so he didn't request another 'Beer Run.' Near campus, Fred parked his car and everyone called it a night. Jonathan got in his car with Maxwell and willingly headed for the Ponderosa Apartments.

CHAPTER 53 TIME TO GET GAS

Since they were on the west side of the USC campus, Fred decided to drive up Vermont
Avenue. Jonathan found that the heavy traffic that one usually encounters was non-existent since it was 2:00 a.m. As he approached the Interstate 10 Freeway, he glanced at his gas gauge and noticed that he was low on fuel. This was a part of town one didn't want to find oneself stranded without gas. Jonathan scanned the landscape and his eyes became fixed on a Chevron service station sign. Like a homing pigeon, he headed directly for it, and as he got closer he could see that it was still open for business. He pulled in and stopped at the far pumps. Maxwell got out and headed for the office. To his disappointment, this service station didn't sell beer.

Both of them exited the vehicle. Jonathan was pleased that he found an open gas station, while Maxwell was unhappy that he hadn't been able to buy some beer. After filling up the gas tank, they drove up to Washington Boulevard and turned right to proceed north on Figueroa Street, which would take them to Maxwell's apartment house. Just as they reached the intersection of Washington and Figueroa, Maxwell noticed another Chevron service station that was all lit up. Abruptly he shouted out to Jonathan, "Pull in to that service station since it looks like it's still open." Again Maxwell, like a man on a mission, darted out of the car to the office to see if they sold beer. To his delight, he saw a cabinet full of frosty beer cans. His enthusiasm was similar to a homeless person learning he had won the lottery.

It was amazing he didn't shout out, "Eureka, I have found it!" Maxwell didn't waste any time; he grabbed the nearest six-pack and proudly marched up to the cashier with his wallet and his ID in hand. Maxwell's eagerness was met with a curt retort from the clerk. "Hey kid, put that beer back. Are you are trying to get me busted by the ABC?" (Alcohol Beverage Commission) Maxwell didn't have a watch on so he didn't realize it had passed the 2:00 a.m. witching hour when the state of California prohibits the sale of alcoholic beverages. As a child, everyone learns that when the clock chimes 12:00 a.m. Cinderella runs out of the ball, losing her glass slipper. Interestingly, as young people grow up in California, they have etched into their brain the fact of life that one has to buy their booze before 2:00 a.m.

Maxwell was embarrassed and contritely carried the six packs back to the beer cooler. He abruptly placed it with the other containers and gazed at the beer like a friend bidding farewell to a dear companion. When Maxwell got back to the car he approached his friend Jonathan and told him the sad story that it was too late to purchase beer. As Jonathan shook his head, Maxwell could see that his friend was tired of driving him around in search of beer. He made a decision that he would continue his quest for beer on his own, not dragging Jonathan along with him. Maxwell told his friend that he would walk the rest of the way to his apartment.

Jonathan was tired and realized that he wasn't going to talk his friend out of his hunt for some cold brew. Jonathan said, "Okay, I will check on you later to make sure you got home." Maxwell gave his friend a half smile and said, "Well, wish me luck," as he turned to walk up Figueroa Street. Johnathon turned his head to see his frustrated friend fade into the dark of the night.

Human beings make less-than-wise decisions when they are young. Nonetheless, Maxwell's decision turned out to be the worst decision he could have ever made. First, it was after 2:00 a.m. and no store or bar was legally going to sell beer to him. Second, he didn't realize that he was being dropped off at Washington and Figueroa, which was a long, long way from his apartment.

Maxwell started walking northbound on Figueroa and crossed under the I-10 Freeway, which cuts through the bottom portion of the downtown area. He had managed to go only two blocks when he had a reality check that his venture for beer wasn't such a bright idea. Walking along the empty sidewalk with no one around, he sobered up to the fact that he was in for a long walk.

Since he had his cellphone, which was well charged up, he reflected on who he could call to drive him home. He couldn't think of anyone who could pick him up at that hour. If this had been New York, all he would have to do is wave his hand in the air and he would have had a taxi at his service. But this was Los Angeles, where taxi service is quite different. One could stand on the corner of Figueroa and Washington, which is a major intersection for Los Angeles, and wait for hours and never see a taxi.

Maxwell had learned that in Los Angeles one had to call for a taxicab. Since he didn't know what number to call, he had enough sense to dial "411" and get an operator that forwarded his call to a taxicab dispatcher. He told the dispatcher where he was and that he needed a cab. He was told that a taxi would soon be on its way. Although it was April in L.A. it was still cold at that hour in the morning. By 2:23 a.m. he still hadn't seen any cab and he was becoming impatient. He called his roommate Marc, who was not at their apartment but was still at his girlfriend's place. It had been over 20 minutes that he had been waiting for the cab. By this time he was starting to feel a sense of desperation. Now all he wanted was to go home and get in his bed. His burning desire for a cold beer was now a mere distant memory.

He decided to give the taxi company one more chance. He called "411" and again talked to an operator and eventually was transferred to a taxi dispatcher. He was given the same information that a taxi would soon arrive. He was frustrated and didn't know what to believe. His head was beginning to hurt from constantly turning to look up and down Figueroa. All he could do was stand on the curb waiting and hoping a taxi would soon come along to pick him up.

CHAPTER 54 THE STRANGEST ROBBERY

This story could have had a happy ending. A taxicab in fact did arrive at the corner of Washington and Figueroa and the driver looked for Maxwell but couldn't find him. The cabbie pulled over to the side of the road and used his cellphone to call the "call back" number for Maxwell's cellphone. It was 2:36 a.m. and no one answered Maxwell's cellphone. Later records indicated that Maxwell's cellphone was somewhere in the vicinity of the Staple Center on Figueroa three blocks north of where the cabbie was calling from.

This becomes a mystery in that we don't know exactly what happened to Maxwell. The facts would indicate that Maxwell got into a stranger's car. Either he had given up on the taxi and was willing to trust a stranger to drive him north on Figueroa to his apartment, or a stranger drove up alongside Maxwell and pointed a gun at him and told him to get in and he was robbed. The end result was that Maxwell Hazlett got into a 1992 white Nissan Altima driven by Angel Cruz. One of the things that make this scenario interesting is the fact that Angel Cruz is a paraplegic who had special controls installed on his vehicle so he could drive it.

Angel Cruz

There are more questions than answers as to what happened between 2:25 a.m. and 3:09 a.m. Sometime during that period Angel Cruz, the driver, shot and killed Maxwell Hazlett, who was seated in the passenger seat. The next known fact is that Angel Cruz was using Maxwell's cellphone to call Angel's friends to ask for help in getting Maxwell's dead body out of Angel's car. Since Angel was paralyzed from the waist down, he couldn't reach over to the passenger door to open it so he could push Maxwell's body out of the car.

Angel became desperate to think of people he could trust at 3:00 a.m. to dispose of a dead body. His best hope was calling Julio D., whom Angel had known for years. Angel drove all the way down Western Blvd to Julio's place on 95th Street. Angel was parked out in front of Julio's place, desperately trying to get Julio to answer the phone. Angel came to the conclusion that Julio wasn't going to answer his call. By now Angel was becoming frantic as he sat in his car with a dead body next to him.

His mind was racing frantically trying to remember his other friends' phone numbers, and he feverishly attempted to dial their numbers on Maxwell's cellphone. He tried dialing another friend's phone at 3:21 a.m. and still no one answered.

Utter panic came over Angel. He couldn't continue to drive around much longer. Soon it would be dawn, and he would look suspicious driving around with a lifeless body with its head tilted back against the headrest. Who is the one person that one could call at 3:22 a.m. in the morning to help one dispose of a dead body? Of course, that person is your mother! Your mother brought you into this cruel world, so she was the one person you can count on to help you when you are in trouble.

Angel's problem was how to contact his mother at this hour. She didn't have a cellphone. Fortunately for Angel, he remembered that his mother's lesbian lover had a cellphone. He realized that his mother would be in bed with her lesbian lover, Maria Adams (Pseudonym). By calling Maria on her cellphone, he wouldn't wake up his dad. The reason was that his dad would be sleeping on the living room sofa. He wouldn't be in his bed with his wife since his wife was in the bed with her lesbian lover. (To some this might seem confusing, like in the Abbot and Costello skit about the baseball game in which they try to describe who is on each base.)

Most people wouldn't be able to follow who was in bed with whom. Fortunately for Angel, he had figured out the sleeping arrangement. He used the victim's cellphone to call Maria's phone, which his mother answered. Angel's mom was surprised to be hearing from her son at that hour. His mother listened to Angel tell a story about how he was driving along and picked up a person that he realized was a person who was out to get him. Angel explained how this person took a screwdriver and tried to attack him as he was driving. However, Angel outsmarted the attacker and grabbed a gun that he luckily had in his lap and shot the attacker two times.

He told his mother that he only shot in self-defense and was afraid the police wouldn't believe him. He needed help in disposing of the body so the police wouldn't know he was involved. His mother listened patiently and finally told him to come home and she and his father would help him out. His mother Amanda woke up her husband and they put on their clothes, including latex gloves. She grabbed a bucket and with her husband proceeded outside to meet their son, Angel, who arrived shortly in his vehicle.

Without any hesitation, Angel's mother got in the backseat behind the dead body. His father seated himself in the backseat behind their son, who was driving. Without much discussion, this family drove off as if they were going to the park for a picnic. Angel proceeded to drive up Lucas Street past the Good Samaritan Hospital, which was one block from their apartment. They drove directly by the old emergency entrance of the hospital where Robert Kennedy was taken after he had been shot by Sirhan Sirhan at the Ambassador Hotel. They didn't stop of slow down to drop the body off at the hospital. They continued further north on Lucas Street four more blocks, looking for an isolated area that would be the perfect spot to dump a body.

CHAPTER 55 EARLIER SHOOTING AT MARGARITA JONES

What Angel Cruz had failed to mention to his parents was the fact that before the shooting he had been involved in another shooting incident. He may have regarded that shooting insignificant because to him it was merely a lark. In his mind, it wasn't a real shooting since all he had done was shoot his gun in the air when he was seated in his car at the Margarita Jones bar and restaurant near the USC campus. Margarita Jones was an old "Watering Hole" that had been used by the older USC students who could legally drink or even the younger students who had questionable IDs that made them appear to be 21 years old. This bar had gone by many different names over the years. During the football season, the USC alumni used Margarita Jones as a meeting place before and after the big games. Since it is directly across the street from the Los Angeles Coliseum, it is a great gathering place. It was convenient for the older alumni to stagger over to see the games and afterward for celebrating the numerous Trojan victories.

After the football season, other elements of society utilized the restaurant. During those times members of the Mara Salvatrucha gang congregated there and could be seen hanging out in the parking lot. On April 3rd Angel had been at the bar to see friends. Around 2:30 a.m. he went outside and got into his car. As he was driving out, one of his acquaintances walked up to his passenger window and started talking to him. Not far away was a security guard who worked for the restaurant. The guard was standing near the front of the bar, casually talking to two young ladies who were waiting for a ride.

For no apparent reason, Angel Cruz started firing a semi-automatic gun out of the driver's window. He seemed to be pointing the gun in the direction of the Harbor Freeway, which runs along the eastside. This surprised and frightened the security guard. There hadn't been any confrontations or arguments to justify the use of a firearm. The security guard didn't know how to react to the shooting. He approached Angel's car and noticed it moving toward the exit of the parking lot. The guard couldn't catch up to Angel's car, so he quickly wrote down the license number. Being a little confused as to what the proper response should be, the guard went inside the restaurant and told the manager that there had been some type of shooting of a firearm in the restaurant parking lot.

The manager was concerned, as he didn't want the bar to gain the reputation of being a gang hangout. He told his security guard that he would contact the police and for him to wait outside for them to come to take a report. The guard returned outside and walked over to where the shooting had occurred. He noticed on the pavement that there were several shell casings. He picked up one to get a closer look at it. He looked at the bottom of the shell casing and could see the numbers "380." He held on to several of the shell casings, hoping to give them to the police when they arrived. The guard waited and waited and no one from the police department arrived, so he threw the casings away and at the end of his shift he went home.

The whole Margarita Jones matter was of little concern to Angel Cruz and three nights later he returned to the restaurant. The same security guard was working at that time and noticed him come inside and start talking to other patrons. The guard didn't want a repeat of the other night so he called the police and asked them to respond. A police unit from Southwest Bureau responded and the officers detained Angel and obtained some basic information for their report and then released him.

Angel realized this detention by the police was a close call. He was concerned that the police might be suspicious of him in the murder investigation of victim Maxwell Hazlett. He was greatly relieved when they released him and sent him on his way. He thought he was the luckiest man in the world. However, he had attracted enough attention that a Detective Parra from the gang unit at the Southwest station started looking into the report about the negligent shooting at the Margarita Jones bar. Three days later, the detective went to Angel's apartment looking for him. Angel wasn't around but his car was, so the detective took some photos of the car. Three days after that, the detective returned with a search warrant for his apartment; however, Angel and his family weren't home.

His mother, Amanda, owned and operated a party supply store. Angel Cruz was out with his girlfriend, and later in the afternoon they both dropped by the store to see his mother. Angel had parked his white Nissan Altima outside the store on the street. He was with his girlfriend, Carolina Morgan, who lived with her parents in the Long Beach area. Right after the shooting of Maxwell, Angel had gone to Carolina's placed to stay with her family. Everything seemed to be going well for all concerned. Angel felt elated that he had gotten away with murder almost to the point that he felt a degree of cockiness about his accomplishment. How many paraplegics could rob and murder someone and get away with it? Angel was a member of the notorious Mara Salvatrucha (MS) gang, which is made up of El Salvadorians. Within this vicious gang, he would be regarded as a hero for his brave deeds.

Then the phone rang at his mother's party supply store. The manager of their apartment on Ingraham Street called and said that the police had been to their apartment #109 looking for Angel Cruz and Amanda. This sent shock waves through the family. What were they to do? They agreed that Angel Cruz should stay with his girlfriend in Long Beach until the whole thing blew over. The family then decided that Angel's car had to disappear. Then the question was how to get rid of the car so the police couldn't search it for evidence of the victim's blood and possible ballistic identification. Angel's family came up with the idea of having Carolina's dad take and dispose of the car.

Carolina called her dad and told him that someone tried to assault her and she defended herself and the attacker got killed. She explained that for her sake, the car had to disappear so it couldn't be traced back to her or Angel. Her father agreed to help out and arrived at the party supply store at 5:00 p.m. He was driven there by his son-in-law, who went by the name of "Shady." Her father got the keys to Angel's car and walked out to where it was parked. The first thing he did was remove the license plates and then he got in the car and drove off. Shady followed in his yellow Chevy Blazer.

The next day Angel was told that the VIN plate had been removed with a chisel and his car had been set on fire in the Echo Park area, near a freeway overpass. It was now April 13th, ten days after the shooting and the fire department responded to a car on fire. It didn't take long for them to put the fire out, yet the car was sufficiently burned so no evidence could ever be retrieved from it. After extinguishing the fire, they turned the matter over to the police officers assigned to the Rampart Station. Since there was no license plate or vehicle identification number, there was no one that the investigators could contact to determine if the car had been stolen or somehow used in a crime. The police didn't know who owned the burnt-out hulk of a car, so they had it towed to an impound lot to determine what to do with it.

CHAPTER 56 TWO SEPARATE POLICE INVESTIGATIONS

The Rampart Division was investigating the murder of Maxwell Hazlett. At the same time, they were investigating an arson of a vehicle with no knowledge of who the owner was. No one was aware of any connection between the two crimes. At the exact time, Southwest Division of LAPD was investigating a negligent shooting in the parking lot of the Margarita Jones Bar on April 3rd. No one in either division had any idea that both shootings were connected and that the burnt car was the same vehicle that was used in both crimes.

Photos of Rampart Division on previous page and Southwest Divisions is above.

The search warrant of Angel's residence didn't turn up any weapons or any evidence connecting him to the Margarita Jones negligent-shooting incident. However, the detective still wanted to talk to Angel to get his side of the story about the negligent shooting. Finally, on April 23rd, Angel got up enough nerve to go to Southwest station to talk to Detective Parra. Angel wasn't sure if the detectives had any suspicion of his involvement in the killing of Maxwell Hazlett.

Angel was so relieved when all Detective Parra wanted to talk about was the stupid shooting of his gun in the air at the Margarita Jones. Angel would have been more than happy to admit to the insignificant shooting. Nevertheless, Angel knew that since he was a convicted felon he could not admit to the possession of a firearm. To protect himself, he denied having any gun or shooting any such gun. He was willing to admit that he had been at Margarita Jones Bar on April 3rd with his girlfriend, Carolina Morgan. He told Detective Parra that he had driven there in his white Nissan Altima. However, he and his girlfriend left around 1:30 a.m. and weren't present when this so-called negligent shooting occurred.

Detective Parra wasn't completely convinced, and he asked to see Angel's car. Angel responded that his car had been stolen and he no longer had it. Detective Parra then asked when had he reported it stolen. Angel stated he hadn't contacted the police about the theft of the car. Detective Parra told him that he should immediately file a police report. Detective Parra knew he didn't have enough evidence to get any prosecutor to file charges against Angel, a paraplegic, for shooting off a gun for no apparent reason.

Detective Para didn't ask Angel any questions about the murder of Maxwell Hazlett. Angel was ecstatic and he felt it was the greatest day in his life. He didn't want to create any suspicion to himself, so he immediately filed a stolen vehicle report of his car there in the Southwest station. In making such a report, Angel would trip himself up in his own lies. When making the stolen vehicle report to the police he stated clearly that he had parked his car on April 19th and when he came out of his residence on April 21st he discovered that his car was missing. At the time, no one questioned what Angel had stated. He was trying to make it appear that his car was stolen just two days before his interview with Detective Parra. But what he had done was trap himself in a big lie that was easily exposed. A year later, the detectives from the Rampart station discovered that Angel's car had been completely burnt up on April 13th, which was six days prior to the last day that Angel reportedly parked his car behind his apartment.

On August 3rd the Rampart Division stolen vehicle crew went out to the impound lot to look for the secondary VIN on Angel's car. Every car has a hidden secondary vehicle identification number. It is placed in a location that can only be seen by using mirrors looking under the frame of the vehicle. There are experts who have been entrusted with the information as to where each vehicle's secondary number is located. On that date, the expert located the secondary number and gave it to the Auto Thief detective. When that number was run through the DMV records it came back registered to Angel Cruz.

This new revelation didn't trigger anything immediately as to any connection that vehicle had to the killing of Maxwell Hazlett. As a result, the old burnt-out hulk of a car was sold by the impound yard to a metal recycling plant. In other words, Angel's car was melted down before it could ever be examined by the CSI team. This fact certainly would be beneficial for Angel.

It was the summer of 2004, and Angel had to be feeling very confident that he had escaped being charged for the Hazlett murder. The detectives working the case weren't getting anywhere. All that was left was trying to unravel the phone calls made on the victim's cellphone.

Also, the investigation of the negligent shooting at the Margarita Jones Bar wasn't going anywhere. The police were hoping that the search warrant of Angel Cruz's place would uncover a weapon that might be enough to have his parole violated. There were so many other shooting cases that were much more serious; therefore, this matter was placed on the back burner.

CHAPTER 57 THE CELLPHONE TELLS A STORY

The Rampart Division's homicide detectives weren't finding any easy leads in solving Maxwell Hazlett's murder. The detectives had served a search warrant on the phone company and received a list of all the activity on the victim's cellphone. The phone records reflected the calls to the taxi company and enumerated the times they were made. However, there were many more phone calls that had been made even after Maxwell had been killed.

The detectives looked at all those numbers to see if there was a pattern or any recognizable parties. Not seeing any clues in the phone list, the detectives obtained a search warrant as to each phone subscriber whose number had been called from Maxwell's cellphone. One number called twice was listed to a Rosa Adams (pseudonym). Out of desperation (and to some extent curiosity), the detectives contacted her. They asked her if she could remember ten months earlier during the early morning hours after the murder. Their inquiry was whether she received a phone call from anyone—possibly from a person by the name of Maxwell.

Rosa looked at the phone records that the police showed her. She hesitated for a moment and had a perplexed expression on her face. Then she blurted out, "That isn't my phone number you have there. That's the phone I gave to my sister, Maria." She seemed delighted that she wasn't the person the detectives were interested in. The detectives now had a name of a Maria Adams. They were coming up with nothing but zeros, but they realized they had better follow up on the sister Maria Adams. Before turning to leave, the older detective turned and handed Rosa his business card. With a stern, authoritative voice, he said, "Have your sister Maria come to the station."

On March 10, 2005, the biggest break of the case occurred. Maria Adams humbly, and with some trepidation, came to the station and agreed to talk to the detectives. The detectives could not have anticipated what she was about to tell them. First she surprised the detectives by being completely candid about having a lesbian relationship with Amanda Cruz, Angel's mother. Without any reluctance, she began telling a tale that these seasoned homicide detectives couldn't have predicted.

Maria related that she went over to the Cruz residence, where she met Amanda outside the apartment and they walked inside. Amanda had had her husband go to sleep on the couch so that she and Maria could use the couple's bedroom. They both went into the bedroom and got ready for bed. Around 3:00 a.m., Maria was using the bathroom when she overheard Amanda, her lover, talking on Maria's cellphone. Amanda often answered Maria's cellphone. While standing in the bedroom, Maria could decipher that the caller was Angel Cruz. From the one-sided conversation, she could comprehend that he was in some type of trouble and seemed to be pleading for his mother to help him out.

Several times the detectives ask Maria to slow down so they could process what she was saying. She went on to describe what she had been told happened during those early morning hours. The detectives now had a suspect to focus on: Angel Cruz. The detectives then contacted the next person's number that had been called several times by Maxwell's cellphone. That number was for a Julio D., who couldn't explain why calls were made to his cellphone during the early hours of April 3rd. He admitted that he knew Angel Cruz, but said he hadn't seen him recently. The detectives continued down the list of other numbers called on Maxwell's cellphone. They quickly learned that every phone number came back to someone who knew or had contact with Angel Cruz.

After analyzing all the phone evidence that pointed to Angel, the detective arranged for him to come to the Rampart Division station. On March 25th, Angel got up enough nerve to go to the station. The detectives advised him that they were doing an investigation of a homicide and would like to talk to him about what he knew. Angel had gained confidence that he was able to talk his way out of any and everything. Then one of the detectives pulled out his Miranda card and started reciting all of Angel's rights. Angel listened and had to think that he had been free as a bird for almost a year so it wasn't likely they had anything on him.

When the detective concluded the Miranda rights and asked if he was willing to waive those rights and talk, Angel in a confident voice stated, "Yeah, why not." This was a pivotal moment for Angel. If he hadn't agreed to talk, he most likely would never have been prosecuted for murder. The detectives wanted to slowly work their way into the facts of the homicide and started talking about the negligent shooting in the parking lot of the Margarita Jones Bar on August 3rd. Angel had to think that ten months earlier he had been asked the same questions by Det. Parra. Obviously, the answers he gave at that time must have been satisfactory because the police never charged him with the Negligent Shooting.

Angel without any hesitation stated that he had been at the Margarita Jones Bar on April 3rd. He admitted that there had been someone shooting a gun off around 1:00 a.m. Again, just like he had stated to Detective Parra ten months earlier, he wasn't the shooter. However, Angel changed his story from his earlier one by claiming that he hadn't driven his car to Margarita Jones. Angel started changing his story for some unknown reason. This new version indicated he hadn't driven to the restaurant but had been dropped off by some mythical person by the name of "Jose Gutierrez." From that point on Angel started digging a hole for himself.

Ten months earlier, the security guard and his good friend Jorge V. had placed Angel as being seen seated in his white Nissan Altima. It was Angel who corroborated the statements of these two witnesses when Angel told Det. Parra that he had driven there in his Nissan Altima with his girlfriend, Carolina. Angel should have stopped at that point, but he continued to tell a tale that was so unbelievable. It was as if he were weaving a web of deceit that was going to eventually strangle him.

CHAPTER 58 THE INCREDIBLE GUTIERREZ STORY

Angel went on to say that a Jose Gutierrez character picked him up and that there was another passenger in his car by the name of Maxwell Hazlett. He placed the time as being around 1:00 a.m. Angel was unaware that Maxwell at that time was in the company of five USC students at the Ivar Nightclub in Hollywood. It wasn't until 2:07 a.m. that Jonathan P. dropped Maxwell off on Figueroa and Washington. Angel went on to dig an even deeper hole for himself by claiming that it took three hours to drive directly home. The detectives questioned him as to how it could take three hours to go a distance of 1.9 miles. Angel wanted to show that he was a quick thinker so he rebounded by saying that his old friend Gutierrez's car broke down on the way to his house and they had to find someone to jump-start it.

Angel claimed that he really got to his place around 3:00 a.m. and it took another 50 minutes for his mother to come down and help him into the apartment. He contended that he remained with his friend Gutierrez and Maxwell all this time until 4:30 a.m. To justify that length of time he indicated that he wanted to help his good friend out so he agreed to let Gutierrez drive his car. Of course, since he was a paraplegic, it took him a considerable amount of time to remove all of his special controls from his vehicle so it could be driven by Gutierrez.

Since it was getting late, he used Maxwell's cellphone to make a phone call at 4:30 a.m. Undoubtedly, Angel thought this would be smart for him to explain why he would have used Maxwell's cellphone. However, Angel should have given a little more thought as to what he was saying. Cellphones rely on local phone towers to transmit the signal to the cellphone. Therefore, cellphone records can show the general area where the cellphone was being used. What the phone records showed was that no phone call was made in the area of Angel's apartment at 4:30 a.m. Furthermore, Maxwell's body was found shortly after 5:00 a.m. He had been dead for several hours, thereby making it impossible that Maxwell loaned his cellphone to Angel to use at 4:30 a.m.

Angel thought that he could talk his way out of anything. Well, this time Angel had talked himself into the BIG LIE. The fact that someone lies to the police doesn't mean he or she is guilty of the crime of murder. Later Angel tried to explain why he had lied to the police. Even though the lies wouldn't convict him, it certainly put him on the defensive. That would mean that Angel at the time of his trial would have to take the witness stand to explain why he lied to the detectives. At the same time, he would have to convince the jury that he was telling the truth when he was testifying under oath.

This case involves incredible strategies on both the part of the Defense and the prosecution. The prosecution had the very difficult task of proving that a paraplegic could be a robber. The public image of a robber is a person who is menacing by his or her threatening appearance or the fact that a weapon is used. However, a 5' 8", 140-pound paraplegic doesn't project the persona of someone to fear. In this case, the victim was a healthy young man who certainly was able to defend himself.

In other words, Angel didn't look like a robber and Maxwell didn't appear to be an easy target of a robbery. None of this conjured up the appearance of a defendant who was capable of committing a robbery. Another problem for the prosecution was the fact that parents and educators teach everyone from a young age that disabled individuals should be respected and given sympathy for their plight in life. Without a doubt, the prosecution would have to find a way of overcoming the natural sympathy that a paraplegic would engender in the jurors.

In this case, the prosecution had no direct evidence to put the victim and the defendant together. There were no witnesses who saw the defendant shoot the victim. Furthermore, no one ever saw the defendant in the company of the victim. There was no weapon ever recovered, so there was no direct ballistics evidence that would connect the defendant to the shooting. The defendant's car was no longer available to be examined for DNA, fingerprints, or any other "trace" evidence to prove that the victim was ever in the defendant's car.

CHAPTER 59 NEED FOR A SHREWD PROSECUTOR

The District Attorney's Office recognized the challenge of prosecuting a paraplegic robber/murderer. This wasn't going to be a simple walk in the park. The DA's Office needed a prosecutor who had the skill set to handle such a delicate case let alone the time to build a solid case that would be convincing to a jury. When confronted with such an unsympathetic case to prosecute, the DA administrators turned to Major Crimes Division to see if they could spare a prosecutor for such a case.

Fortunately, Major Crimes was finishing up several high-profile cases and Hoon Chun could squeeze in another one as long as it didn't require an immediate trial. Since Angel's case was still in the early development stage, it didn't have a trial date. Hoon Chun had been in Major Crimes for several years, and he had learned that there was no such thing as an orthodox approach to preparing Major Crimes cases. The fact that a case is assigned to Major Crimes Division generally means that there is something about the case that requires special attention.

Hoon Chun had unique qualifications that made him a perfect fit for Major Crimes. His academic achievement of being a graduate of Harvard Law School meant that he was sharp as a tack. What that meant was that he wasn't merely a quick learner but he could assimilate a massive amount of facts into retrievable categories. Some cases can be so huge that the usual attorney can become lost in all the weeds. It takes an especially talented person who can make sense of all the documents and reports.

Hoon also possessed another characteristic that made him an effective litigator in the courtroom. He projects the Asian cultural trait of being polite and circumspect;

however, when his case is attacked, he can revert to Mr. NO FEAR. He can rise to the occasion and not give an inch to the other side. He has the innate ability to select just the right words to respond to a Defense attack. He finds the precise words to disarm his opponent while he remains composed in the heat of battle.

At times there appear to be two Hoon Chuns. When in court, he uses the formal nomenclature, but when in a more relaxed setting, he can be disarming by using the latest hip terms and jargon. The same is true with his dress attire in court, which gives a formal appearance with a dark navy-blue suit and a splashy tie that shows a degree of independence. At other times he gives the impression of a younger version of Jackie Chan.

When in the presence of Hoon, one can't avoid feeling his confident demeanor. To him the glass is always half full, not half empty. Even when a jury comes in with a hung jury, he will claim that since he now knows the Defense, he will be able next time to nail the defendant. He isn't a naysayer since he has learned through experience that with hard work, he can build a case that can withstand any type of attacks. Hoon realizes that jurors have a short interest span and that visual aids in the form of diagrams and charts can help convey the information that the jurors need to know and remember. As arduous as it is to dot the eyes and cross the tees, he knows that half of the work for any trial is done in the preparation phase.

His meticulous construction of every detail in his cases gives him the advantage in the courtroom since he knows where he is going with each witness and what comes next. In all cases there are some shockers that come up that can't be anticipated, but Hoon's cases seldom have surprises. With Hoon's experience, eye for detail, and willingness to put in the time necessary, he was a perfect choice to take on the prosecution of the Angel Cruz's case.

CHAPTER 60 PARENTS ARE DANGLING IN THE WIND

It didn't go unnoticed by the prosecutor, Hoon, that the only evidence to connect the defendant to the victim, Maxwell Hazlett, came from the most unlikely source, that being the defendant and his parents. The prosecution could show that the defendant had given several inconsistent statements. However, as previously stated, the mere fact that a defendant is a liar doesn't prove he is a murderer. The parent's statement clearly stated that their son shot and killed Maxwell, albeit in self-defense. Of course, the parents thought they were being helpful to their son when they told the detectives that he pulled the trigger to save his life from being beaten to death.

They both said that Angel during the early morning hours came by their place with a dead body in the car and asked them to help him dump the body. This was a two-edged sword for the prosecution. Their statements supplied the connection of the defendant to the victim. The prosecution hoped that the jury would infer that if one were driving around with a dead body in one's car then it was likely that the driver had something to do with the victim's death.

However, what hurt the prosecution was the defendant's statement to his parents. The statement was that the victim was a gangster who was trying to get him for something that happened in the past. Further, the defendant told his parents that the victim was attacking him and he luckily had a gun nearby, so he defended himself by shooting the attacker. This statement provided the defendant with an excuse for shooting the victim. The legal result was that if the jury believed this, it would be a justifiable homicide in which the defendant would go free.

Hoon realized the only way the case could be won by the prosecution was if he could get the parents to testify to their statement that they had given to the detectives. However, the parents claimed they couldn't testify against their son without incriminating themselves. Therefore, if Hoon called the parents to the witness stand in Angel's case they would invoke their Fifth Amendment right not to self-incriminate themselves. Hoon was in a Catch 22, and the only way around it was to file the 'Accessory After the Fact' charges against the parents. This was a legitimate charge to file against the parents since they admitted to assisting their son in getting rid of the victim's body. Several months after the main case was filed against Angel Cruz, their son, Hoon filed the 'Accessory After the Fact' charges against his parents.

Some prosecutors might be reluctant to file criminal charges against a 69-year-old father who is a frail 5' tall and weighs 120 pounds. Without a doubt, he was the most henpecked husband in the world. His wife was 54 years old and obviously wore the pants in the family. However, Hoon had to file criminal charges if justice was going to be served in Angel's murder trial.

What the prosecution was counting on was that Angel's case, being a murder case, would not move along as quickly as his parent's new case. After several months the parents were willing to plead no contest to the 'Accessory After the Facts' charges in exchange for a sentence of five years' probation.

As a result, the parent's case was disposed of in short order, and within 60 days from time of sentence the parents' time to appeal had run. The end result was that at this stage the parents couldn't object to testifying in their son's murder trial on the basis that they were invoking the Right not to Self-incriminate themselves. What that meant was that the prosecution could subpoena the parents to testify at their son's trial. Without any delay, Hoon had both parents subpoenaed. Since they were both on probation, they weren't free to leave the area or the country, so they had to obey the subpoena and make themselves available for their son's trial.

CHAPTER 61 OPENING STATEMENT

The prosecution, in its Opening Statement to the jury, indicated that it would prove circumstantially that the defendant stopped to pick up the victim, who was waiting for a taxi. The prosecution explained that the defendant intended to rob the victim and in fact took his cellphone, his ID, and his shoes. Hoon knew that the jurors were going to have a complicated task of trying to keep track of so many people who they would hear about during this trial. If the jurors became confused, they wouldn't understand the significance of each and every phone call made to certain individuals. Therefore, Hoon created a poster, which was like a road map of all the people the jurors would be hearing about. In his Opening Statement, he used this Relationship of Parties visual aid to show how all the people were interconnected to each other.

Another puzzling aspect of this Cruz case was the fact that there are so many different locations in the greater Los Angeles that the witnesses would be talking about. The jurors would have to remember the various locations that Maxwell went to as well as remember everywhere the defendant drove trying to get rid of the body. Hoon wanted the jurors oriented as to what happened and where it occurred, so he used a map highlighting some of the points the jurors would hear about.

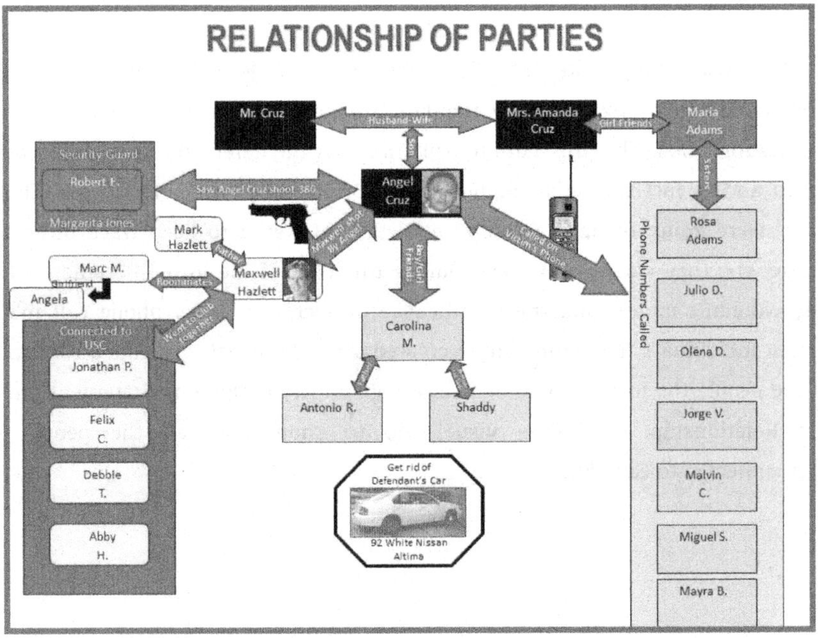

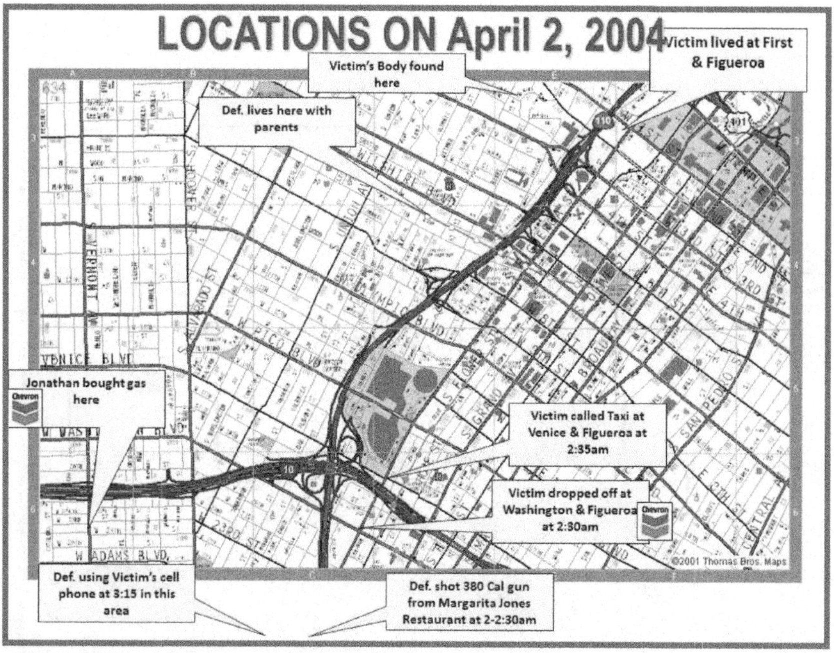

The last preliminary item he wanted the jurors to thoroughly understand was when the actual events occurred. In order for Hoon to keep the various times and dates straight, he liked to use Timelines.

He created a Timeline on a poster that he could continually refer to during his Opening Statement as well as later during the Argument.

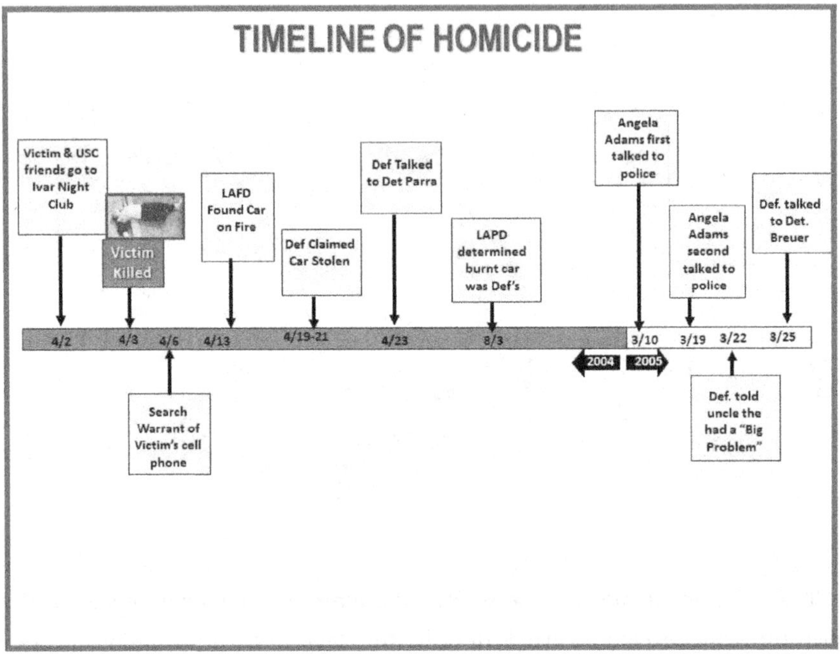

The prosecution went on to tell the jury that this was a Robbery that went BAD. To illustrate his point, the prosecutor had placed two chairs next to each other in the courtroom, which the jurors could see. He had placed a mannequin in the right seat that was to represent the passenger's seat, and the prosecutor sat in the left-hand seat, which he said was the driver's seat. Hoon demonstrated how a person with their left hand could shoot the mannequin. He had placed trajectory rods through the mannequin's body exactly the way the coroner had indicated in the autopsy report as to the direction of each of the shots.

He used the coroner's diagram to show the direction of the trajectory and placed wood rods through the mannequin's body to illustrate how the defendant with his left hand was able to shoot the victim seated next to him in the front seat.

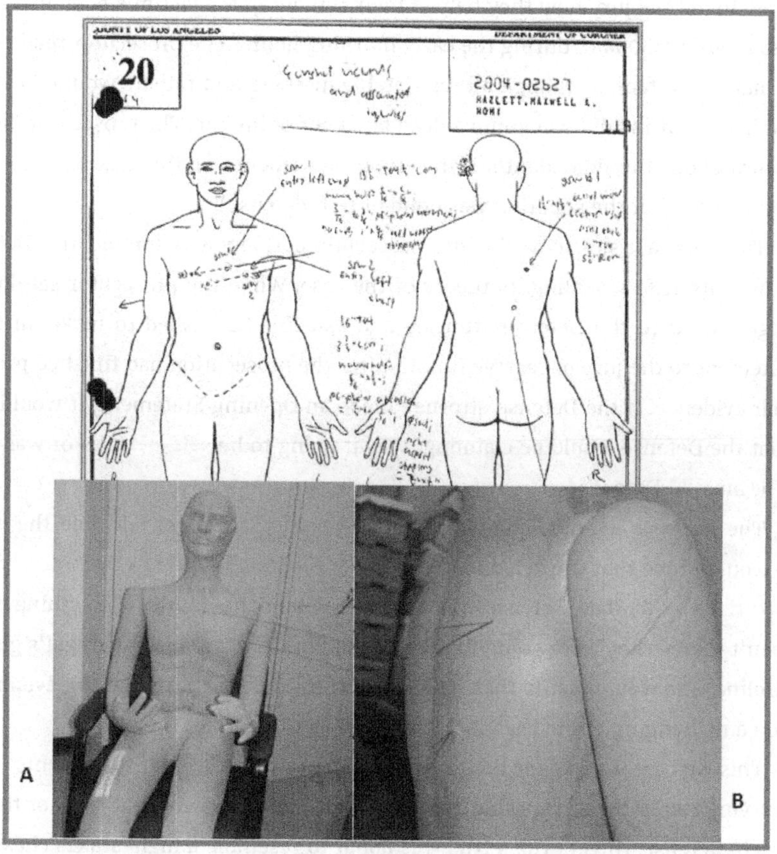

Through this demonstration, the jurors could see how the shooting occurred. The prosecutor went on to explain that they were calling the security guard from the Margarita Jones Bar to testify that shortly before the robbery of the victim the defendant was seen holding a gun in his left hand and firing it out the driver's window in the direction of the 110 Freeway. Not only was he using his left hand to fire the gun but he was using .380 ammunition just like that which was used to shoot the victim. Also, bullets that were removed from the victim's body indicated that he had been shot by a .380 type weapon, which was consistent with what the security guard testified to.

The prosecutor went on to explain that the parents of the defendant would be called to tell the jury how they helped their son dump the victim's body in a secluded area around 4:00 a.m. during the early morning hours. The prosecutor made it sound so matter-of-fact, as though all respectable mothers and fathers would do the same and help their invalid son dump a dead body out of his car. The prosecutor didn't say a word about the defendant's self-serving statements or the parents' self-serving statements (that the shooting was done in self-defense).

This was a risky move by the prosecution. Hoon was forcing the Defense to commit itself to revealing its theory of the case. When the prosecutor sat down, the judge looked to the Defense attorney and asked if he wished to make an Opening Statement to the jury or reserve it until after the prosecution had finished presenting their evidence. If the Defense attorney made an Opening Statement, it would divulge what the Defense would be claiming. Was it going to be self-defense or was it going to be an alibi Defense?

The Defense attorney commenced his Opening Statement and told the jury that he would prove that the defendant had never met the victim nor had any connection with the victim. The Defense was that the defendant didn't do anything since he wasn't there. They were going to rely on an alibi to be supplied by Angel's girlfriend, Carolina. She would testify that she was with the defendant that entire evening up to 4:00 a.m. hanging out in the Margarita Jones parking lot.

This was great news for the prosecution since it meant that the parents wouldn't be trying to tell their story that the defendant had told them that he shot the victim in self-defense. Angel Cruz's trial was about to resemble a high-stakes chess match. After the Defense's Opening Statement implied that it was relying on an ALIBI Defense, Hoon, the prosecutor, wanted to yell the word 'CHECKMATE.' All of Hoon's hard work was paying off.

CHAPTER 62 THE TRIAL BEGINS

Both sides finished their Opening Statements, and the prosecution then called their witnesses.

Mark Hazlett, the father of the victim, testified for a short time, providing basic information about his son going to school at USC and deciding to live at the Promenade apartments. It was very intriguing that the parents of both the victim and the suspect sat almost next to each other on the hard wooden benches in the back of the courtroom. What a contrast between these two families, since they both wanted the best for their sons. The Hazlett's had had great hopes for Maxwell becoming an international businessman. However, the Cruz family's aspiration was that their son wouldn't be found guilty of MURDER.

Marc M., the victim's roommate, testified that the two of them shared an apartment unit at Promenade Towers. He decided to spend Friday and Saturday with his new girlfriend instead of going out with Maxwell. He related to the jury that Maxwell called him several times during the evening just to check in to see how he was doing. When Maxwell didn't return to the apartment, he started calling around to see where he might be. By late afternoon, Marc was sufficiently concerned to go to LAPD Central Division to file a Missing Person's Report, which he did. The next day he contacted Maxwell's parents about the disappearance of Maxwell.

Jonathan P. testified that he picked up Maxwell and they met friends from school and went to the Ivar Nightclub. He explained to the jurors that after returning from the nightclub, Maxwell wanted to purchase some beer and stopped at a 7-Eleven to purchase the beer. There he discovered he had left his ID at the nightclub. They all returned to the nightclub, where he retrieved his ID. Maxwell didn't want to delay the others so they took everyone back to the USC area. Jonathan explained that he needed to get gas and they stopped at a service station to get gas but it didn't sell beer. As they headed back to Maxwell's apartment, they saw another Chevron service station, where they stopped. Maxwell went in to buy the beer, only to learn it was after 2:00 a.m. and they couldn't sell it to him. That was where Maxwell told Jonathan to leave him at Washington and Figueroa and he would walk the rest of the way back to his apartment. That was the last time and place that Jonathan saw or heard from Maxwell.

Other USC students briefly testified that they went with Maxwell to the Ivar Nightclub. He had a Nokia cellphone and was wearing black suede shoes, a metallic gray Guess jacket, a black collar shirt, black pants, and a black belt. He had a wallet with money since he had withdrawn money from the ATM machine. They testified that they were dropped off at USC and had no further contact with Maxwell.

A Taxi supervisor testified that the taxi cab dispatching service records showed that Maxwell had requested a cab and they were in the process of sending a taxi when they received another call requesting a taxi. They took the phone number of the caller and assured him a taxi was on its way. Their records showed that a cab did arrive at the location at Washington and Figueroa but the cabbie couldn't find the caller. The taxi cab driver called the callback phone number they had and he was unable to make contact with the caller.

Officer Finding the Body testified that he had received a radio call to go to a location off Emerald Street and Second Street to check out a possible dead body. When he arrived, he did find a dead body lying on his back with his head partially in the street and rest of his body on the grassy median of the sidewalk. When his shirt was opened, there were two gunshot wounds to his chest. The victim had pants on but no belt, and had only socks on his feet. The officer contacted the dispatcher to notify the homicide detectives.

Homicide Detectives Mota and Breuer testified that they conducted an investigation. Each testified that they noticed that the victim didn't have any jewelry, wallet, shoes, watch, or cellphone. It appeared it could have been a robbery gone bad. There were no shell casings or any weapon found in the area. Later they learned that the victim, Maxwell Hazlett, was a student from USC whose permanent address was in Hawaii. The detectives were able to track down his father in Hawaii and notified him of his son's death.

They learned that the victim always used his cellphone, and they obtained a search warrant for the victim's phone records. There were numerous phone calls before 3:00 a.m. that involved the victim calling his friends. However, there were numerous calls after 3:09 a.m. to parties who didn't know the victim. At that point, the detectives obtained search warrants for each of the numbers called after 3:09 a.m. When they learned the names and addresses of these other callers, they contacted those parties. That was when they requested those parties come to the police station for interviews.

The Custodian of Phone Records was called to testify, and that person brought in the relevant cellphone records for the victim and all the parties called after 3:09 a.m. The phone records were placed into evidence by the court. This witness also was able to tell the jurors where the phone calls were made from. Although they couldn't show the precise location, they could show the vicinity within two blocks of the cellphone towers.

Julio D. testified that he was a friend of the defendant. His phone was called at the following times: 3:09; 3:13; and 3:15. He didn't answer the first two calls but did answer the last one. That was when the defendant asked him to help get rid of a body and he told the defendant he didn't want to get involved. Later in the day he talked to the defendant, who told him that he shot someone in his car and he needed help to get rid of the body.

Mayra B. was willing to testify that she may have received a phone call from the defendant during the early morning hours but she didn't answer it. She stated that Julio told her that the defendant had called him and asked him to help him out since he was in trouble. Later in the day Julio called again and said that the defendant told him that he shot someone in his car.

She further testified that the defendant claimed he was an active member of the Mara Salvatrucha gang. He often drove around looking to do drive-bys. On one occasion the defendant asked her to act as a decoy to get a drug dealer to open his door so his gang members could rob him.

Jorge V. testified that his phone may have been called at 3:21 a.m. but he didn't answer it. Later he was contacted by Julio, who said that Angel told him that he shot someone in his car. Also, he testified that on the night in question he was at Margarita Jones and saw the defendant shoot into the air. On other occasions, he saw the defendant carrying a gun in his lap. He testified that the defendant liked to commit robberies and had a mask and gloves in his car.

Det. Parra testified he was the detective assigned to the negligent firing case that occurred at the Margarita Jones Bar. He received the license number from the security guard and he was able to ascertain that the car was registered to the defendant. He obtained a Search Warrant for his residence and recovered 15 cellphones and items of other people's identification. He interviewed the defendant at the Southwest station and the defendant denied doing the shooting. When asked where his car was he told him that his car had been stolen. The detective told him that he should file a stolen auto report.

Women whose cellphones were taken were called as witnesses and they testified that a man in a wheelchair was present when their cellphones disappeared. One woman confronted him about taking her phone. He pulled a gun on this woman and eventually threw her phone back to her.

Robert E. was the security guard at the Margarita Jones Bar and testified that he saw the defendant discharge a semi-automatic weapon from his car. He held the gun with his left hand while firing it toward the Harbor Freeway. He wrote down the license plate number of the defendant's car and later examined the shell casing, which was marked with .380.

A Fire Department Representative testified that he received a call regarding a car on fire under the Echo Park Bridge. They responded and put the fire out. Afterwards, they had it towed over to an Auto Storage Lot where it was kept for the Auto Theft Detail.

An Auto Thief Expert testified that since the VIN had been chiseled out, they had to locate the secret secondary VIN. When they ran the VIN of the burnt car, it came back registered to Angel Cruz.

A Stolen Car Report Officer testified that Angel Cruz came to Southwest Division and reported that he parked his car on April 19th and went to pick it up on April 22, 2004, but found it missing.

Officer Zeigler was Qualified as a Gang Expert and testified that Angel Cruz lived in the gang territory of Mara Salvatrucha. That Margarita Jones nightclub was one of the gang's hangouts in 2004. He stated that Cruz's devil tattoo, text display on Cruz's cellphone, writings on the walls in Cruz's room, as well as a gang notebook were all consistent with membership in the Mara Salvatrucha gang. Based on the photographs and writings, tattoo, and incidents of making gang hand signs at Margarita Jones Bar, it was his opinion that the defendant was an active member of the Mara Salvatrucha gang.

Medical Examiner-Coroner testified that the cause of death was multiple gunshot wounds. The victim was shot two times and there was stippling around both entrance wounds. One bullet entered the center of his chest and penetrated the upper lobe of his right lung. A second bullet entered the left side of the victim's chest and penetrated his heart and lower lobe of his right lung.

Maria Adams testified that she was a close friend of Amanda Cruz, the defendant's mother. She explained how she got a cellphone from her sister Rosa. On April 3, 2004, she went to the Cruz residence to spend the weekend with her companion, Amanda. She was in bed with Amanda and around 3:30 a.m. she woke up and heard Amanda talking to her son Angel on Maria's cellphone.

They had further discussion and when finished Amanda went and woke up her husband, who was sleeping in the living room. Amanda was looking for some latex gloves to wear. Maria remembers Amanda and her husband going downstairs and leaving with their son. Later in the morning, Maria got up and heard Amanda and Angel arguing. Amanda stated that as far as she was concerned it was Angel's problem and not hers.

Amanda told Maria that they went with their son and got into his car. In the front passenger seat was a dead body. They drove several blocks and Angel stopped his vehicle and Amanda's husband got out of the car. He went to the front passenger door and opened it. Then he pulled the dead body out of the car. This witness Maria went on to testify that later in the day Amanda and her husband took cleaning products down to the car and tried to clean out the blood in the front seat. Amanda told her how hard they tried to clean the car. Later on during the day, the husband told Maria that he had helped remove a body from Angel's car.

CHAPTER 63 USING PARENTS AND GIRLFRIEND

Eventually, it was time to call the defendant's parents. The father was called by the prosecution first since he wasn't quite as hostile to the prosecution as the mother was. The investigating officer went out into the hallway to escort him into the courtroom. The father was a pathetic looking soul with his velvet hat rolled up in his hand. He looked down as he shuffled his feet along the carpet on the courtroom floor. An interpreter followed him to the witness stand and took a seat directly behind the father. The clerk in a loud voice asked the elderly man whether he would tell the whole truth so help him God. The father quietly said, "Si" as the interpreter bellowed out the word "Yes."

Sadly, no one in the courtroom expected that he would tell the whole truth or any part of the truth. It was a peculiar situation in which the prosecutor didn't expect him to tell the truth. No one knew what the father would say. Obviously, he didn't want to be the one to convict his son of murder. The questioning by the prosecutor started out pleasant with neutral type questions. He was asked if he and his wife owned a party supply store. He answered, "No." This foundational question wasn't meant to be adversarial. The prosecutor asked the question again slightly differently and again the answer was "No." The one thing the prosecutor had to do was to get the father to be responsive to the questions. Then the prosecutor took a more direct attack and asked a leading question. This wasn't usually permitted on direct examination of one's own witness. However, there was the exception in the case of a hostile witness. Everyone in the courtroom would have to agree that the father would fall into the category of being a hostile witness.

Finally, the prosecutor was able to get the father to concede that he and his wife did have a party supply business back in 2004. The next question was just as agonizing when the father was asked if he and his wife lived at 1241 Ingraham Street, Apartment #109, on April 2, 2004, which was the morning of the shooting. The father's answer was "No." Then the prosecutor, out of frustration, asked a leading question stating that in fact he and his wife and son all lived at that address. Then the answer was "Yes."

It appeared that the father was going to be as uncooperative as he could be, possibly in hopes that the prosecutor would give up on him. What the father didn't understand was that the prosecutor desperately needed him to testify so that the prosecutor could play the tape recording of him and his wife admitting to helping the defendant dump the body of the victim. The prosecutor needed to pull out of the father that he in fact did talk to the detectives. The prosecutor tried another approach. He thought that maybe the father was too embarrassed by the fact that his wife had a lesbian lover who slept in his bed, which required him to sleep on the sofa.

The prosecutor tried to tactfully address this issue by saying that no one in the courtroom was prejudging his wife's lifestyle of having a lesbian lover who spent the weekends with his wife while he was present. The father sat crunched down on the witness stand with the frightened look of a deer staring into the bright headlights of an oncoming car. The prosecutor's attempt to put him at ease didn't seem to have hit a sympathetic chord with him. Hoon seemed stymied as to what he could say and do to make the father more responsive in his answers.

The prosecutor thought the best thing was to ask the father the most basic question that no one could dispute. He asked the father whether he and his wife were convicted of Accessory After the Fact of the murder. To everyone's surprise in the courtroom, the father meekly shook his head and said, "No." The prosecutor reached for the court docket of his conviction and showed it to the witness. The father looked at the docket and continued to deny that he had ever been convicted of anything. At this point, the prosecutor walked the father through the docket showing him his name printed on it and the fact that he had pleaded "No Contest" to the charges. At that point, the father said that he had pleaded "No Contest" but still wouldn't acknowledge that he had been convicted and sentenced to probation.

The prosecutor, without looking at the father, asked him, "Do you love your son?" And to that question the father in a timid voice said, "Sure, sure." Hoon could see that this case was starting to slip away from the prosecution. If the father stated that he didn't remember making statements to the police, the tape-recorded statement wouldn't be admissible before the jury.

The prosecutor started to probe the fundamental question, which was whether the father had told the detectives that he had helped his son dump the victim's body. The father started out saying he didn't remember. It looked as if the Defense had out-smarted the prosecution. There was a reason why Hoon was called the 'No Fear Prosecutor,' in that he doesn't give up when a witness goes South on him. Hoon persisted to ask the father additional questions in hopes of finding the elusive answer. He reworded his question by asking if he might have said to the detectives that his son had a dead body in the car when he came over. Eventually, in frustration, the prosecutor pressed the father whether he said that Angel had a dead person in his car. For whatever reason, the father fired back stating, "I told the police that but that wasn't true." The father had just given the prosecutor the words he needed in order for the court to permit the prosecution to play the tape recording of that conversation he gave to the police.

The prosecutor didn't care what the father was going to say as long as he admitted that he had made the prior inconsistent statement to the detectives. All the prosecutor cared about was the fact that the jury would hear his taped statement. The statement had been edited to take out any references to what the defendant had told the father about the reason he had a dead body in his car. The strategy had worked, and the defendant was going to have to find another way to explain why his folks were saying that he came home with a dead body and that they helped him dump the body. When he was asked about cleaning the blood out of the car, the father said that he was drawing a blank. Then when pressed he said that he had said it but it was false.

This was a big win for the prosecution. However, the true test would be how well the prosecutor would do in prying information out of the mother. Without a doubt, she would be a witness who would be more challenging and definitely more hostile. When she took the witness stand, Hoon was trying to make himself the most ingratiating person in the world. He purposely asked simple questions that only required a "Yes or No" answer. However, her response was a long tirade in which she explained it was all a setup and a bunch of lies while verbally attacking one of the prosecution's witnesses. To everyone in the courtroom it was obvious that her answer was not responsive. It seemed that someone had told her to get all sorts of information in front of the jury by blurting it out while appearing to answer the prosecution's questions. She seemed to have her own agenda of what she wanted to tell the jury. Her answers were unrelated to the questions being asked by the prosecutor, but she didn't seem to care.

She claimed that she didn't talk to the detectives about the case. Then the prosecutor asked her if she would change her statement of not talking to the detectives if she knew there was a tape recording of her interview. She remained defiant and claimed that she hadn't talked to the police and she knew of no tape recording.

At that point, Hoon decided to take another approach and started asking the mother about someone named "Shady" who came over and take the car to be destroyed. She denied that she had ever known a person by the nickname of "Shady." When she was shown in a transcript where she had talked about "Shady" she said that she had blanked the entire event out of her mind. Then she said that God had allowed her to remember some things about "Shady." But her main claim about the taped statement was that it was the result of her being forced to make those statements after she had been deprived of food and water for such a long time.

She said the only reason that she made those statements about her son having a dead body in the car and dumping the body was to get some nourishment. She said that the detectives promised her and her husband cookies if they would make those statements that were recorded. What it sounded like was that she and her husband had sold out their son for several cookies that the detectives had given them.

It is amazing at times, the web of deceit witnesses weave to explain what they initially told the police. By the end of the mother's testimony, she had made it clear to everyone in the courtroom that she had talked to the detectives. As a result, her taped statement was definitely going to be heard by the jury.

Later in the trial, one of the detectives was called to authenticate the tapes of the parents. Hoon played the tapes and asked the detective if what was heard on the tape was true and accurate. The detective identified the tapes to be true and correct and they became part of the court's record of evidence.

When Angel's girlfriend, Carolina, was called, she was supposed to testify to the destruction of the car that Angel had been driving. However, the Defense wanted to use her to provide an alibi for Angel. She testified that she was with Angel the evening of the shooting. She testified that she was with him until 4:00 a.m. that fateful morning. She further explained that she and Angel were just hanging out with friends in the parking lot at the Margarita Jones Bar. The Defense had to be pleased that Carolina was doing a great job of building a solid alibi for Angel.

The prosecutor began asking her some pointed questions as to what she had done the night before and the night after. She apparently didn't realize how important it was for her to be absolutely certain that it was the morning of April 2, 2004, that she was talking about, further that she was with Angel late at the Margarita Jones Bar. She apparently wanted to outsmart the prosecution and didn't want to get pinned down on her dates. Then she started answering that she wasn't certain about the date but that it could have been April 2nd or some other date. That was devastating for the Defense since they needed her to be unwavering as to being with the defendant on that particular date until 4:00 in the morning.

CHAPTER 64 THE DEFENSE

The prosecution finally rested its case and had all its exhibits received into evidence. The moment of truth had arrived for the Defense. Would they call the defendant to be a witness? However, that would have to wait since they recalled Angel's mother to say that she recognized one of the prosecution witnesses. That was a surprise since no one could decipher what difference that made. This didn't add anything for either side. It appeared that the defendant's mother had some personal issue with this person in the audience. She convinced the Defense attorney to allow her to testify to her dislike for that person.

The Defense then called one of the LAPD officers to testify as to his encounter with Angel several nights later when the officer had come in contact with Angel, who was in his car at the Margarita Jones Bar. The Defense attorney asked if he had noticed any blood or dampness on the passenger side of defendant's car. The Defense was trying to show that there was no one who had been shot in the car several days earlier. The officer admitted to looking for a gun in the car and didn't find one. He testified that he didn't pay attention to the passenger seat and didn't notice if it was moist. He was further asked if he noticed any bullet holes in the back of the passenger's seat. Again the officer testified that he wasn't looking for bullet holes so he couldn't say with any certainty that there were or weren't bullet holes.

If the Defense was looking for a bull's-eye, it had missed the target. Everyone in the courtroom was waiting for the big anticipated event, which was the defendant taking the witness stand and telling his story to the jury. Throughout the beginning of the trial, the Defense was forever alluding to the fact that the defendant would answer certain questions when it was his turn to testify.

The LAPD officer having completed his testimony, the Defense attorney stood up. Everyone expected him to announce the fact that his client was about to take the witness stand. However, all the Defense attorney said was, "The Defense rests its case." Apparently, this fearless gang member was going to take the safe way out and not take the witnesses stand. His attorney didn't want the jurors to hear about his client's past. If he had testified, the prosecution would have been able to impeach him with his prior felony convictions.

One prior conviction was for Manslaughter, which some of the jurors would have found interesting since now he was charged with killing another person. Also, if Angel had testified, the prosecution could have asked him about all the different stories he had told the detectives. After hearing so many different stories, the jurors would have come to the conclusion that he was an outright liar. After weighing the downside if the defendant testified, it was clear that the Defense wouldn't be better off. He could have fallen into the prosecution's trap. The Defense's emphasis would have to be attacking the prosecution's case.

CHAPTER 65 TIME FOR ARGUMENT

Both sides had rested, and it was time for the Argument from both sides. It had been a long, confrontational trial with a lot of disjointed pieces of evidence. Now it was the prosecution's task to connect all the pieces and show what he had proved. First, Hoon wanted to get out of the way some of the technical questions. The legal issue of the Felony Murder Rule needed to be explained to the jurors in order to get them to apply it to this case. The law states the following:

FELONY - MURDER RULE:

1. **Unlawful killing,**
2. **During commission or attempted commission of a specified felony,**
3. **Def. had the intent to commit or aid & abet the commission or attempted commission of the underlying specified felony.**
   - **Does not matter which of the participants did the actual killing.**
   - **Does not matter whether the killing was intentional or accidental.**

If the Felony Murder Rule applied, it elevated the killing to a First-Degree Murder if the defendant intended to commit a felony and in the process someone was killed. In this case, the prosecution couldn't prove that Angel said, "Give me your money." It is possible that Angel didn't even utter a word about a robbery. What if Angel was being the cocky gangster who liked to act threatening? Since he had fired his gun minutes before in the parking lot of the Margarita Jones Bar, Angel could have stuck the gun into Maxwell's face just to scare a wealthy college student. One defense could have been that the gun went off accidentally. Or another might be that Maxwell in a panic grabbed the gun and Angel had to fire it to prevent Maxwell from using it against him.

Hoon used the below Visual as a way of showing how all the pieces when put together were Evidence of Robbery.

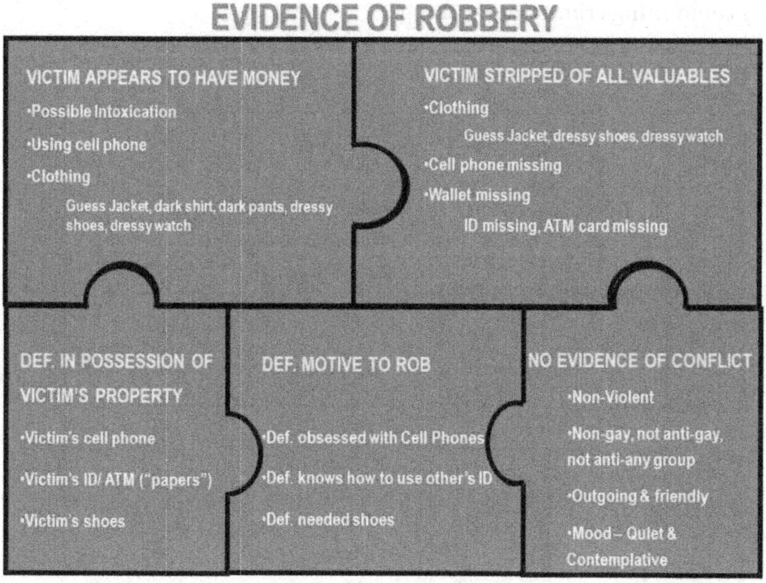

In other words, where is the evidence that Angel had formed the intent to rob the victim? If the idea to rob was a second thought after the shooting, then the Felony Murder Rule wouldn't apply. The prosecution wanted the jury to infer that Angel had formed the intent to rob from the totality of the situation. Obviously, Angel saw that Maxwell was well dressed, wearing expensive shoes, and of course he had the latest cellphone. The parents' tape recording to the detectives indicated that after they had dumped the victim's body, the defendant later threw the victim's shoes out of the car. However, the strongest argument to prove a 'Robbery' was the fact that Angel was in possession of the victim's cellphone since he was calling his relatives and friends with it.

The biggest attack by the Defense was regarding the Gang Allegation, which claimed that the robbery was committed for the benefit of Angel's gang. During the prosecution's case, they presented evidence that Angel was an active gang member. To prove this, the prosecution introduced a photo of the defendant's bedroom, which was covered with graffiti of the Mara Salvatrucha gang. Another photo showed the defendant giving gang hand signs while seated in his wheelchair in his bedroom.

Hoon used the below visual to prove that the defendant was a gang member and still actively committing crimes for the Gang.

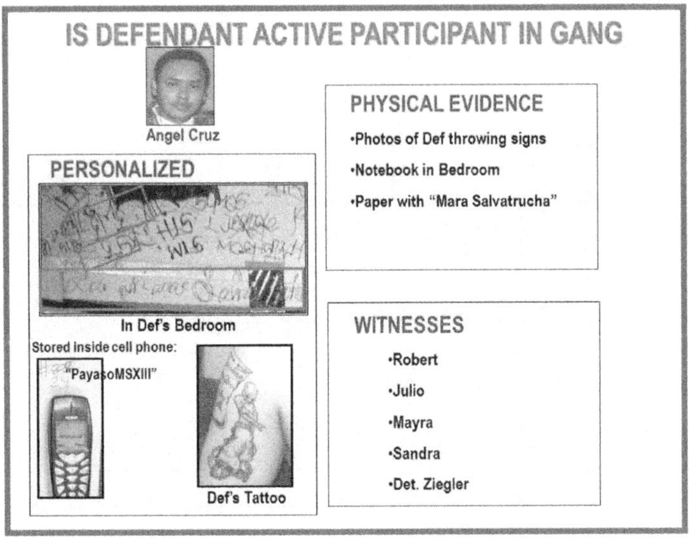

Angel's Defense attorney vigorously argued that the prosecution was trying to paint with a broad brush to show that Angel was still active in his old gang after an earlier shooting that made him a paraplegic. The Defense claimed that his gang banging days were over. And certainly he didn't do this Mickey Mouse robbery for the benefit of his old gang. Angel's Defense attorney recognized the importance of attacking the Gang Allegation since if he were convicted of it he would never have a chance of being paroled.

Hoon wanted to discuss with the jurors all the lies Angel had told the detectives. The prosecutor fully recognized that this case was extremely complicated since it involved two separate investigations into two separate crimes. The Ramparts Division detectives were focused on the Maxwell Hazlett homicide, while the Southwest Division detectives were investigating a possible gang shooting at the Margarita Jones Bar. Although the crimes occurred within minutes of each other, they both occurred in different LAPD jurisdictions.

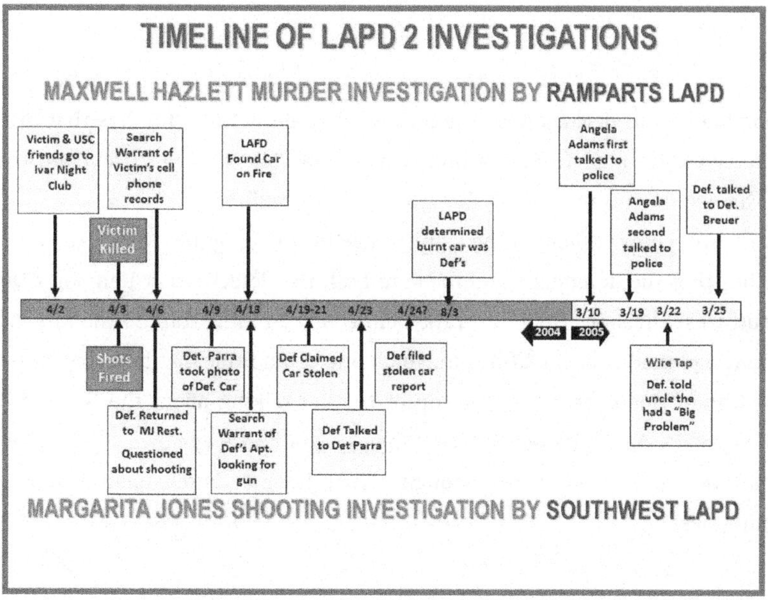

Hoon used this timeline that had all the Rampart events on the top and all the Southwest events on the bottom portion. In this way, the jurors could easily make a distinction as to what each detective knew about their case.

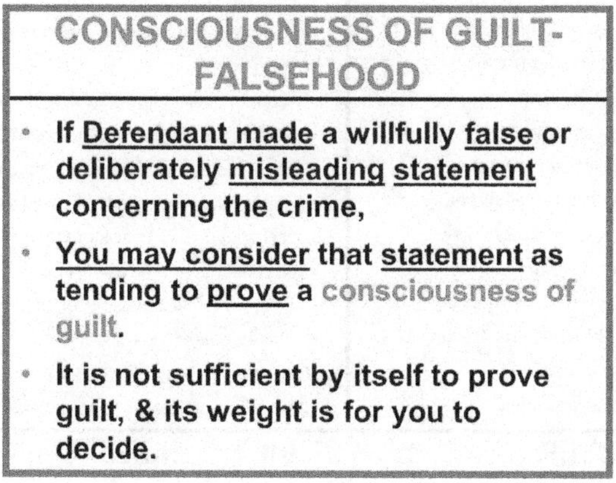

Hoon wanted to discuss with the jury what to do with all the lies that Cruz told the detectives. He read from the jury instructions (above), which explain that the jurors can use the lies in proving the defendant was guilty.

After the prosecutor explained the significance of the lying, he wanted to go through all the lies that the defendant had made to both the detectives at Ramparts Division and Southwest Division. Hoon used the below visual to illustrate to the jury that the defendant had made dozens of lies in which one could infer that he is trying to cover up something. Hoon started at the top of the list talking about the lie, and on the right he explained why it wasn't true. When he got half way down the list, he could see that the jurors had heard enough. Then he just barely skimmed over the remaining lies.

WHY DEFENDANT LIED ABOUT 4/2-3/04?

DEFENDANT'S STATEMENT	FACTS
•Claimed not a Gang Member	•Def. is a MS Gang Member
•Claimed didn't drive to Margarita Jones	•Def. was seen in his car at Margarita Jones
•Claimed Jose Gutierrez dropped him off	•Def. was seen in his car
•Claimed he didn't shot any gun in parking lot	•Def was seen shooting from his car
•Claimed there was fighting & bottles thrown	•There was no fighting or bottle throwing
•Claimed shots came from black cars	•There wasn't six cars that sped away
•Claimed Gutierrez picked him up 1:00-1:40am	•Def. wasn't pick up by anyone
•Claimed Victim Hazlett was in Gutierrez car	•Victim Hazlett was with his friend Pong
•Claimed they went straight to his place	•Def lived less than 3 miles away
•Claimed they got there at 3:00am	•It wouldn't take 3 hours to drive 3 miles to his house
•Then claimed Gutierrez' car broke down	•Def. changed story to add in break downs
•Then claimed waited 50mins for mother	•Def. could have had his friend help him to his house
•Claimed at 4:30am used victim's cell phone	•Victim's cell phone was being used in South Central
•Then claimed disconnected controls to his car	•Def changed story to account for longer time
•Claimed he gave his car to Gutierrez to use	•Def. could have taken friend home
•Claimed nothing unusual when car returned	•If victim was killed in Def's car, there would be blood
•Claimed with Gutierrez & Victim until 4:30am	•Victim was dead by 4:30am
•Claimed his car was later stolen	•Def. is still making payments on his "stolen car"
•Claimed he hasn't considered leaving home	•Def. told uncle he had "big Problems"

= LIED TO COVER UP MURDER OF VICTIM HAZLETT

Hoon knew that the jurors were going to have to rely on the testimony of the security guard at Margarita Jones. The events that the security guard testified to occurred over a year earlier. He used this poster to show that the guard had written down the license plate number on a wood railing, which was preserved in a police report. Although the number recorded was R4974, Cruz's license plate number was DPR 4947. Even if it was missing a few digits, the jurors could see how close it was. The inference was that Angel Cruz had been at the restaurant.

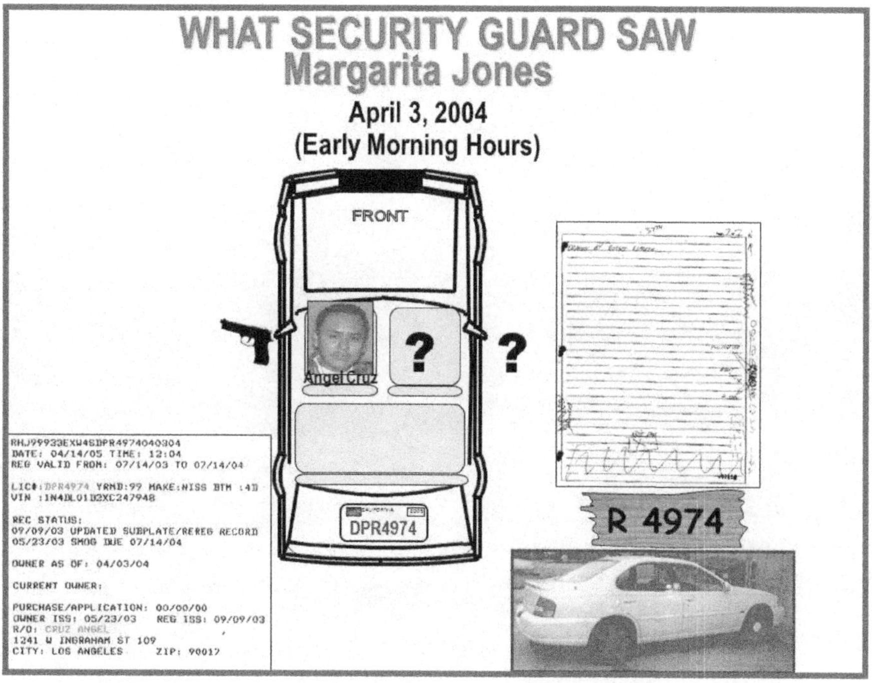

CHAPTER 66 ARGUING IMPORTANCE OF CELLPHONE RECORDS

The defendant's use of the victim's cellphone was critical in proving that this was a robbery. However, the cellphone records showed how the victim was using the cellphone up until 2:46 a.m., and by 3:09 a.m. the phone calls were being made to Cruz's friend Julio. Those latter calls were coming from a cell tower near where Julio lived. Additional calls were made to Cruz's friends Mayra and Jorge. These cellphone records corroborate the phone calls to his mother when he was seeking his parents' help in getting rid of the body.

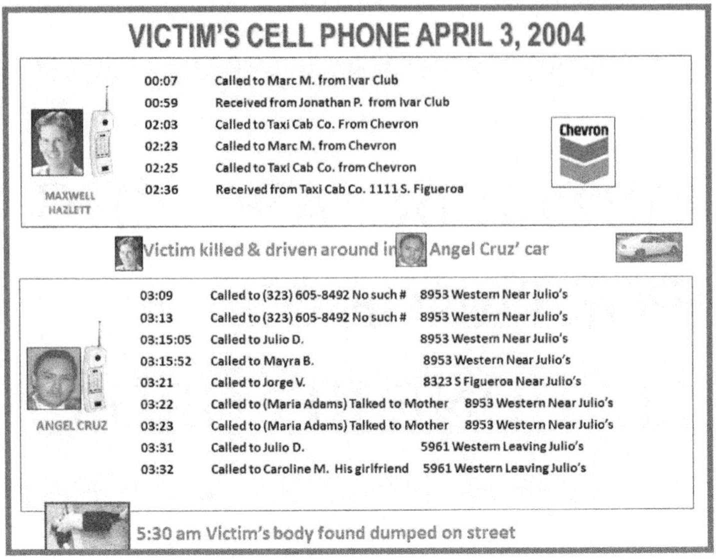
VICTIM'S CELL PHONE APRIL 3, 2004
00:07 Called to Marc M. from Ivar Club
00:59 Received from Jonathan P. from Ivar Club
02:03 Called to Taxi Cab Co. From Chevron
02:23 Called to Marc M. from Chevron
02:25 Called to Taxi Cab Co. from Chevron
02:36 Received from Taxi Cab Co. 1111 S. Figueroa
MAXWELL HAZLETT
Chevron
Victim killed & driven around in Angel Cruz' car
03:09 Called to (323) 605-8492 No such # 8953 Western Near Julio's
03:13 Called to (323) 605-8492 No such # 8953 Western Near Julio's
03:15:05 Called to Julio D. 8953 Western Near Julio's
03:15:52 Called to Mayra B. 8953 Western Near Julio's
03:21 Called to Jorge V. 8323 S Figueroa Near Julio's
03:22 Called to (Maria Adams) Talked to Mother 8953 Western Near Julio's
03:23 Called to (Maria Adams) Talked to Mother 8953 Western Near Julio's
03:31 Called to Julio D. 5961 Western Leaving Julio's
03:32 Called to Caroline M. His girlfriend 5961 Western Leaving Julio's
ANGEL CRUZ
5:30 am Victim's body found dumped on street

The question was how to convey to each of the jurors the importance of the change in the phone calls around 3:00 a.m. Since the case hinged on that single point, Hoon thought up the idea of illustrating the various calls by using the face of a clock. In this way jurors could better visualize when those phone calls were made. However, this type of visual didn't reflect the location (cell tower) where the calls were being made.

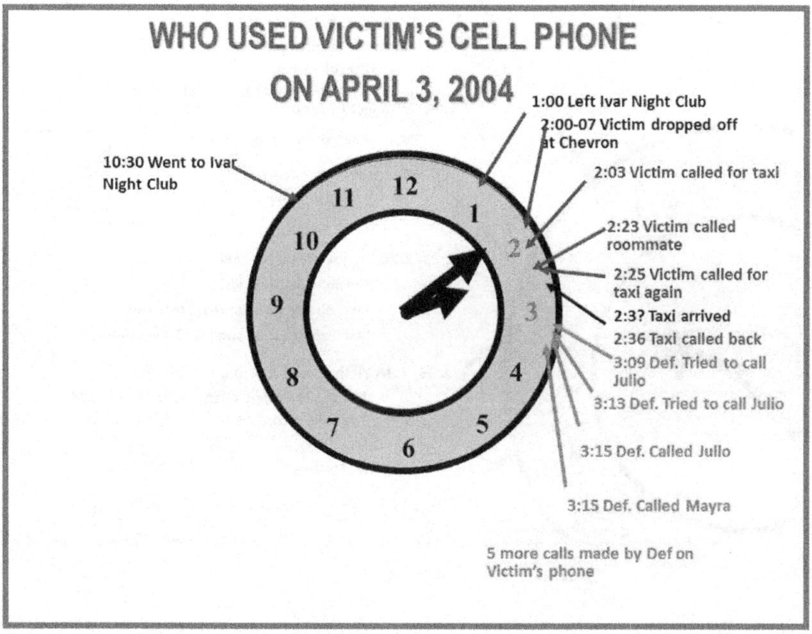

Near the end of his Argument, Hoon used another type of Clock Timeline. This one showed what the victim and the suspect were doing at certain specific times. It was important the jurors knew and understood that. Hoon went line by line down the poster as though he was trying to etch the specific times in the jurors' minds.

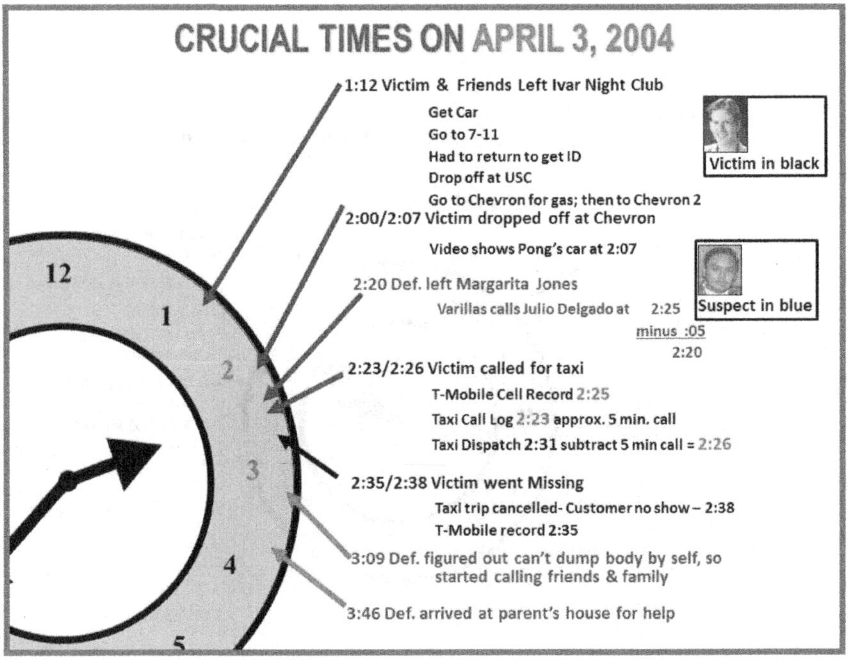

Finally, Hoon wanted to take each of the points he had discussed with the jury and try to show that all those facts pointed to one person, and that was the defendant, Angel Cruz. All the evidence proving the homicide was Circumstantial Evidence. As to the shooting at the Margarita Jones Bar, that was partly Direct Evidence since the security guard saw Angel do it.

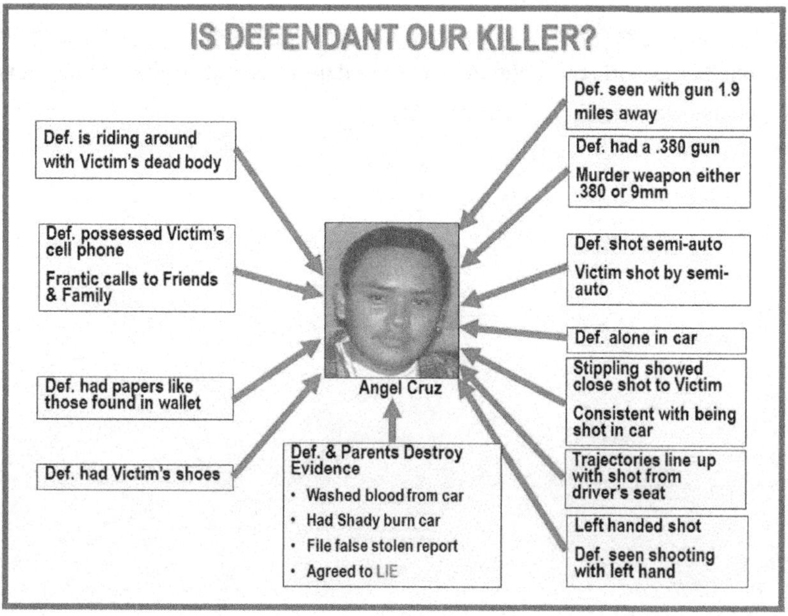

Hoon finished his Argument and wondered what he might have forgotten to tell the jurors. After a brief pause, he couldn't think of anything he missed and Hoon took his seat at counsel table.

The Defense attorney got up in front of the jurors and began arguing that the prosecution hadn't proved their case. He claimed that the prosecution was unfairly making the defendant look bad by all the information about the defendant's gang activities. The Defense attorney relied on Cruz's girlfriend to claim she was with him and they didn't come in contact with or see the victim during the early morning hours of the murder.

After the Defense ended his Argument, Hoon got up and went down the list of all the witnesses that would have to be lying as to the killing of the victim, such as Jorge, Julio, and Mayra, as well as Maria Adams. As to the shooting at the Margarita Jones Bar, the Defense had no way of impeaching the security guard. Hoon reminded the jury that the defendant's girlfriend tried her best to claim she didn't see any firing of a weapon at Margarita Jones bar. However, when she was asked how certain she was as to the date of the shooting, she wavered by saying she wasn't absolutely certain about being with the defendant on the date of the shooting. Hoon showed that the Defense was based on shaky ground.

CHAPTER 67 RESULT OF ANGEL'S CASE

When both sides had finished their Arguments, the judge read the final instructions. The judge had the jurors sent to the jury room to commence their deliberations. Their first act was to select a foreperson, and after which they started discussing the case. After two hours they were told by the bailiff that they were adjourned for the day and to return in the morning at 9:00 a.m.

On Friday morning, all twelve jurors were present and they resumed their deliberation. At noon, the jury was excused for lunch and returned at 1:30 p.m.to resume deliberating. Then at 2:00 p.m. the jury's buzzer rang to everyone's surprise. This seemed too early for a jury verdict unless it was a not-guilty verdict. Occasionally, a jury will feel sympathy toward a defendant and come back immediately to show their support for the defendant. Could that be true in Angel's case? Was there an overwhelming sympathy for a poor 30-year-old who was confined to a wheelchair for the rest of his life?

Hoon had a worried look on his face as he sat alone at counsel table wondering what he could have done or should have done. Angel's attorney had a half-hearted expression, wanting to believe that a quick verdict usually favored the defendant. The judge asked the foreperson to hand the verdict forms to the bailiff. The passing of the verdict forms eventually ended in the hands of the courtroom clerk. Of course, every clerk enjoys being the center of attention and tries to prolong it by clearing her throat. Finally, the moment arrived and in Angel's case the clerk read, "We the jury find the defendant GUILTY of MURDER in the FIRST DEGREE."

However, the jury did throw a crumb to Angel by finding the gang allegation had not been sufficiently proven to be true. Throughout the trial, the Defense wanted the jury to understand that the defendant had a difficult life by merely being a paraplegic. The Defense was hoping that the defendant would come across as a sympathetic character that the jurors could feel sorry for. This would mean that the defendant couldn't look like or come across as a gangster. Unfortunately, the defendant was a gang banger at heart and couldn't completely play the sympathetic role that his Defense attorney was trying to convey to the jurors.

The prosecution was hoping that the jury would be able to see the real Angel—a gangster with a prior conviction for Robbery and a separate conviction for Manslaughter. Throughout the entire trial the question was, which perception would the jury see? Would it be the Defense version that Angel was merely an unlucky paraplegic that the police were harassing, or the Prosecution image, in which he was a predator who was trying to rob anyone he could find? Apparently, in the end the prosecution's image of Angel seemed to prevail.

CHAPTER 68 WHAT HAVE WE LEARNED?

JURORS' SYMPATHY FOR A PARAPLEGIC

The question in this Angel Cruz case was whether the jurors were going to be influenced by the fact that the defendant was a paraplegic. Would the average juror be swayed by their emotions and not be able to convict a paraplegic to a sentence of spending the rest of his life behind bars? Some jurors would take the position that Angel's propensity to rob was caused by the fact he had been cheated in life by not having the opportunities that a rich college kid from Hawaii had. However, the quick verdict of guilty may mean that jurors discounted the paraplegic factor since it was his gang activity that caused him to end up in a wheelchair.

TRANSFERRING CASE TO THE DA'S MAJOR CRIMES DIVISION

The DA's Office made the right decision in transferring this case to Major Crimes Division. The time required to develop a strategy for the case and all the days of preparation could only be available to a prosecutor who had a limited case load. If the case had been allowed to proceed in the usual manner there was no way that Angel would have been convicted.

FAIRNESS OF DA'S STRATEGY

Some legal scholars claim that a trial is the SEARCH FOR THE TRUTH. However, that may be a naïve approach when considering our criminal justice system. The entire strategy of the Defense was not to be convicted. That may mean hiding the ball or in some cases not telling the complete truth. As in this case, the parents didn't want to testify to the truth (that their son had them help him dispose of the victim's body). The parents didn't want to admit to making such an incriminating statements to the detectives, even though there was a tape recording which showed them saying it in their own voices.

The prosecution's strategy was to force the parents to testify so the tape recording could be played before the jurors. Was it fair to use the defendant's parents to basically convict their son? This is more a philosophical question since the rules of evidence aren't based on fairness but are more concerned with reliability. The tape recordings of the parents' statements to the detectives are an undisputed fact, therefore they are highly reliable. It was the defendant who decided to change his story from Self-Defense to Alibi. All the prosecution was trying to do was show the jury that they should be suspect of his new alibi defense since the defendant originally had told his parents he was forced to shoot the victim in self-defense.

This case is a good example as to how a trial is more like a chess mate game in which strategy plays a vital role in the final outcome.

HOON'S USE OF VISUALS

Many attorneys are overly impressed with their verbal skills in explaining the facts and law to a jury. However, Hoon's experience had taught him that the most effective way of communicating with a jury is by inserting visual aids in the attorney's presentation. By viewing the visuals in this case, you the reader can see how helpful they were in explaining the facts to the jurors. This was especially true as to the importance of the cellphone calls and their locations. Merely having a phone company custodian read or present dozens of phone records is hard for jurors to understand their significance. By using a visual Hoon was able to crystallize in the minds of the jurors what they needed to consider.

TURNING POINTS IN CASE

This case had more twist and turns that could have completely changed the outcome in this case. The perseverance of the homicide detectives was amazing. If the prosecution hadn't continually pursued the victim's cellphone records to discover the numbers called after the victim's death, the case wouldn't have been solved. Their follow-up revealed who was the one using the victim's phone.

Another surprise was how candid Maria Adams was in talking to the detectives. If she had remained silent, the detectives would never have uncovered the method of the disposal of the victim's body.

Another turning point of the case involved the security guard at the Margarita Jones Bar. He made a great witness by supplying the prosecution with information that the defendant could shoot with his left hand and used .380 ammunition.

Without a doubt, the parents were pivotal to this case. When they talked to the detectives, who would ever think they would admit to helping their son get rid of the victim's body and later to cleaning up the car?

The defendant was unbelievable when he went to the Ramparts Division and was willing to waive his Miranda Rights and talk freely about the shooting as a matter of self-defense. The more he talked, the deeper the hole got until he had completely buried himself.

There was plenty of evidence that Angel did have a bruise to his left eye, which might have come from Maxwell trying to hit Angel. However, we will never know for certain if the defendant would have been more successful if he had continued to claim Self-Defense. This was truly a case that could have gone a different way depending on any of the above factors.

CHAPTER 69 SUMMARY OF ALL THE CASES

This book tried to give you, the reader, a close up look at two incredible prosecutors. It may be helpful to review what we have discussed and hopefully learned from this particular book.

GOVIN & GRAJEDA CASE

After reading about this case, you will always make sure you pay your taxes on time. As much as some of you don't want the IRS knocking on your door, that might not be as bad as the Mexican Mafia knocking on your door. Although I say this in a humorous vein, think of how many people live in constant fear that they may have done something to offend one of the Carnales, like not paying enough taxes or paying the wrong person.

You have learned about the importance of the Green Light list. Can you imagine how a person feels when they see their name on such a list? How do you continue to live without wondering about everyone around you who might be waiting to kill you? What most readers take away from this case is that you don't want to be a part of the gang or drug dealer's world.

MEGA MEXICAN MAFIA CASE

However, this case gave us another perspective about the Mexican Mafia's Green Light. Who knew that a person who is Green Lighted would be the perfect witness for the prosecutor? Since they are as good as dead, they realize their only hope for survival is to go into the Witness Protection Program. After testifying for the prosecution, this dead man gets a new life in some other part of the world.

In this case we learned about poor Muppet, the teenage drug dealer who thought he could talk his way out of the charges by telling the cops who had killed the Sanchez Brothers. The detectives told him that they would keep his information confidential and they sincerely meant it. However, nowadays the courts require the prosecutor to turn over all reports and evidence that they receive from the police regarding a criminal case.

Who knew that someone would forget to redact Muppet's name from a police report turned over to the Defense attorney? To this very day, everyone is still pointing fingers as to who was the person who screwed up. Was it some intern with the DA's Office, or was it some staffer in the police department that missed crossing out Muppet's name? What have we, the readers, learned? Most of us in this day and age realize there is no such thing as total confidentiality with the internet, especially with so many hackers. However, sometimes the breach is a simple 'oops' mistake.

MONSTER OF ATWATER—TIMOTHY MCGHEE

How do you execute a young lady who two days earlier helped you search for your cell phone you dropped at one of the shootings? Also, when he stood at the glass door of the Shell service station and without any hesitation shot at a kid he grew up with. It would seem that McGhee is extremely Cold Hearted, or possibly he has no heart at all. For years McGhee was untouchable since he was so good at killing off any potential witnesses against him. The strange thing about his undoing was that it took a cell phone to bring him down. Since phone records and cell phones aren't alive, they had no fear of suffering the wrath of McGhee. McGhee would win hands down the most despicable person award.

When I heard about the detectives being involved in the horrendous traffic accident, I had to think that McGhee was definitely the Teflon Man. I had to think how unfair life was when he continued to escape justice. Thankfully, the woman he met at the Losers Lounge turned out to be a winner for the prosecution. The other young lady, Monica, was willing to testify and identify McGhee as the person looking for the lost cellphone. Fortunately, these two women made a difference in bringing McGhee's reign of terror to an end.

THE PARAPLEGIC ROBBER—CRUZ

I, the author, must admit that I was one of the many people who told prosecutor Hoon that he couldn't convince 12 jurors that a paraplegic could be a robber/murderer. I marvel how Hoon went to work proving me wrong. His idea of using the parents as witnesses against their son the killer never entered my mind. His brilliant idea paid off in that the parents' Aiding and Abetting case finished long before the murder case was tried. Noon waited until the appeal time had run out before he subpoenaed the parents. At trial, Hoon played the parents' tape recording in which they admitted that they helped their son get rid of the dead body in the car.

As much as the parents disliked testifying against their son, they had to. What the defendant learned on the night of the robbery was the fact that none of his friends were willing to help him out to get the dead body out of the car. It wasn't until he called his mother that he received help from anyone. The old adage that blood is thicker than water continues to be true. When you are in a desperate situation, 'You can always count on your dear mom to help you out.'

THANKS TO THESE TWO TENACIOUS AND DEDICATED PROSECUTORS

Tony Manzella

He was a rare breed of prosecutor since he didn't have to work to make a living. Being a prosecutor was more of a hobby he outright enjoyed in doing. His satisfaction in prosecuting a case was to see if he could overcome all the legal obstacles in order to convict the killer. Winning wasn't a personal thing for Tony. For him it was a contest of him pitting his litigation skills and strategic techniques against his opponent.

Tony was the ultimate professional who enjoyed the journey more the destination. His 40-year legal career had taught him the importance of PREPARATION. When he started a trial, he had already dictated his final Argument. Without a doubt he was the consummate prosecutor of all times. I am proud to have had the opportunity to work alongside Tony. I can only wish we could clone him in order to have his type still working with in the DA's Office.

Nowadays Tony is enjoying his retirement charting new courses in his gigantic sailboat as he sails the tranquil Coast of California.

Hoon Chun

How many attorneys do you know who have an attitude that the 'glass is half full'? Hoon has been given more cases with the word 'LOSER' invisibly spelled out on their files than anyone else I have worked with in Major Crimes. Hoon doesn't dwell on all the obstacles but concentrates on the various solutions to overcome the challenges in his cases. Many attorneys want to complain how unfair it is for them to receive such a loser of a case, but not Hoon.

Hoon's strong suit is that he is a detail person. He delights in walking jurors through the maze of obstacles and shows them the way out. He effectively uses visuals to make sure the jurors are in lockstep with him to reach the guilty verdict. He is deadly serious about his cases in court, but out of the courtroom in the DA's Office he is very congenial person who doesn't take himself too seriously. He has an understanding that you have to enjoy what you are doing in order to be the best at it. Without a doubt, Hoon Chun is a rare breed who made a significant contribution to the Major Crimes Division.

Hoon has moved on from trials to being a DA supervisor.

MESSAGE TO FUTURE

The Los Angeles County District Attorney's Office has been blessed with so many remarkable prosecutors especially those assigned to the Major Crimes Division. I was pleased to have the opportunity to work with this unbelievably talented group. The Golden Age of the Major Crimes Division was the first decade of the new millennium, in which they truly reached the pinnacle of what this Division was established to do.

One of the reasons I wrote this DA DELTRA FORCE series was to inspire future generations of prosecutors to understand what makes for a great DA's Office. It's an extraordinary group of prosecutors who are bright, highly skilled, tenacious, and dedicated to putting in whatever amount of time and energy it takes to see that Justice is done.

I believe the public has a right to know who are the BEST OF THE BEST DAs.

Made in the USA
Monee, IL
04 November 2026

67376812R00203